Motivating Every Learner

Motivating Every Learner

Alan McLean

Los Angeles | London | New Delhi
Singapore | Washington DC

First published 2009

Apart from any fair dealing for the purposes of
research or private study, or criticism or review, as
permitted under the Copyright, Designs and Patents Act
1988, this publication may be reproduced, stored or
transmitted in any form, or by any means, only with
the prior permission in writing of the publishers,
or in the case of reprographic reproduction, in accordance
with the terms of licences issued by the Copyright Licensing
Agency. Enquiries concerning reproduction outside those
terms should be sent to the publishers.

SAGE Publications Ltd
1 Oliver's Yard
55 City Road
London EC1Y 1SP

SAGE Publications Inc.
2455 Teller Road
Thousand Oaks, California 91320

SAGE Publications India Pvt Ltd
B 1/I 1 Mohan Cooperative Industrial Area
Mathura Road
New Delhi 110 044

SAGE Publications Asia-Pacific Pte Ltd
33 Pekin Street #02-01
Far East Square
Singapore 048763

Library of Congress Control Number: 2008938673

British Library Cataloguing in Publication data

A catalogue record for this book is available from the British Library

ISBN 978-1-84860-181-9
ISBN 978-1-84860-182-6 (pbk)

Typeset by C&M Digitals (P) Ltd, Chennai, India
Printed in Great Britain by TJ International, Padstow, Cornwall
Printed on paper from sustainable resources

Contents

This book is dedicated to the memory of my mother, Mary McLean and my sister, Maureen Morrison, the two personal motivators with whom I was blessed throughout my childhood.

Acknowledgements

This book would not have been possible without the support, advice, encouragement and interest of many people. I am grateful to the teachers, parents and young people with whom I have had the pleasure to have worked, particularly in St Charles, St Blanes and St Marnocks. I am indebted to all my colleagues in the North East Psychological Service for putting up with my obsession over the years and for their helpful criticism. I am especially indebted to my colleagues who were willing to experiment with the Matrix as it developed and gave encouraging feedback, particularly Mary Bendermacher, Elaine Miller, Fiona Williams, Yvonne Bushnell, Sam March and Fergal Doherty. Special thanks go to Gillian McVittie for her creative cartoons and to Angie Gray for her excellent work on the graphics. Helen Fairlie, my editor at Sage, gave unstinting encouragement from the earliest forms of the book as well as honest and wise feedback throughout its development. Finally I am most grateful to Chris Smith, Kate Whiteley, Sharman Muir and Bob Cook for their great patience and constructive criticism that has been so significant in helping to transform my early drafts into this book.

About the Author

Alan McLean is a Principal Psychologist in a large education authority in Scotland. He taught in a Secondary school and a Special School for students with emotional and behavioural problems. He is the author of the staff development programmes. *Promoting Positive Behaviour in the Primary School, Promoting Positive Behaviour in the Secondary School* and the award-winning *Bullyproofing Our School*. He had a weekly column in *The Scotsman* for several years and has been a regular contributor to the *Times Educational Supplement Scotland*. His latest training programme on Motivation was commissioned by the Scottish Government and has been used in schools throughout Scotland.

Route map of the book

Part I   What makes pupils tick

Chapter 1 discusses what motivation is. 'What makes pupils tick' is all about how they get their needs met, and Chapter 2 outlines what these needs are. These learner needs provide the foundation for the motivation matrix.

Part II   What pupils do to motivate themselves

What helps or hinders pupils getting their needs met? Anything that helps is an *energizer* and anything that hinders is a *drainer*. There are internal (pupil) and external (classroom) energizers and drainers. Part II considers the internal energizers, including, for example, self-esteem and emotional intelligence. These energizers drive motivation from within and shape pupils' capacity to get their needs met from within their own resources. Chapter 3 outlines how pupils' needs organize their personality, followed by Chapter 4 which discusses how pupils meet their needs for themselves. Chapter 5 considers how personality, in particular resilience, shapes the way pupils meet their needs and, finally, Chapter 6 looks at how pupils feel about themselves.

Do not panic! This may sound a bit overwhelming but stay with it and all will be revealed and will fall into place.

Part III   What teachers do

Chapter 7 describes *what* teachers do to motivate pupils through the external (*classroom*) *energizers*. Chapter 8 explores teachers' own motivations and perceptions that shape *how* they use the classroom energizers, that is, their teaching styles. It concludes with a discussion of what it feels like for pupils, that is, *the classroom climates*. The teaching styles and classroom climates are presented as layers of the motivation matrix.

Part IV   How pupils adapt

Part IV considers how pupils adapt to the classroom climates, as expressed through their learning stances. The learning stances layer of the matrix is developed in Chapter 9. Chapter 10 summarizes the different layers of the matrix. It concludes with an overview of the development of learning stances through the key motivational milestones.

Part V   How teachers need to adapt to different stances

Part V explores how teachers might adapt their styles and classroom energizers to the different learning stances. It aims to help teachers find the right *buttons to press*. Four pupil defensive reactions are introduced. In separate chapters, profiles of each reaction are provided along with an exploration of why pupils might react in these ways. Each chapter puts forward examples of particular energizers that work well with these reactions, as well as examples of drainers that make them worse. This part concludes with a chapter on the positive stances and examines why pupils choose to engage and how to keep them engaged. The final chapter recaps on how the learner needs matrix has been built up, identifies some recurring themes and draws some conclusions.

Introduction

Motivation is a personal business. It is appropriate therefore to start a book on motivation with an explanation of my personal motivation.

My interest in motivation was triggered when, as a parent, I found myself struggling to motivate my 10-year-old and 8-year-old sons to take up the guitar. I'll never forget catching myself saying: 'That guitar is getting thrown out in the morning and that's £100 I've wasted.' After six years' training in psychology and 20 years' experience as a psychologist, the only way I knew how to motivate my sons was to try to make them feel guilty.

I realized then I knew little about motivation. I had been working in education too long! I knew how to control, manipulate, reward and punish pupils but I did not know how to motivate them. That came as a bit of a shock to a psychologist who was supposed to know about motivation.

Around the same time, I was becoming increasingly dissatisfied with behavioural models of school discipline. I had done a lot of work over many previous years on promoting positive behaviour and felt we had taken that paradigm as far as we could.

This personal experience as a father also made me realize that self-motivation had been a lifelong personal interest. I am the youngest of six children. When I was 16 I was the first person in my family to sit national examinations. In fact I was the only person in my street in a Glasgow housing estate to be studying for exams. It was this that got me interested in psychology, to find out what made me different from the rest of my family and friends, particularly what made me motivated to work hard at school. As you can see, exploring self-motivation has been something of a lifelong quest.

I have been working on developing my model of motivation for 10 years. In that time I have had many setbacks in trying to make sense of it and communicate it to teachers and others in an accessible and practical way. This journey has been like raising a child, a journey of emotional highs and lows where, no matter what, I could never give up. I hope my obstinacy and persistence has paid off.

One of my sons has, at the age of 17, decided to start learning to play the guitar. Maybe patience is necessary for those of us who seek to motivate.

Part One
What makes pupils tick

1

What makes pupils tick

This chapter outlines the aims and focus of the book, and explores what motivation is about. It gives a preview of the motivation matrix. It argues that misbehaviour is a function of poor motivation and concludes with a description of motivation as a two-way process between teachers and pupils.

This book has been written mainly for teachers but it will be of interest to anyone who wants to develop their ability to motivate others to learn. This depends on the following:

- How do you feel about yourself in your particular role?
- What is your capacity to tune in to people?
- How flexible are you?

The teacher's tool kit has traditionally consisted of pedagogy to teach the curriculum and disciplinary techniques to control behaviour. This book is not about controlling pupils or shaping their learning progress. It is about understanding what makes them want to engage in learning. The overarching aim of the book is to develop a motivational matrix that synthesizes current thinking about motivation to help generate new knowledge. This matrix enables a deeper understanding of motivation by

- affording you the opportunity for self-reflection
- examining the types of learning environments that can exist in a classroom
- exploring the core conditions for learning and teaching.

The motivation matrix takes the lid off classroom life and develops your understanding of yourself and your pupils. The main priority is to help you to make sense of your own ideas and experiences. The matrix will make connections between ideas and show how the different components relate to each other and fit into the bigger picture. For example, popular concepts such as confidence, emotional intelligence and self-esteem will be integrated into the matrix.

Motivating teaching is intuitive and hard to articulate. The matrix will help you identify where there is scope for improvement. For example, you may not be aware of your teaching style and its impact on your pupils. Hopefully the book will increase your self-awareness and therefore your resilience.

The focus of the book

The central focus of the book is teacher–pupil interactions and how they can promote pupils' engagement in learning and *motivational resilience*. Motivational resilience is the capacity to cope with setbacks, adversity, pressure and power. Engagement refers to the intensity and quality of a pupil's involvement during a task.[1] Engaged pupils express their voice and take initiative in trying to produce changes in their environment.[2] Disengaged pupils, in contrast, are passive or let external forces control their involvement. Engagement is important because it predicts achievement.[3] Young people's engagement in learning declines over the school years,[4] in part due to the way teachers teach.[5] On a more positive note, however, pupils' motivation is easily malleable.[6]

This book tries to capture the importance of motivation, an issue that 'stems from the complex interactions between individual psychology, the relationship between teacher and pupil, peer group interactions and the link between school and the outside world'.[7] The more you are willing to immerse yourself in the matrix and, in particular, reflect on your own teaching style, the more useful this book will be to you.

Stop and think

What is the biggest lesson you have learned about motivating pupils? Why do pupils engage differently in different classes?

You may be looking for tips on how to motivate pupils, especially those who are difficult to engage. Motivational teaching, however, cannot be 'manualized'. The difference between teachers is not down to tips and gimmicks but what kind of teaching style they use. What kind of tip would work for all teachers with all pupils? Consider, for example, the use of praise. Not all teachers are able or willing to give praise and not all pupils are motivated by praise.

Here are some reasonable tips:

- Give high profile responsibilities.
- Negotiate private challenges.
- Maintain familiar routines.
- Surprise them.

Taken together, these tips do not make a lot of sense and contradict each other. Each will work well with some pupils but will drain others. What is the answer? The matrix makes sense of the strategies developed over the years and will also, hopefully, help you generate some new approaches.

The foundation of the matrix is provided by the learner needs. These needs are fundamental to being human and are what pupils are all about. The matrix also describes how teachers and pupils engage with each other, that is, the teaching styles and the learning stances. There is also a layer of the matrix that describes classroom climates and includes a set of general dos, called *classroom energizers,* and don'ts, called *classroom drainers*. It also provides a set of *stance-specific dos and don'ts*.

Stop and think

Think of a range of pupils you know well, or a whole class. Write each pupil's name on a separate Post-it™. Try to get as wide a range of pupils as possible in terms of what we will call *engage-ability*.
Now rank order the pupils from high to low *engage-ability*.
Now cluster them into high, low and average engage-ability.
Consider now what the pupils in your high engage-ability group have in common. What is it about them that made you think of them, that makes them so readily engage-able? Write down your descriptions.
Finally do the same for your low group.
This exercise will enable you to outline and share your understanding of high and low engage-ability. It will be particularly useful to focus on a class and compare your perceptions with colleagues who also teach that class.

When pupils walk into your classroom, they need to feel enthused to learn. Your biggest challenge is that all pupils are motivated in different ways. How can teachers tune into their pupils? The answer lies in recognizing their learning stances. This is your *sim card* connecting you with the learning network in your classroom.

The learning stances reflect the key difference between pupils, namely, how they feel about themselves as learners. They characterize 'engage-ability'. The learning stances matrix develops a greater understanding of learners and generates personalized responses. It captures how the individual changes not only in response to the different classrooms but also as a result of the individual's moods. Teachers do not need to develop different strategies for every individual. Fortunately pupils are more similar than they are different.[8] To engage every pupil, teachers need to adapt their teaching style to the number of stances instead of the number of pupils in their class.

The differentiating characteristics of each stance together with the *internal energizers* underpinning them provide the essential clues needed to discover the most appropriate *classroom energizers* for each stance.

The essential feature of the learning stances is their dynamism, which underscores the need for teachers to be flexible in their response to the changing stances. The wider the range of energizers in a teacher's repertoire, the more flexible their teaching style will be. This flexibility to change what you are doing, if it is not working, is one of the hallmarks of motivating teaching. The motivating teacher gains influence by demonstrating an ability to adjust to the needs of pupils.

What is motivation about?

 Stop and think

How would you define what motivation is?

Motivation is a relatively modern term that was introduced from America in the 1940s. Motivation is all the reasons behind why we behave as we do and revolves around intentionality. We are all motivated by many different things. It is influenced by our past, present and the future.

> Motivation is the pilot light for learning. (Learning support teacher)

Textbook definitions suggest that motivation is what moves us to action: why we start, go on with or stop an activity; giving a motive to do something; internal processes and external incentives that spur us to satisfy a need; the response we make to challenges and threats in situations where success or failure is possible; the marshalling of enthusiasm, confidence and persistence.

 Stop and think

Who is the most motivated person you know?
What are the hallmarks of a motivated person?
Who is the most demotivated person you know?
How motivated are you?

The arrival of the new chemistry teacher resulted in 100% attendance rate by the girls.

When people are asked, *'How motivated are you?'*, they automatically ask, 'How motivated am I *to do what?'*, or *'In what context?'*. That is the only way they can answer the question. And yet, teachers regularly complain, in general terms, about a pupil or a class being 'demotivated'. But we cannot actually say a pupil is not motivated; we can only say the pupil is not motivated to work in, for example, my mathematics class. The mistake teachers make is that they think motivation is a feature of the learner. Motivation is not a feature of the learner but of the transaction between the learner and the context. Motivation, like trust, occurs between people rather than within people.

Now rate yourself on how motivated you are in your current job, on a scale of 1 to 10, with 10 being high. We will return to this later.

Interviewer: You have been talking about motivation, but motivation to do what?

Robert, a 10-year-old pupil (at the end of a 12 week motivation programme): Everything.

Interviewer: What do you mean? I'm motivated to play golf but not to do housework.

Pupil: Well, what you need to do when doing housework is to put some music on, or treat it as exercise, find something that makes it more enjoyable, that's what being in control of your own motivation means.

The dark and light side of motivation

 Stop and think

What negative emotions can pull behaviour from you?

When I have asked teachers and pupils to talk about what they think motivation is, they invariably paint a positive picture of motivation as some kind of drive to achieve, fulfil a desire and so on. Motivation, however, is more complex than this. Every pupil is motivated. It is just that some of them are motivated to wind the teacher up, to get their revenge, to impress a member of the opposite sex or to avoid more failure, and so on. Motivation can be either positive or negative.

The main theoretical perspective of this book is taken from self-determination theory, developed over the past 30 years, that has enhanced our understanding of the conditions which allow individuals to operate at their best.[9] Self-determination theory highlights the needs that give our goals their motivational power. If our needs are met our motivation will be self-determined. While all pupils share the same basic needs, they all have unique personalities and backgrounds that lead them to meet their needs in different ways.

If our needs are thwarted we may become driven to get them met in inappropriate ways. Defensive motives come into play following blocks to our basic needs.[10] These defensive motives then create need substitutes that can have negative consequences. Boredom, for example, may be a motivating force that makes us engage in challenge-seeking behaviour.[11] We know intuitively about negative motivation, as seen in our wariness about making *emotive* comments, in case we motivate negatively.

The shower metaphor

The metaphor provided by a shower is useful for describing the learning stances taken by pupils as well as the different styles of teachers.

The two variables we can manipulate to control a shower are temperature and pressure. The vertical dimension of Figure 1.1 represents the temperature variable with warm at the top and cold at the bottom. The horizontal dimension represents the pressure variable, with weak at the left and powerful at the right side. Warmth and power are fundamental dimensions in the classroom.

 Stop and think

1 How does it feel to be in a shower that is very warm and quite powerful?
2 How does it feel in a shower that is reasonably warm and very powerful?
3 What is it like in a shower that is very cold and powerful?
4 How does it feel in a shower that is warm but very weak?
5 What kind of shared feeling do 1 and 2 have?
6 What kind of shared feeling do 3 and 4 have in contrast to 1 and 2?
7 What is the feeling generated by a shower that is inconsistent, one minute hot and the next minute cold, in response to someone putting the washing machine on?

The answers:

1 Most people would describe a shower that is warm and quite powerful as 'soothing'.
2 Most people would describe a shower that is reasonably warm and very powerful as 'invigorating'.
3 Most people would describe a shower that is very cold and powerful as 'shocking'.
4 Most people would describe a shower that is warm but very weak as something like 'unfulfilling'.
5 Both the soothing and invigorating showers have 'energizing' qualities.
6 The shocking and unfulfilling showers might be experienced as the opposite of energizing, that is, 'draining'.
7 Finally, everyone will have experienced a shower that is inconsistent as 'exasperating'.

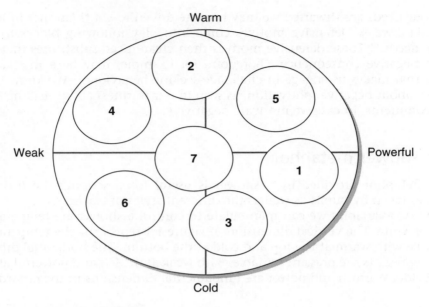

Figure 1.1   The shower metaphor i

These seven descriptors are presented in Figure 1.2. This simple matrix help-fully describes not just the shower experience but also how teachers perceive different pupil responses, that is, learning stances as well as teaching styles and also different classroom climates.

 Stop and think

Using these shower metaphor labels:

How would you describe your typical contribution to staff meetings?
How would your pupils describe your teaching style?
How would pupils describe the climate in your class?

Preview of the motivation matrix

The interplay between the three learner needs of affiliation, agency and autonomy will be used to create the *learner needs matrix*. *Affiliation* is the need to feel a sense of belonging. *Agency* is the need to feel that you can meet the demands of the task. Affiliation forms the vertical axis and Agency forms the horizontal axis of the matrix, displayed in Figure 1.3.

Autonomy is the need to be self-determining. It is in large part, a function of how our needs for affiliation and agency are met. Affiliation encourages us to be co-operative and agency encourages us to be ambitious. Autonomy allows us to be both. Autonomy is conceptualized as an arc that balances affiliation and agency. The optimal point is the midpoint of the arc, but you can exercise

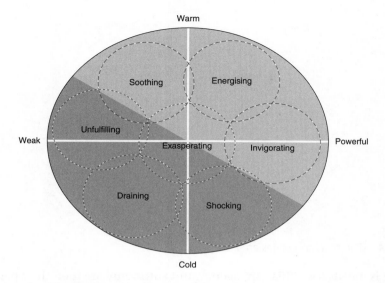

Figure 1.2   The shower metaphor ii

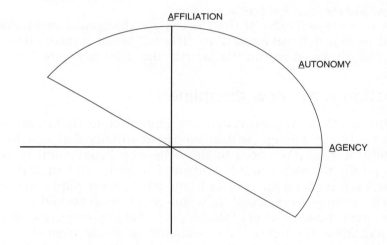

Figure 1.3   The learner needs matrix i

some autonomy from anywhere on the arc. As such, autonomy is a more expansive concept than the other two needs.

This 3A layer provides the foundation for the motivation matrix, a layer of which will be used to describe how teachers motivate pupils. The teaching styles matrix is also conceptualized as an arc, mirroring the autonomy arc. It contains three overlapping teaching styles, as shown in Figure 1.4.

The fundamental goal for the teacher is to attune to pupils and communicate that they are open to compromise. Teaching styles can vary between being soothing and pushing. The trick is to get the balance right, to be flexible rather than too loose or too tight.

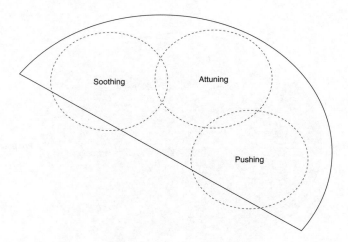

Figure 1.4   The teaching styles arc i

If pupils' needs for affiliation, agency and autonomy are met, their personality flourishes and expresses itself through the positive learning stances. A further layer of the matrix will include the three stances, displayed in Figure 1.5, which reflects variants of high levels of autonomy.

Pupils become defensive if their needs are threatened or blocked. This can lead to four defensive reactions. The full set of stances and reactions can now be displayed within the matrix, displayed in Figure 1.6.

Motivation is the new discipline

Discipline, in its literal context deriving from disciple, that is, one who follows, is no longer enough within modern curricula that aim to nurture responsible learners. We need to move beyond behavioural models that control pupils through rewards and punishments, and increase the distance between teachers and pupils to models that see pupils' needs, goals, beliefs and feelings as the important sources of motivational power.

Despite a constant stream of initiatives, aimed at improving discipline, indiscipline remains at the top of the educational agenda in most countries. Our partial understanding of the motives behind difficult behaviour leads to 'hit or miss' interventions whose outcomes are poorly evaluated and therefore teach us little. It can also lead to unhelpful feedback to pupils. Being told you are disruptive will not increase your self-awareness or self-control. Understanding is the hallmark of a motivated school. We need to match our new insights into how pupils learn with a better understanding of how they engage with school.

Progress in behaviour management has given us a good foundation to look at the context of learning. The strategies schools are using, however, including star charts, behaviour target cards and time out, are not always effective, with the same pupils targeted over and over again. The challenge is to get beyond the mechanics of behaviour management to better understand pupil motives. Most misbehaviour is a function of poor or inappropriately directed motivation. In particular, as we will discover later on, most behaviour problems are a result of self-determination, not self-esteem issues as is often assumed.

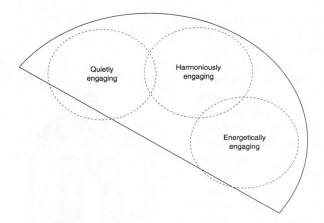

Figure 1.5   The learning stances i

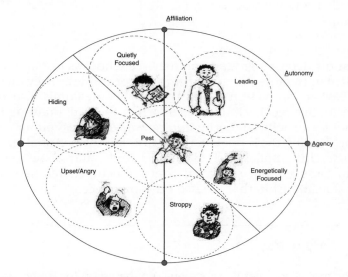

Figure 1.6   The learning stances and reactions i

Behavioural approaches have taken us as far as they can. We need to transcend the coercive relationships that try to redirect unwanted behaviour. The message in traditional discipline is – here are the rules; if you comply you will be rewarded; if you break them you will be punished. If you persistently break the rules you will be excluded. The learning stances matrix is more optimistic and empowering. It recognizes that pupils are actively seeking control and responsibility, and it offers them an opportunity to achieve this.

Motivation is a two-way street

After considering the implications of motivation I realize that I have to make my students aware of the benefits of motivation. There is no point me knowing all this stuff and them not knowing, since after all, it relates to both of us. (Further education lecturer)

The teacher's motivation is downloaded to pupils but pupil motivation can also be uploaded to the teacher. Pupils have a crucial but seldom acknowledged role in creating the classroom climate and supporting teacher morale. They often, however, have little awareness of the teacher's predicament and may not see their part in this dynamic. For example, they do not realize it is their reactions that force the teacher to behave in oppressive ways and not in their preferred teaching style. They think that grumpy teachers are just grumpy people.

Pupils whose motivation is limited have not been exposed to a motivation-rich background and may see school as just an endless set of imposed demands rather than learning opportunities. They need help to understand what motivation to learn is all about. Pupils also need to be encouraged to give feedback to teachers when they are draining their motivation. Schools can achieve this by finding ways to access pupils' views about how they are finding the school, perhaps through the personal learning planning process. This implies a significant attitude shift about the nature of authority towards a more reciprocal contract between teachers and pupils, rather than a relationship that is based on compliance.

Summary of key points

- The motivation matrix will be built up, based on the 3A needs, and will consist of many layers mirroring this pattern.
- Engagement is important because it predicts achievement.
- Motivation is not a quality of the individual learner but of the transaction between the learner and the learning climate.

2

What pupils need

This chapter outlines the needs of affiliation, agency and autonomy (the 3As). Schools must nurture these in their pupils in order to engage them. The interplay between these needs is used to create a *learner needs matrix*. This matrix also profiles the motivational toxins that can pull young people into the dark side of motivation.

A need is something that, when met appropriately, promotes our well-being. Our needs signal the nutrients that are necessary for our well-being. We are not necessarily conscious of them.

The first learner need is for *affiliation,* which is the need to feel a sense of belonging within their class and school. The second, *agency,* is the need to feel competent in meeting the demands of school. Both these needs form binary or two-tailed dimensions. Affiliation and its opposite *alienation* form the vertical axis, and agency and its opposite, *apathy,* form the horizontal axis of the learner needs matrix, as displayed in Figure 2.1. Alienation and apathy are two common routes into disengagement.

Pupils learn within peer groups and these groups have pecking orders which are very important to learners. They call on two main motives to drive pupil behaviour: first, getting along, that is, affiliation and, second, getting

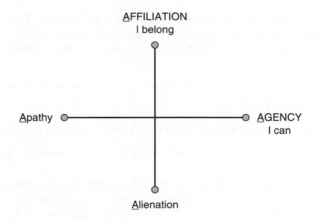

Figure 2.1   The learner needs matrix ii

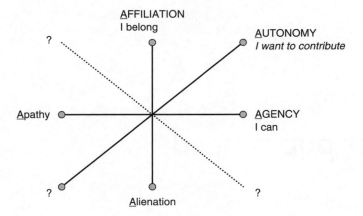

Figure 2.2   The learner needs matrix iii

ahead, that is, agency.[1] Girls are socialized more for affiliation, whereas boys are socialized more for agency.[2]

Affiliation and agency work together to nurture the third need, namely, autonomy, the need to be self-determining. Our autonomy benefits from the support of others, affiliation and our growing competencies, agency.

The 3A needs are displayed in Figure 2.2. At this stage, the matrix presents a picture of high and low motivation, the light and dark sides of motivation. Pupils with high satisfaction levels of affiliation, agency and autonomy will have high motivation to learn, and those with low satisfaction will have low motivation. However, motivation is not as simple as this and the question marks in the diagram need to be explained to reveal the full picture. An exploration of the multipolar concept of autonomy will help in this quest.

The 3A needs in detail

Teachers engage pupils by meeting their 3A needs, namely:

- affiliation – a sense of connectedness, creating '*I belong*' feelings
- agency – beliefs about competence, triggering '*can do*' feelings
- autonomy – 'I'm trusted' feelings, generating '*want to contribute*' attitudes.

Stop and think

How well are your 3A needs realized in your working context?

Each of these needs must be considered to understand pupil motivation in a holistic way. Each makes its own independent contribution to how pupils feel about themselves as learners. Pupils have a combination of these needs, with some pupils showing a stronger preference for a particular need.

The 3As also work as a team and can be seen in many aspects of life. For example, as one political commentator has noted, voters consider three things in deciding on a politician:

- Does he care about people like us? (affiliation)
- Does he know what he is doing? (agency)
- Can you trust him? (autonomy)

Stop and think

Use these dimensions to consider your working relationship with your line manager.

So far, brief definitions of the 3As have been outlined. However, these concepts are so central to our role as teachers in creating the energizing classroom that they need to be explored more fully.

Stop and think

What is the best job you have ever had? We will use this context to look at how the 3As work.

Affiliation

Affiliation is a sense of being valued and understood, of feeling part of a team, of feeling an emotional bonding.[3] We need affiliation to develop our sense of security. Motivational resilience rests on a strong connection with at least one supportive caregiver in the early years.[4] People with high affiliation needs are keen to be liked and enjoy friendships and teamwork. This sense of affiliation is what makes soldiers sacrifice their lives in battle.[5] For learners, a sense of belonging involves allegiance to the values and goals of schooling, as well as a feeling of connection with peers, teachers and other staff.

Stop and think

How did your best job meet your affiliation needs?
What is your most memorable experience of affiliation in a learning situation?
What are the hallmarks of high and low affiliation in a pupil or teacher?
How much affiliation did you have when you started your current job and how much do you have now?

Some 11-year-old pupils were asked: what is a sense of belonging? Their answers were illuminating:

- The environment suits you.
- It feels like home.
- You feel comfortable.
- It's welcoming.
- Nobody judges you.

Miss Driver my Mum says I don't need to play in the hockey team today 'cos my affiliation levels are rock-bottom.

Affiliation to teachers is particularly critical.[6] Pupils who feel appreciated and supported by their teachers feel positive about school, and this feeling is not just a by-product but a core ingredient of their engagement. Affiliation elicits more support from others that in turn further builds affiliation. Efforts to improve engagement in learning must start with attention to pupils' affiliation needs. Those with the lowest level, but the greatest need, tend to be hostile towards school. They feel rejected (often by their parents) and they become alienated from school, and this leads to more isolation.[7] Unfortunately they are often excluded from affiliation-building experiences, like school trips and residential camps, and this pushes them further away. It is perhaps ironic that many initiatives to combat antisocial behaviour try to prevent young people congregating and so deny this genuine need.

Pupils are likely to take on board the values of those teachers who help them meet their affiliation needs.[8] Through identifying closely with teachers these school values gradually change from feeling imposed and externally controlling to internally motivating.

When a group is stressed, members tend to narrow their affiliation to a smaller faction and stop being part of a wider group.[9] Thus the stressed staffroom becomes riddled with cliques. School mergers present a huge challenge to the staff's sense of belonging and it is not surprising that over half of school mergers result in a decline in standards.[10] Successful mergers are built on a shared vision and a speedy sorting of conflicts, that is, good affiliation maintenance.

> I can't cope with the staff room, it has changed from one big conversation to lots of little (private) conversations, where I feel left out. (Teacher, after a recent school merger)

Stop and think

Who might be the main source of affiliation for pupils in your school? (When a colleague put this question to a group of senior high school pupils, the answer was the dinner ladies.)

The opposite of good affiliation, social exclusion, has a large negative impact on educational progress.[11] The low attainment of many pupils who are *looked after* by the local authority bears testimony to the impact of rejection. Rejection triggers aggression and hostility.[12] It also causes self-defeating behaviour, such as paying less attention, taking poorly judged risks, seeking immediate rewards and making bad choices. It damages self-control and reasoning.

> Rejection strikes at the heart of what our psyche is all about.[13]

Rejection makes us lose self-awareness and increases our blind spots, which that in turn exacerbates poor self-control. It is interesting that the brain's response to rejection and pain are the same. They both lead to a numbing, physically and emotionally. The brain bears pain by masking it, but at the cost of reduced awareness. These pain mechanisms reflect patterns that operate in our psychological life. The brain deals with physical pain and emotional hurt by muting awareness.[14]

Self-control is encouraged by our affiliation need, that is, we restrain ourselves in order to be valued by others. Those with poor self-control end up being rejected. At the same time, rejection damages our motivation for self-control. Rejected pupils therefore need to be given an early opportunity to rebuild a sense of belonging, through positive affirmations to help them regain positive self-awareness and self-control.[15]

> The problem with detention is you just sit and do nothing. So it just makes you feel worse. You just get more agitated. It doesn't help you think. You end up feeling like doing something even worse. Punishment needs to help you think. (Robert, aged 12)

Stop and think

How have you felt when you have been turned down for a job?
How are pupils in your school helped to re-establish a sense of belonging on return to school after an exclusion from school?

> How do you create affiliation-building routines in your school and classroom that generate a sense of togetherness?
> Which one thing would improve the affiliation levels in your school?

Agency

Agency is a sense of confidence and self-belief, feeling up to the task, in control and able to contribute. It is an intrinsic satisfaction that reflects personal growth and promotes learning. The opposite is a feeling of hopelessness that leads to *apathy*.

 ### Stop and think

How did your best job meet your agency needs?
What are the hallmarks of high and low agency in a pupil or teacher?
What is your most memorable experience of agency in a learning situation?
How much agency did you have when you started your current job and how much do you have now?

Agency enables us to strive for success as opposed to respond passively. It includes a constructive use of anger. Agency becomes particularly important when variations in ability level can be easily observed, for example, in physical education.

A sense of high agency is reflected in a desire to experiment and innovate, and is marked by curiosity and creativity. Those with a high agency drive enjoy making progress in their goals and are open to new learning. They are motivated by status and welcome feedback that lets them know how well they are doing.

Status is determined by many factors, but significantly by a person's agency. Female status has been found to be determined particularly by beauty and male status by height.[16] Boys' height at 16 has been found to predict adult status. Height influences status indirectly through participation in extra-curricular activities, especially sport which confers high status that in turn boosts boys' confidence.[17,18]

An individual's beliefs about the causes of success and failure are the building blocks of their sense of agency.[19] Pessimistic pupils tend to explain failure in terms of personal, permanent and pervasive causes, like a lack of ability. They put down any success to external, unstable and specific causes, such as luck or an easy task. Conversely, optimistic learners think that failure is due to external, unstable and specific causes, and that success is due to personal, permanent and pervasive factors. This leaves them feeling that success is within their control.[20]

Autonomy

Autonomy is the capacity to take responsibility for ourselves and be in charge of our own learning. It is feeling un-pressured in our actions. Autonomous behaviour feels freely chosen and reflects personal values and self-determination.[21]

Stop and think

How might you measure a pupil's or class's level of autonomy?

The capacity to assert ourselves to achieve our goals within the requirements to conform is a key aspect of success in school. It is with this desire for pupils to assert themselves that teachers have the biggest problem. Some teachers think it would be better if pupils were to suppress this drive, but it is critically important in the development of autonomy.

Exercising autonomy involves responsibilities as well as rights. The classroom needs to give opportunities for autonomy but pupils also need to develop their capacity to exercise it. Autonomy is like wealth or health; it is largely down to how you use it. Also it is not equally distributed.

Those who want autonomy are keen to make an impact and enjoy taking the lead. Pupils' capacity for choice and decision-making is a key indicator of their autonomy.

Stop and think

How did your best job meet your autonomy needs?

What is your most memorable experience of autonomy in a learning situation?

How much autonomy did you have when you started your current job and how much do you have now?

Does your boss trust you? Do you trust your boss?

Who has the most autonomy in your school?

Autonomous pupils take a proactive role in their learning, generating ideas and availing themselves of learning opportunities, rather than simply reacting to the teacher. They take their learning seriously, share in the setting of their learning goals, take the initiative in planning and review their learning to evaluate their progress. Autonomous learning means that the learner has much of the responsibility for assessing its value. There are degrees of learner autonomy and it is a dynamic process rather than a state that is reached once and for all. Autonomy is, like political devolution, a process not an event.

Stop and think

Are you maximizing your own autonomy?

What is limiting your autonomy?

What scope do you have to give pupils autonomy?

Are you maximizing the autonomy you give your classes?

The dark side of the 3As

 Stop and think

What are the different ways people can be irresponsible?

Motivation does not come solely from getting what you want from others or your environment. Neither does it come entirely from within. It comes from the interactions between yourself and others, the task and your surroundings.[22] The 3A needs must all be in alignment. Vitality is a feeling of personal energy and is nurtured by activities that meet these three needs.[23] Just as healthy skin reflects physical well-being, so our vitality or energy level reflects how positively we feel about ourselves. In contrast some feelings can pull our behaviour from us. These are the *motivational toxins* that form the dark side of motivation.

Affiliation and agency are, as already stated, binary dimensions, each with one opposite. The optimal point for both is at the high end of each bipolar continuum. Autonomy is, in large part, a function of how our needs for affiliation and agency are met. While agency drives autonomy on, affiliation, like the partner in a political coalition, acts as a moderating influence and holds autonomy in check. Affiliation, however, should not be smothering. It needs to allow autonomy. Growth in autonomy does not require cutting the emotional ties with others; it needs others to provide support.

Affiliation encourages us to be co-operative and agency encourages us to be ambitious. Autonomy allows us to be both. Autonomy is sometimes confused with independence and some people question the appropriateness of encouraging it in pupils. Autonomy however is not independence, rather it is the essential step towards collaboration, not an end in itself. Collaborative learning is impossible for non-autonomous learners.

Autonomy is conceptualized and displayed in Figure 2.3 as an arc that balances affiliation and agency. The optimal point is the midpoint of the arc, but you can exercise some autonomy from anywhere on the arc. As such, autonomy is a more expansive concept than the other two needs that are conceptualized as bipolar continua. Autonomy is also the most interactive of the 3As and is especially catalytic. You can give yourself affiliation and agency but not autonomy, as it is generated within a power relationship.

If the 3A needs are blocked, pupils may become driven to get their needs met in inappropriate ways. While all pupils share the same needs, they all have unique personalities, experiences and backgrounds that lead them to meet those needs in different ways. Most pupils want to do their best but, for some, their goals can become restricted, distorted or overwhelmed through a combination of personal problems, peer relationships and how they feel they are being treated within the classroom.

Pupils become defensive if their needs are threatened or blocked[24] and defensive motives lie behind such behaviour as vandalism, graffiti and knife-carrying. Defensive motives create an unhealthy motivation. Deprivations of, or conflicts between, the 3A needs underpin various clinical issues, such as eating and obsessive-compulsive disorders.[25]

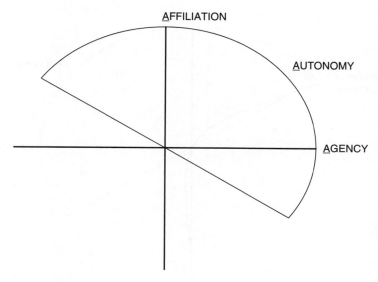

Figure 2.3   The arc of autonomy i

Low agency, with reasonable levels of affiliation, tends to restrict autonomy while low affiliation, with reasonable agency, tends to distort autonomy.

Low agency + reasonable affiliation = restricted autonomy

Low affiliation + reasonable agency = distorted autonomy

We will return to the interplay between the 3As and the pivotal role of autonomy in Chapter 3, when we look at how our resilience shapes how we meet our needs, and again in Chapter 7, when we look at how autonomy forms the circle for the matrix. For the moment we will examine how affiliation and agency can be corrupted.

Acquiescent affiliation

Meeting their need for affiliation requires pupils to make adaptations as they try to get along with others. They also need to achieve autonomy which has potential to conflict with their need for affiliation. However the need to feel both autonomy and affiliation is the basis through which the mutual solution is achieved.[26]

Good affiliation reflects a caring orientation, balanced 'give and take' relationships, and a healthy focus on others in a way that does not have negative implications for the self. Some people can develop an acquiescent form of affiliation that is unrestrained by agency and involves a focus on others to the neglect of the self.[27,28] It is displayed in Figure 2.4. It shows itself in imbalanced relationships where people masochistically give but do not take. They do not want to burden others with their problems and feel they do not

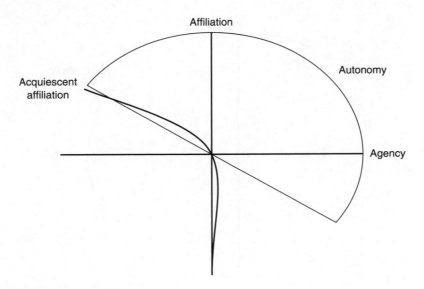

Figure 2.4   Acquiescent affiliation

deserve support. In fact they may take on others' problems as their own. They try to create a positive self-image in the eyes of others.

> Martha was a 10-year-old pupil who loved to please her teachers. She lacked confidence in her academic abilities and had a very cautious approach to school work. Consequently she preferred to spend most of her time doing simple class jobs for the teacher.

Acquiescent affiliation is also illustrated in over-conformity in, for example, territoriality and in 'group think'. Another common example is when people comply with others' values, even if it means compromising their own. In this way autonomy loses out to affiliation and such *people-pleasing* restricts growth. Parent-pleasing young people are usually highly attuned to their parents' spoken or unspoken aspirations. They can, for example, spend many years training for a particular profession only to realize they have achieved someone else's ambition.

Antagonistic agency

Agency is a healthy focus on the self. An antagonistic form of agency is a focus on the self to the exclusion of others.[27,28] It is agency that is not restrained by affiliation. It is displayed in Figure 2.5. It is reflected in an arrogant, calculating, confrontational interpersonal style that reflects difficulties experiencing and expressing emotions and an often destructive use of anger.

> Tommy was an intelligent and good-looking, but underachieving, 13-year-old pupil. He spent most of his energy in class showing off to his girlfriend and arguing with the teachers.

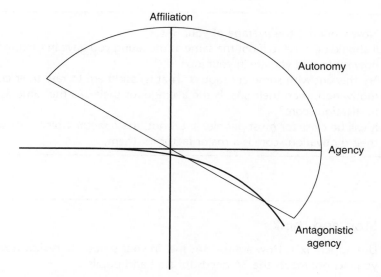

Figure 2.5   Antagonistic agency

Antagonistic agency can be seen in overambition and workaholism. We can pursue agency as a means of feeling worthwhile, but because self-worth lies in knowing that you are worthwhile regardless of the outcomes, such achievement does not satisfy but often takes on an addictive quality. It is also seen in people who are materialistic and seek high-profile signs to show their worth. This, however, does not give them the well-being they are searching for.[29,30] They tend to come from cold and controlling backgrounds that have limited their ability to develop empathy. Their materialism does little for their empathy and causes them to treat others as objects to be manipulated.[31]

> Designer labels are miniature life rafts for people whose personalities lack buoyancy. People who are obsessed with labels generally have one permanently sewn to their back: inadequate.[32]

Teachers with unrestrained agency may, for example, focus exclusively on the pedagogical side of the job and prioritize dominating the classroom at the expense of relationship-building.

Stop and think

On a scale of 1 to 10, with 10 being high, rate yourself in the context of your current job on each of the 3As:

- Affiliation
- Agency
- Autonomy

Now work out the average of your 3As.

It should be close to if not the same as the rating you gave in Chapter 1 for how motivated you are in your job.

Try this out with some colleagues. That is, ask them to rate their current motivation, then their 3As. Is the average for their 3As the same as their motivation score?

It will be close for most people. If it is not, the A factor which is closest to their motivation score is a major factor for them.

 Stop and think

Use Appendix 1, How are the 3As met in your school, to review how well your school meets the 3A needs for staff and pupils.

How the mind is organized to meet our needs

The mind is considered now to be a system of specialized modules, rather than a single entity.[33,34] Modules have been proposed that motivate people to meet each of the 3A needs.[35] They are:

1 *The relationships system (affiliation).* This is what gives us a built-in curiosity about individual differences. Our affiliation need motivates us to work out how to get along with others, and so we need to work out what to expect of them. Consequently, we are keen to size up and collect information about other people.

2 *The status system (agency).* Our agency need motivates us to tailor our behaviour to our aptitudes and to compete with our rivals. This module specializes in collecting information about the self, particularly how we compare with peers, through, for example, feedback and competition.

3 *The socialization system (autonomy).* Our autonomy need motivates us to learn the rules, adapt to the culture and group, to find out how to behave appropriately in order to be allowed to participate.

Motivating teaching will take into account the motivation provided by the modular mind and go with the grain of pupils' positive motives, and, for example:

- let pupils get to know each other as much as possible to build affiliation
- let pupils know how well they are doing in relation to peers to develop agency. (Clearly it would not be helpful to openly compare pupils, but teachers can harness this motive by providing model answers that give a benchmark of the typical pupil in the class, with which pupils can compare their performance.)
- make them feel accepted and encouraged to participate to nurture autonomy.

Stop and think

Focus on a particular class you know well.

Rate on a scale of 1 to 10 how well you meet this group's needs for affiliation, agency and autonomy. Average the 3As and this should give you a general rating on how motivating you think you are with this group.

What evidence can you think of for your ratings? Ask a colleague who knows your work well to rate you. Why not ask your pupils?

Summary of key points

- A need is something that when met appropriately promotes our well-being.
- Needs are what give goals their power and direction.
- If the needs for affiliation, agency and autonomy are met, pupils will be self-motivated.
- Most pupils want to do their best but, for some, their goals can become restricted, distorted or overwhelmed through a combination of personal problems, peer relationships and how they feel within the classroom.

Part Two

What pupils do to motivate themselves

> What a piece of work is a man. (Shakespeare) Who knows why we do the things we do. (Coleridge)?

All pupils are different. What are the key differences, open to teacher influence, that shape their *'engage-ability'*? The answer is how they feel about themselves and their *motivational resilience*, their capacity to get their needs met and cope with setbacks. This is in part shaped by what pupils do to motivate themselves, that is their internal energizers and drainers (their 'motivational baggage'). Figure II.1 presents the learning stances as the tip of an iceberg, with the internal energizers that underpin them lying unseen below the water.

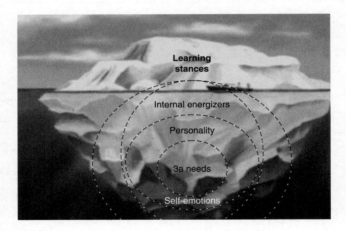

Figure II.1   The learning stances and internal energizers

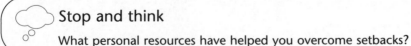

Stop and think

What personal resources have helped you overcome setbacks?

While there is much to be gained by a deeper understanding of these internal energizers, it is important to remember that motivation is not a quality of the individual learner but of the transaction between the learner and the learning climate. The 3As, affiliation, agency and autonomy, in the classroom are not so much personal qualities of learners as the fruits of teacher – pupil interactions.

Part II defines what personality is before describing how our needs shape our personality. It then outlines the key personality traits that are pointers to preferred environments. It also looks at how schools develop pupil personality. It then looks at how pupils meet their own 3A needs. This is followed by a discussion about how personality, particularly resilience, shapes how pupils meet their needs. Part II concludes with a consideration of how well our need satisfaction in turn shapes our personality and is expressed through the *self-emotions*, how we feel about ourselves.

What pupils do to motivate themselves

What is personality?

 Stop and think

What aspects of your personality do you like and dislike?

Our personality is how we adapt to different situations. It is our personal organizer that influences how we think and feel about ourselves. Pupils share the same emotions and needs. Their individuality comes from their unique personality that shapes the different ways each pupil tries to meet their needs.

Differences in pupils' personalities become apparent early in life and have pervasive influences upon and throughout their school career. From the young person's perspective, personality is their identity, who they are, shaped in terms of how they adapt to the demands of school and other aspects of their lives. From the teachers' and peers' view, personality is the young person's reputation, what kind of pupil they are, defined in terms of traits, such as helpful and calm. Reputations describe pupil behaviour and identity explains it.[1]

Personality traits and the learning stances

It is our personality traits that make us unique and consistent.[2] Individual differences in personality traits exist in degrees. Traits are stable over time and situations, and they let us predict how people are likely to behave.[3]

Personality is organized in a hierarchy, with broad traits at the highest level, for example, extraversion, and more specific traits at lower levels, for example, sociability, that are made up of particular behaviours, for example, being talkative. Pupils express their personalities in classrooms through the behaviour they exhibit in a given situation, that is, their learning stances.

Personality does not predict academic achievement very well. Personality types (how we categorize people who share similar personalities) have been found to be better at predicting achievement than personality traits (the main labels we use to describe personality). Personality type at the start of primary school predicts later behaviour problems.[4] These associations, however, are small.[5]

Achievement is more closely related to individual pupils' approaches to learning than to their personality, such as learning styles (and learning stances) that are a learned component of pupil personality.[6,7] Approaches to learning are changeable over time, which explains why they may be better predictors of achievement than personality.[8]

Research has identified five broad traits that we use to describe personality. The traits, known as the 'Big 5', are described below. Each of the traits is bidirectional, for example, agreeable–disagreeable.

1   Extraversion

Extraversion and introversion reflect how people are energized. Extraverts are energized by interacting with the world, while introverts draw from their inner world. Introverts avoid too much external stimulation because they are already stimulated enough. Extraversion is shown by being communicative, optimistic, cheerful and assertive. Extraverts are drawn to competitive sports and enterprise.[9] Extraversion is reflected in pupils' sociability and positive activity.[10] Extraverts tend to be better at doing more than one thing at a time and are more resistant to distraction on verbal tasks. They have good conversation skills because they can think up topics of conversation and speak fluently. Extraverts are also advantaged when speed is more important than accuracy. These factors make extravert pupils likely to adopt the energetically engaging stance.

The downside of extraversion includes

- impulsivity
- excitement-seeking
- recklessness
- poor tolerance of monotony and boredom
- overconfidence
- a tendency to be self-important.[11]

Extraverts find it harder to think deeply and may be better equipped to handle stimulating environments, whereas introverts cope better with monotony and boredom. Introverts perform better when attention needs to be sustained or when reflection and caution are required. Introverts are perhaps more likely to adopt the quietly engaging stance.

2   Agreeableness

Agreeableness involves being respectful, co-operative, empathic and trusting.[12] It is a key trait for getting on well at school and predicts the positive stances, particularly the harmoniously engaging stance. It is linked to being likeable. Even the biggest rogue in the class can be 'forgiven' if they are likeable. Agreeable people, however, may be less ambitious. When stressed they tend to self-sacrifice rather than try to outdo others.

A lack of agreeableness is reflected in being

- antagonistic
- dominant
- competitive
- selfish.[13,14]

It is also marked by a tough-minded, self-reliant and impatient approach. Low agreeableness will often be linked to the opposing reaction. An early childhood precursor of low agreeableness is a frequent and intense expression of negative emotions.

3   Conscientiousness

Conscientiousness refers to determined efforts to succeed, including being efficient, predictable and purposeful. It is crucial for the internalization of values and rules. It is an important contributor to long-term achievement, independent of ability.[15] It has been termed the 'will to achieve'[16] and is an asset that encourages positive learning stances.

While some elements of conscientiousness relate to achievement, others relate to dependability, that is, orderliness, conformity and high need for structure. Conscientiousness may be constraining when linked to an excessive need for order. Another downside is when highly conscientious people are short on agreeableness; they can be inflexible and unreasonably demanding.[17]

4   Emotional stability

Emotional stability is the tendency to experience positive emotions. It is reflected in a calm, assertive and optimistic approach along with a keenness to take the lead and seek autonomy. The opposite tendency to experience negative emotions leaves the individual vulnerable to stress. Pupils low in emotional stability tend to be pessimistic and unsure of themselves and so dislike decision-making and become nervous presenting themselves. Low emotional stability damages both self-belief and self-esteem[18] reflecting a lack of perceived control. It leads to passive and emotion-focused ways of coping.[19]

Anger and fear are emotional tendencies that are separable by the end of a child's first year. Fear is related to later shyness, while anger is linked to later aggression.[20] These two kinds of negative affect predict these two types of behaviour problems in the early school years. Fearful pupils turn in on themselves, common in the hiding reaction, while pupils who show irritable distress turn in on themselves but also against the world, typical of the alarming and draining reaction. The alarming and draining reaction reflects how anger and fear gradually merge later into the broad trait of emotional instability.[20]

5   Openness to experience

Being 'open to experience' is being reflective, creative, unconventional, willing to question authority and champion change. People high in openness are intrinsically motivated, idealistic and find rules constricting. They are commonly found in the harmoniously engaging stance.

Openness is linked to, but broader than, intelligence[21] and includes receptivity to one's feelings. It is similar to interpersonal intelligence.[22] Achievement is correlated with openness.[23] Openness is a mixed blessing as it can lead, through high sensitivity, to distress as well as happiness. Low openness reflects a conforming, risk-averse, cautious person who adapts to convention.

Stop and think

What are the demands that school makes on pupils' personalities?
When and how do you take pupils' personalities into account?
When can pupils' personalities become a barrier to engagement?
When can pupils' personalities become an asset to engagement?

How our needs shape our personality

> To get a big reputation in this school you need to be tough and popular. (George, 11 years old)

Pupils learn in peer groups structured in terms of status hierarchies and this creates two main drives, namely to get along, that is, to seek affiliation, and to get ahead, that is, to seek status through agency.[24] They also have to seek acceptance and be allowed to participate, that is, to seek autonomy.

Achievement may be the desired outcome for our curricula but, as articulated by George, the energizers within many peer groups (and political parties) are popularity, acceptance and toughness. Motivating teachers manage to align these energizers to their learning goals.

How our personality traits help us meet our 3A needs

Affiliation
Agreeableness is the personality trait that most significantly shapes how pupils meet their needs for affiliation. Affiliation also benefits from a high degree of emotional stability and conscientiousness, making pupils easy to get on with.

Agency
Getting ahead benefits from high levels of emotional stability, conscientiousness and openness to experience. These traits help to instil confidence, ambition and an eagerness to learn. Striving for status is also linked to extraversion, which makes pupils keen to excel and to achieve rewards.[25]

Autonomy
Autonomy, the capacity to balance our motives to get along and get ahead, is nurtured by all five traits, but in particular by emotional stability and openness.

Traits as pointers to preferred environments

 Stop and think

Does your personality make you more comfortable in particular settings?

Personality traits help us to thrive in particular kinds of environments and, as such, are pointers to our most suitable environments. Low emotional stability, for example, leaves pupils vulnerable to anxiety in evaluative settings.[26] It is especially draining to be exposed to threat to your self-worth in social settings.[27] All teachers will know anxious pupils who are distractible in stressful circumstances and who do better when the environment is reassuring.

The traits consist of helpful and unhelpful aspects. For example:

- Extraverts are more useful to have around when a rapid response is needed but introverts perform better when reflection is required.
- The sociability of extraverts helps teamwork but their impulsivity can make them over-competitive.
- Extraverts prefer competitive climates whereas introverts prefer co-operative climates.[30]
- Extraverts seek excitement and group involvement, whereas introverts prefer environments with lower stimulation and cope well with working alone.[31]
- Extraverts respond best to fast pace, novelty, rewards and competition, while introverts prefer order and set their own pace.
- Agreeable pupils are popular but they can be disadvantaged in competitive, pressured or conflict situations, because of their tendency to be deferential or dependent. Agreeableness leads to distress following conflict.[28] High agreeableness together with emotional instability creates dependency.[29] Highly agreeable pupils will therefore be better suited to co-operative than competitive group work.
- Conscientiousness is essential for achievement but can stifle enterprise and creativity.
- Low emotional stability can be problematic but it can also help keep us alert to threats.

The advantages and disadvantages of extraverts compared to introverts are summarized in Table 3.1.

How schools develop pupil personality

Many education systems see personality development as an important purpose of the curriculum. For example, the Standards in Scotland's Schools Act, 2000 states that

> The purpose of education is to encourage the development of the *personality*, talents and abilities of pupils to their fullest potential.

Table 3.1   Introverts and extraverts: who has the edge in school?

	Introverts	Extraverts
Advantages	find it easier to think are seen as more mature are quieter, more reflective are conforming are good listeners show good concentration do not need much feedback persevere are creative think independently cope well with monotony enjoy routine seek order and precision approach tasks carefully focus deeply	perform better in public are more sociable and enjoy groups are confident communicators express themselves easily enjoy action concentrate on results are enterprising are happier have more influence over others are better at dual tasks are better at verbal/symbol processing are better if speed is needed

Disadvantages	find it hard to think in groups
	struggle in groups
	are less outgoing
	are less rewarding to teach
	can become isolated
	cope badly with public
	    class tests
	are indecisive and risk
	    aversive
		are poor listeners
		are on 'transmission only'
		are high maintenance
		need a lot of attention
		can lose self in frenzied activities
		are easily bored
		enjoy socializing over learning

Stop and think

What does developing personality mean?
What aspects of personality development can a school influence?
Is there a tension between the role of education in personality development
and its role in socialization?

Paradoxically, personality has been somewhat ignored in educational thinking, probably because of the widespread assumption that it is hard-wired and
there is little we can do about it. But we need to understand the significant
role personality plays, see it in context, and support young people to adapt
and make the best of their personality. Developing personality means helping
to bring out the best in pupils. Motivation becomes more stable as people age
but it is far from fully crystallized, even by late adolescence.[32]

Young people's sense of progress influences how their personality develops.
Success or failure at one stage is likely to shape the mastery of later tasks, and
repeated failures may pave the way for later problems.[33] For example, pupils
with low achievement and high levels of antisocial behaviour experience
increasingly high levels of negative emotionality as they grow older.

Pupil personality develops through their two-way interactions with the classroom. Just as we as adults shape our jobs to suit ourselves, pupils mould their

classroom into environments that suit them.[34] Their personalities also elicit distinctive reactions, thus continually reinforcing their qualities. For example, teachers of overactive pupils may become hostile to them, while easily engaged pupils evoke more positive responses. Pupils also seek out peers who are like themselves. Friends resemble each other because we choose to mix with people like ourselves. Aggressive pupils, for example, choose to mix with other aggressive pupils.

Childhood personality has been found to predict early adult competence in coherent ways.[35] For example, conscientiousness and agreeableness predict success in adulthood. Pupils high (or low) on these traits eventually reached better (or worse) attainment than would have been predicted based solely on their childhood attainment.

However the correlations between childhood and adult personality are moderate. Continuity estimates suggest some degree of stability but much less than that found in adults, suggesting personality is only beginning to stabilize in childhood.[36] Substantial change takes place across the years. Personality is dynamic and responds to environmental changes.[37] For example, pupils with family risk factors are more likely to change from being resilient to impulsive.[38] Extreme negative emotions, caused, for example, by protracted bullying can also trigger personality change.[39]

Adaptation, and therefore personality, is never permanent. There are always new challenges, vulnerabilities and strengths emerging.[40] Personality integrates our well-being, therefore it must be open to change to allow us to profit from experience.[41,42]

The classroom provides the context in which pupils express their personality through their learning stances. Pupils should be helped to function within the best part of their personality. Personality development is a journey towards increasing autonomy.[43] As such, schools are well placed to support their pupils' personality development.

Pupils express their personalities differently as a function of the degree of support for their needs, particularly autonomy. This is because support for autonomy is all about support for being oneself.[44] The more autonomy-supportive the climate, the more pupils will express their personality and be more extraverted, agreeable, open, conscientious and emotionally stable. The more they feel controlled, the more they become closed, less caring, less outgoing and energetic, and more tense and unstable.[45]

Late adolescence offers possibly the greatest potential for transformation and the first real opportunity for individuals to take charge of their lives.[45] Sexual maturity changes pupils' identity and motivates young people to evaluate themselves. Adolescents' competence at meeting their needs creates the possibility for them to move away from their childhood relationships and choose the environments in which they will develop. This creates the opportunity for self-directed change, and the emergence of abstract thought makes self-realization a real possibility.

Stop and think

Which aspects of school life resonate with and make the most of your personality?
Which aspects of school life clash with or drain your personality?

What pupils need to meet their needs for themselves

Affiliation

Friendship

A close friend is 'another self'. (Aristotle)

Pupils' affiliation nurtures and is in turn enhanced by friendships. Play among friends also builds lasting affiliations.[1] Friendship is all about giving each other space and autonomy support, and striking a balance between individual and group goals. Pupils who are good at making friends tend to be self-confident and pro-social, and have good social skills such as self-disclosure and emotional attunement as well as good language skills. They will also have good emotional control that helps them resolve conflict. Adolescents' engagement in learning is particularly swayed by the engagement of their friends. A hallmark of adolescent friendship is its emphasis on intimacy that helps teenagers understand themselves.

Secure attachment

The foundation of the capacity to fit in is a *secure attachment* with a parent or carer that nurtures *social competence*. Social competence has its roots in responsive parenting that builds secure attachments. Pupils internalize their early care experiences, which then influence how they relate to others.[2]

Attachment theory tries to explain how personality develops within early relationships and how the quality of these relationships affects pupils' development.[3] Attachment behaviour is any behaviour that looks for comfort and is triggered by distress. Distinct attachment patterns develop in response to different parenting styles. Attachment is all about protection from threat or danger.[4] Patterns of attachment, for example, crying and clinging, are infants' ways of getting carers to protect them. Four attachment patterns have been identified[5,6] and are displayed in Figure 4.1, and provide another section of the internal energizers layer of the matrix.

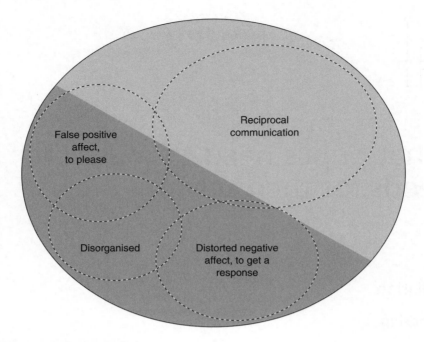

Figure 4.1   Attachment patterns

False positive
The primary carers are predictable but not attuned to their infants and are slow to respond. They think their children need to learn to control themselves. Parental approval is conditional on the suppression of any anger and on the expression of self-reliance. The children learn to please rather than to express themselves. They change any negative affect into *false positive affect*[7] and become emotionally inhibited and rule-bound. This leads to self-containment and wariness about getting involved with others. This pattern is a prototype of the hiding reaction.

Distorted negative
Carers respond to their babies' crying, but unpredictably. This maintains displays of irritable distress for long periods. The parent's behaviour bears no connection to the child's behaviour. The child cannot therefore establish any connection between what he or she does and their mother's response, other than that attention-seeking behaviour seems to get a reaction eventually. They learn to manipulate their parents by exaggerating their own feelings. This pattern is a prototype of the opposing and exasperating reaction.

Reciprocal
A third pattern is based on a consistently responsive communication of expectations and feelings. Relationships between the child and parent have emotional reciprocity that creates a sense of trust. Pupils are given words that

accurately describe their feelings – even when these are negative and express frustration with their parents. This pattern is a prototype of the positive learning stances.

Disorganized

Here carers are frightening, leaving their children increasingly confused. The parent's unpredictable behaviour makes the children afraid of or for them. They are overwhelmed by turbulent emotions. The children are faced with an irresolvable paradox. Those who continue to rely on unreliable parents do themselves some damage. This pattern is the precursor for the alarming and draining reaction.

Emotional intelligence

As just discussed, pupils' early attachments come to form the prototype for later relationships (and learning stances).[8] In particular, these early experiences impact on pupils' social competence. The key skills for group learning are social skills that help pupils get along with their peers. It is social competence that largely determines pupils' affiliations. Social skills are the behaviours that let pupils achieve social goals. Social competence is the effective use of these skills.[9] In contrast, submissiveness leads to sacrificing your needs and aggressiveness leads to trying to get your own way.

Emotional intelligence is the modern way of thinking about social competence. It was defined for the first time in 1989.[10] Traditional measures of intelligence were thought to have failed to tap differences in the ability to manage emotions. What made the biggest difference in life were abilities such as being able to handle frustration, control emotions and get along with other people, or the ability to resist temptation.[11]

Some evidence has been found for the influence of emotional intelligence on achievement.[12] Among low-ability pupils, those with higher emotional intelligence have been found to do much better at school than those with low emotional intelligence.[13] Emotional intelligence seems to come into play when the demands of a situation outweigh a pupil's intellectual resources.

Positive interpersonal emotions

Interpersonal emotions play a crucial role within peer relationships.[14] The key emotion is *empathy*, the ability to understand how another person is feeling. *Sympathy* is feeling concerned about the other person. A third possible response to someone else's plight is *personal distress*, when you focus on how you are feeling about the other person. Pupils need to be able to cope with their own emotional reactions before they can deal with other peoples' emotions.

There are two parts to empathy. First, there is a cognitive element, namely, a *theory of mind*.[15] Pupils' early peer acceptance is linked to their understanding of the mind.[16] Theory of mind is the ability to take another's perspective and predict what they are going to do.[17]

A particular skill that tells us pupils have a good theory of mind is the ability to instil a false belief into another person's mind by telling them something,[18] for example, to pretend not to be interested in something in case your sibling then

wants it, or to pretend that sweets taste disgusting to put the other person off. This kind of deception needs theory-of-mind abilities. Young pupils cannot do this because they are unable to separate what they know from what another person knows. This skill is a landmark development, occurring around 4 years of age.[19] The brain circuits that underlie such perspective-taking skills continue to undergo a lot of development beyond early childhood and into early adolescence.[20]

Second, there is an affective part to empathy. To empathize, you need some degree of affiliation, to be able to realize the other person has feelings that affect your feelings. In an ambiguous situation, for example, when one child bumps into another and it is not clear if it was deliberate or accidental, pupils have to decide how to react. Some pupils are more likely to assume benign intentions and choose constructive solutions rather than aggressive reactions. The stances taken in these situations are critical in determining social relationships and are shaped by pupils' *capacity for perspective-taking*.

Beyond the interpersonal emotions of empathy, sympathy or personal distress, there is also aggression and anxiety. Aggression happens when there is a lack of empathy.[21] Aggressive people focus on how they feel. Both anxiety and aggression result from misjudgements about what is happening. Anxiety is triggered by appraisals of personal threat. Aggression is linked to appraisals of hostile intent in other people.[22] Misjudging another person's intentions is an example of faulty empathizing.[23]

Agency

Two main aspects of pupils' ways of thinking underpin agency, namely their ideas about ability and their explanations of progress. Fortunately, teachers can influence both.

Ideas about ability

Pupils tend to think about ability in one of two ways.[24] Some hold an *entity* theory and see intelligence as fixed, as something they only have so much of and about which there is nothing they can do to increase it, just as we think of the speed of a car being set by its engine capacity. Those who have an *incremental* view, on the other hand, think their ability could be increased through effort, they see intelligence as the sum of what one has learned. Entity pupils tend to see learning as measuring their intelligence while incremental pupils may see the same task as only measuring their current ability at the particular task.

Pupils' theories about how we become intelligent have developed by around 10 to 12 years of age and create a belief system that influences their motivational resilience. Fixed ideas about ability tend to lead to a lack of persistence in the face of setbacks. Fortunately most pupils hold either incremental or mixed ideas. They also hold different beliefs about their ability in different domains.[25]

These relations also apply in the social world.[26] Those who hold an entity theory of personality are more concerned about judgements in social situations than those who hold an incremental view. A fixed notion of personality leads to pessimistic interpretations of any social difficulties and cause a lack of persistence in social interactions.

Very young pupils are more concerned about ideas of goodness and badness than intelligence.[27] This is perhaps because pupils' early socialization focuses on their behaviour and goodness. Some develop, around 5 years of age, a view of goodness and badness as a stable or malleable quality. Praise for goodness, just as for intelligence, can encourage a fixed view that encourages negative ideas about the self when the child does something wrong.

> If a child is told often enough he is bad, he will end up being bad. (Parent of a 5-year-old child)

Pupils who blame failure on their low ability tend to give up in order to avoid further setbacks. Pupils with a fixed view of intelligence are especially sensitive to failure and have a tendency to react defensively, for example, by escaping from the situation or minimizing effort.

Pupils can be taught to understand that their brain is a muscle that gets stronger the more it is used, that learning makes new brain connections and that they are agents of their own brain development.[28]

 Stop and think

Do you believe you are hopeless at certain things and assume you will never improve, for example at spelling, mathematics, singing, dancing, drawing or baking?
Where did these ideas come from?
What is the evidence?
Are you giving out the right messages about your pupils' abilities?

Making sense of progress

Another factor underpinning pupils' agency that schools can influence is how pupils explain their progress to themselves. An attribution is an inference we make about the causes of our behaviour. Such beliefs about the causes of success and failure are the building blocks of achievement[29,30] and influence the individual's sense of agency.[31]

Pupils are more likely to think about the reasons for outcomes when they are in a new or important learning situation or when the outcome is unexpected. They are also more likely to contemplate the causes of failure than of success.

The motivational impact of attributions comes from how we make sense of them. An attribution can be perceived as *personal*, that is, 'it's down to me' or *external*, that is, the environmental conditions. Putting a success down to a personal cause builds self-belief. A cause can also be *permanent* or *unstable* over time. The breadth of attributions can range from *pervasive* to *specific*. Some pupils believe that the cause of any failure undermines their confidence about everything, while others manage to limit this to a narrow skill area. Each of these dimensions affects how much control pupils feel they have over their learning.

Stop and think

Are you an optimist or a pessimist?

Think of a recent success. What would you put it down to? Circle the dimensions of your explanations in the grid below, as appropriate.

Think of a recent failure. What would you put it down to? Circle the dimensions of your explanations in the grid below as appropriate.

Success	Failure
Personal/External	Personal/External
Pervasive/Specific	Pervasive/Specific
Permanent/Unstable	Permanent/Unstable

Pessimism tends to lead pupils to explain failure in terms of the three 'P' dimensions – personal, pervasive and permanent causes – and put down success to external, unstable and specific causes. Feeling in control, in contrast, is an outcome of explaining success in terms of the three 'P' dimensions. Personal, pervasive and permanent explanations are typically controllable. Feeling in control is a key factor in building agency.[32] Permanence is the most important dimension in terms of shaping motivational resilience.[33]

The attribution pattern of success-orientated pupils creates a positive self-energizing spiral. Success gives confidence in one's ability while failure signals the need to try harder. Thus failure can motivate already successful pupils. Failure-avoiding pupils tend to blame themselves for failure but take little credit for success. They are demoralized by a self-draining spiral of failure because they feel unable to do anything about it. Girls generally are more likely to express negative, failure-prone attributions than boys.[34]

Pride is an emotional response to success, most strongly evoked by public praise, and adds another component of motivation beyond those stemming from appraisals of ability. Pride that results from a specific achievement or good deed and comes from attributions that are personal, unstable but controllable causes (*I won because I practised*) is particularly helpful to drive perseverance in long-term goals.[35]

This authentic pride is distinct from self-aggrandizing pride which is associated with narcissism. Such pride in the global self results from attributions to personal, stable, uncontrollable causes (*I won because I'm great*). Such pride is the flip side of shame and both tend to be elicited by personal, permanent and uncontrollable attributions, whereas guilt and authentic pride tend to be elicited by personal, unstable but controllable attributions.

An individual feels guilty when they put down failure to controllable factors that break their own standards. The emotional impact of such guilt is usually limited to the specific behaviour. Shame, in contrast, is more likely to be experienced when failure is seen as due to uncontrollable factors. Pupils who are shame-prone tend to blame themselves. Shame extends beyond the specific behaviour to reflect badly on the entire self. Shame-prone people try to fix themselves rather than the problem, as they blame their whole character. Consequently, this overgeneralization to the whole self makes them particularly vulnerable to the full draining force of failure.[36] They internalize the causes of any failure and do not take advantage of any extenuating circumstances. Shame and perceived low rank make pupils vulnerable to rumination and submissive behaviour[37] that funnels pupils into the hiding or alarming and draining reactions.

 Stop and think

Can this impact of shame give us some insight into the barriers to learning faced by pupils who are looked after and accommodated or have significant medical conditions?

Looked after and accomodated (Laac) pupils want to be treated as the same as everyone else. Can this be achieved within strategies that aim to highlight these pupils and expect all teachers to know who all the Laac pupils are?

In thinking about their progress, *entity* pupils focus on their fixed ability and explain failure in terms of lack of ability. In contrast, *incremental* pupils are more likely to think in terms of effort. When faced with failure they will look for ways to improve through more effort or remedial action. If pupils have faith in their own efforts they develop motivational resilience.[38]

Failure is more ambiguous than success. Success needs everything going well, failure just needs one thing to go wrong and it is hard to say what has happened. Explanations for failure are almost automatic and happen just on the edge of awareness.

Pupils' ways of explaining progress stabilize into a particular pattern by about age 9,[39] by which time they may have got themselves into explanatory ruts.[40] It would be helpful, therefore, to teach pupils to identify their attributions, help them see their consequences and encourage them to think of alternative ways of explaining progress.[41] Once established, the helpless pattern is difficult to break as it leads to a tendency to over-assimilate feedback into a pervasive hopelessness.

Stop and think

How might your formative assessment approaches impact on your pupils' explanations of progress?

Autonomy

Pupils have attitudes towards achievement that influence how they approach learning[42,43] and these attitudes are a reflection of their autonomy. They may, for example, see classroom activities as tests of their ability or as opportunities for learning. These attitudes reflect the two main competence motives: the need to achieve and the need to avoid failure. Achievement behaviour is in turn directed at either developing or demonstrating ability.

Mastery and competitive attitudes

Some pupils adopt a *mastery* or self-improvement attitude and define success in relation to their own progress. They cope well with failure which they see as a necessary part of learning. In contrast a *competitive* attitude focuses on how ability will be judged. The main goal for such pupils is to show they are smarter than others, and so they usually define success in relation to the progress of others. For them failure suggests low ability.

Mastery builds motivational resilience. The competitive goal is to look smart while the mastery goal is to get smarter. Mastery pupils are motivated to achieve *their* best while competitive pupils are motivated to be *the* best. Mastery is in most ways preferable and leads to positive learning stances. The competitive goal leads to pupils trying to prove their worth. The mastery goal is growth-seeking. Competitive pupils feel 'up' when succeeding but 'down' when they fail.[44]

Stop and think

Is there a competitive or mastery culture in your school, or in education as a whole?

You've been doing well in the acting post you have been filling for over a year now, but unfortunately you just didn't perform and sparkle in the interview. (Feedback given to an unsuccessful candidate)

The mastery and competitive mindsets are independent and so it is possible to be high or low in both or to have various high–low combinations. Both goals are necessary and so a mixture might enhance motivation.[45] Mastery goals promote engagement and keep competitive pupils focused on their work. Competitive goals stop mastery pupils from getting lost in their work. However, focusing on proving one's ability can force out learning goals.

Self-protection and learned helplessness

Disengaged pupils may be highly motivated to avoid failure rather than to succeed.[46] One of the main internal energizers underpinning achievement is emotional anticipation. Success-seeking pupils anticipate pride in their accomplishments. On the other hand, pupils with a fear of failure dread further failure. Fear of failure is probably the most common internal drainer of motivation to learn.

Failure-avoiding pupils do not try, as trying and still failing drains further their *self-emotions*. (These are explained in more detail in the next chapter.) Avoiding additional damage to their self-emotions is more important than receiving praise for trying.

Pupils with a fear of failure may develop a *learned helplessness* that reflects a loss of hope when no matter how hard one tries, failure is inevitable.[47] Learned helplessness in the form of lethargy develops not only when events are uncontrollable but also when praise is given regardless of whether the child has actually done well. In this way even well-intentioned unconditionality can undermine mastery. Love can be given unconditionally but praise must fit the effort and success.[48]

> I remember the teacher praising us for sitting in our seats. After that I thought – what's the point in doing anything. (Alison, aged 11)

When poor performance is likely to reflect badly on pupils' ability, some look for circumstances to let them 'off the hook' and put failure down to something other than their ability.[49] Such *self-worth protection* dominates pupils when they anticipate poor performance that they think will be put down to their ability. Much opposing behaviour, for example, is an alternative way of bolstering the self-emotions, seeking status from being the most disruptive pupil in the class, when being the 'cleverest' is not an option.

The four attitudes to achievement are shown in Figure 4.2, providing another section of the internal energizers layer of the matrix.

Friendship, status and acceptance

Friendship, status and acceptance, as displayed in Figure 4.3, all interact and impact independently to shape how each of the 3A needs are met. An individual can be accepted by the group but be poor at making friendships. Acceptance and friendships make independent contributions to well-being.[50] Similarly, gaining acceptance and high status are not the same thing.[51]

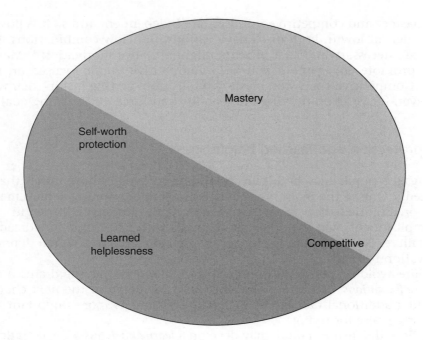

Figure 4.2   Attitudes to achievement

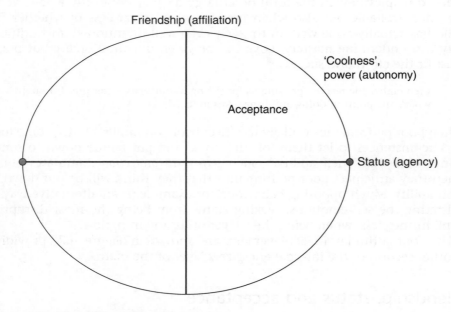

Figure 4.3   Friendship, status and acceptance

As we saw in Chapter 2, the need to be popular can push some pupils to acquiescent affiliation, while the desire to look tough can push them in the opposite direction, towards antagonistic agency. What young people might refer to as *'coolness'* is the prize for resolving this dilemma.

5

How resilience shapes how pupils meet their needs

Motivation to learn is all about what makes pupils tick and that comes down to how well their needs are met. This section explores the way our personality shapes how we meet our 3A needs. In particular, the resilience model of personality type will be used to create an arc of resilience that will form the background for the matrix.

While pupils are all different, they share the same range of emotions and needs. Their motives are the paths they take to meet their needs. It is their unique personality that interprets their needs and shapes how they try to meet them, and so makes them different. Our personality shapes how we think, feel and adapt to our environment.[1] In particular it influences how we think and feel about ourselves. Our need satisfaction in turn shapes our personality.

The arc of resilience

Personality has been characterized in terms of the two interacting processes of resilience and reactivity.[2] Reactivity is our tendency to either contain or express our impulses and feelings. It is shown by the speed and intensity of our reaction to stress. Resilience is how well we can control our reactivity to stress, in particular, how well we bounce back from adversity. Reactivity is an arc of flexible self-control. It has a curved effect in that optimal levels of resilience are achieved at moderate levels of reactivity, with lower levels of resilience at either end of the reactivity arc. As you move around this arc, reactivity becomes increasingly discrete with a tendency towards either of two opposite forms, namely, caution or impulsivity.

The combination of reactivity and resilience leads to three personality types, as shown in Figure 5.1, namely, those who are

- *resilient and have flexible self-control* including the ability to stay focused, shift attention and persist on tasks[3]
- *low in resiliency and impulsive,* under-controlled
- *low in resiliency and cautious,* over-controlled.

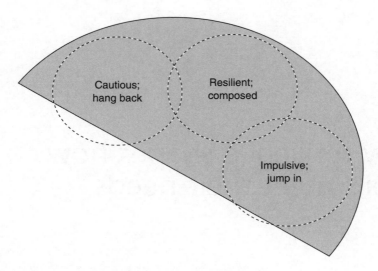

Figure 5.1   The arc of resilience and personality types

Stop and think

Do you have a predominant type or a balance in your classroom?

Resilience in combination with reactivity predicts how we adapt. Any discrepancy between resilience and reactivity has been pinpointed as the core of any adjustment problems.[4] Pupils who are the hardest to engage will have the least resilience and the highest reactivity. They lack the spontaneity to deal with new situations and struggle to manage their emotions. They have particular difficulties maintaining attention, which is a key tool in handling your emotions.[5]

The three personality types

1 Resilient pupils tend to be conscientious, high in emotional stability and open to experience.
2 Impulsive, under-controlled pupils tend to be disagreeable extraverts who lack conscientiousness and emotional stability.[6] This antagonistic orientation towards the world pushes them towards the opposing reaction. Impulsive pupils have been found to have lower achievement than both resilient and cautious pupils, and in fact to show a drop in achievement as they get older.[7,8,9] It is under-control that gets pupils into trouble and their resilience that will decide whether they work through it.[10]

Stop and think

Why do some opposing pupils seem to manage to maintain high esteem?

Pupils with this personality type maintain reasonable self-esteem, even when faced with peer rejection.[11] This is perhaps because of their antagonistic side. Or it may be down to a lack of awareness or just a front they put up. It is possibly also because they confuse their high status with popularity.

Stop and think

Why do hiding pupils fall behind in attainment?

3 Cautious, over-controlled pupils show low levels of emotional stability and extraversion.[12] They tend to be conscientious and agreeable introverts. They start school with relatively good attainment but later fall behind, perhaps because they do not push themselves.[13] They are likely to have restricted classroom interactions and withdraw if there is any risk of failure.[14] Or they may have lower competence that was masked earlier by their compliance. It is an advantage to be compliant at the early stage of schooling but this may reduce as pupils get older.

A fourth personality type is formed by a combination of the two low-resiliency types. Very low resiliency is associated with both internalizing and externalizing problems. Internalizing problems occur when pupils beat themselves up mentally by, for example, blaming themselves for any difficulty. Externalizing problems happen when pupils blame others or act out against objects or other people.

Anger and fear are separable in early infancy then gradually merge later into the broad trait of low emotional stability.[15] The highest levels of difficulty have been found in brittle over- and under-controlled young people.[16]

Stop and think

Do you know pupils who fit these descriptions?

The arc in Figure 5.1, incorporating the three personality types, will be used to form the background to the learner needs matrix. There is nothing problematic about being cautious or impulsive and each has its advantages. This arc therefore represents normal personality. Think about the new classes you meet for the first time. Some pupils settle quickly and impress you with their composure. Others hang back and watch what is happening, while some dive into the action without much thought. Problems only arise when pupils become too cautious or too impulsive, that is when they move into the dark side of personality. An inverted arc is now added to represent this shadow side of personality, as displayed in Figure 5.2.

As one moves around the arc, away from *optimal resilience*, the individual becomes either more cautious or impulsive. The *impulsive/cautious dichotomy* becomes increasingly discrete as people become rigid or chaotic until the two strands merge again at the lowest levels of resilience at the bottom of the shadow arc. As indicated by the two sets of numbers descending from 10 at resilient, to 0 at low resilience, people can slide down, at any time, one of two paths towards low resilience, namely, the impulsive or cautious path. Whichever path they take, the length of that path will have a significant effect on their defensive reactions.

The learner needs matrix

The 3A needs can now be considered within the arc of resilience and its shadow. Two of the needs, affiliation and agency, are shown as axes at right angles to each other, as displayed in Figure 5.3.

The arc of autonomy

The opposite of autonomy and the question marks in the matrix will be explained by the multipolar nature of autonomy. The personality types give us some clues, hinting that the opposite of autonomy will include:

- being cautious or rigid
- being impulsive or chaotic
- having low resilience.

In the same way as resilience, autonomy will be conceptualized as an arc with a shadow side, as displayed in Figure 5.4.

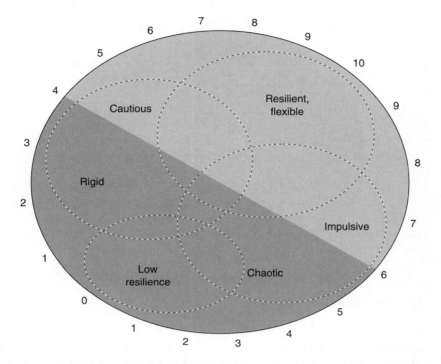

Figure 5.2   The arc of resilience and its shadow

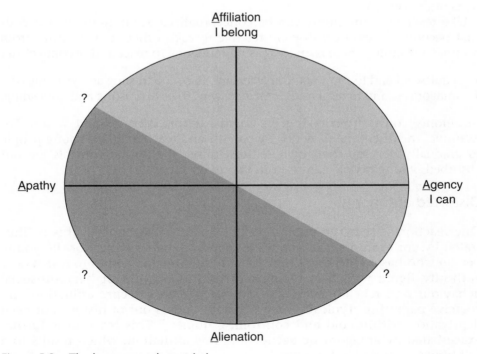

Figure 5.3   The learner needs matrix iv

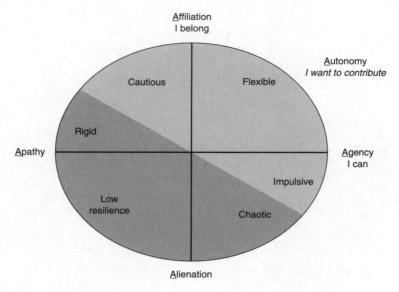

Figure 5.4   The learner needs matrix v

Engage-ability is a function of the mutual interaction between resilience and autonomy. Resilience is the realization that we are not powerless, that we have autonomy. Motivational resilience is the capacity that enables us to exercise the autonomy we are given in any situation, on the elements of any problems under our control.

Like resilience, autonomy can be conceptualized as an arc with two ends that become increasingly discrete relative to each other. As you move from optimal autonomy there is an increasing tendency to react and become either

- acquiescent and to show *restricted autonomy*, to be too trusting and yielding, or
- antagonistic and to display *distorted autonomy*, to be distrusting and unyielding.

Autonomy comes from taking on board external controls and values. For example, the discipline provided by parents and teachers helps young people to gradually develop their own self-discipline. If external controls are not absorbed, young people can react in two main ways.

Distorted autonomy

One reaction is that the pupil develops distorted autonomy. This is illustrated by, for example, the impulsive rebelling that is typical of the young person who has had to bring himself or herself up and comes to resent any authority figure who tries to impose controls on him or her. Antisocial behaviour and rebelliousness are associated with insecure affiliation and coercive parenting. Typically such behaviour arises out of histories of need deprivation within cold and controlling homes.[17] This reaction is further exacerbated by antagonistic agency and low affiliation, which results in a full-blown distorted autonomy.

Assertiveness is an element of autonomy in contrast to defiance that is self-empowerment through negativity for its own sake. Rebelliousness is wanting to do something contrary to that required by an external authority.[18] It needs the external authority. Similarly, dominance can grab control but it is not autonomy, it is actually a need substitute. 'I am happy to be here as long as I get my own way.'

Restricted autonomy

The second reaction that can happen is restricted autonomy. This is typical of the young person who has learned to please adults or to pay lip-service to keep teachers off his or her back. Such a reaction is further exacerbated by limited agency and acquiescent affiliation that leads to a full-blown restricted autonomy: 'I am happy to be here – as long as teachers don't make many demands on me, let me keep colouring in, or just leave me alone.'

The crushed autonomy reaction

This split becomes increasingly discrete until the lowest level of autonomy when the two strands merge to form a third low autonomy reaction at the bottom of the shadow of the arc of autonomy, namely, crushed or over-whelmed autonomy that reflects anxiety. It combines aspects of restricted and distorted autonomy. Pupils, for example, suffering bereavement or abuse may react in this overwhelmed way, where they feel abandoned and think they are losing control: 'Beam me out of here.'

These three *low-autonomy* reactions are displayed in Figure 5.5.

Stop and think

Consider your own motivation. Place yourself on the matrix, when your own motivation has been at its highest and lowest. Does this help you work out what was happening in these situations?

This learner needs matrix will provide the template for the layers of the matrix and will describe both how teachers motivate pupils, that is, the teaching styles, and how pupils engage, that is, the learning stances.

Implications for values

We rightly spend a lot of time considering values. We do not, however, think enough about how we share those values with pupils. Pupils can:

- passively comply with the school's values, perhaps being dutiful, paying lip-service or just going along with things for a quiet life
- take on board and embody the school's values, or
- reject the school's values.

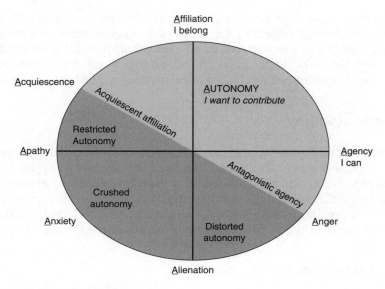

Figure 5.5   The learner needs matrix vi

By considering the dynamics between autonomy and affiliation, we can see how values can be internalized passively through a sense of guilt, adopted positively or rejected, as displayed in the grid below.

Affiliation	Autonomy	Values
Identification	Supported	Adopted positively
Acquiescence	Restricted	Passively complied with
Alienation	Distorted	Rejected

The elements of full autonomy

If we think about the three forms of low autonomy described above as

- wanting our own way (distorted autonomy)
- hiding out (restricted autonomy)
- giving up and tuning out (crushed autonomy)

and consider, in turn, the opposite of each of these, we can identify the three ingredients that are necessary for full autonomy, namely:

- giving and taking
- expressing and asserting self
- wanting to contribute.

These three bipolar components of autonomy are displayed in Figure 5.6.

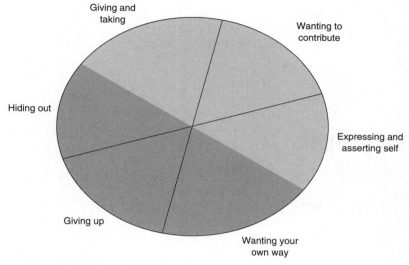

Figure 5.6   The elements of full autonomy

The energy for learning matrix

We can now integrate this subdivision of the dark and light sides of autonomy within the energy for learning matrix formed by autonomy and the other needs of affiliation (getting along) and agency (getting ahead). This matrix now consists of five bipolar dimensions and is displayed in Figure 5.7. It provides a useful format for reflecting on and evaluating the key factors underpinning a pupil's engage-ability.

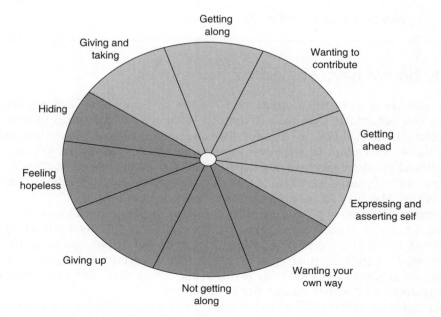

Figure 5.7   The energy for learning matrix

How pupils feel about themselves: their emotions as their personal guide

This chapter explores the important role emotions play in motivation to learn. It contrasts energizing and draining emotions. How well our needs are met is expressed through the *self-emotions*, how we feel about ourselves. The different types of self-emotions are profiled. Finally, we discuss how the different elements of the self-emotions work together.

 Stop and think

Why do we have emotions?

Why do we have emotions?

The main function of our emotions is to tell us how we are coping and to guide our behaviour. Our goals determine what we pay attention to and our emotions help us check on our progress towards these goals. This information motivates us to adapt to whatever context we find ourselves in.[1] We use our emotional radar to appraise our experiences and adjust our behaviour to try to maintain optimal conditions.[2] Worry, for example, motivates us to do something about what we are worried about.

Some pupils have a positive emotional radar, others have a more negative beam. Emotions have a rapid response system. Each appraisal makes pupils inclined towards a certain learning stance or defensive reaction. In the same way, emotions push teachers towards a certain teaching style or defensive reaction. As such, our feelings about ourselves are never neutral. Emotions can be either energizing or draining.

Emotions are always linked to what we are doing, unlike our moods which can seem to be free-floating. Any event in which we have self-interest will generate emotions, and the more self-interest the more intense the emotions. Consequently, classrooms can generate a great deal of emotional heat.

Emotions and thoughts work together to determine pupils' learning stances. As such, emotions are central to classroom behaviour. In fact neuro-psychologists now believe that feelings are the real sources of our actions.[3] Emotions organize learning, and learning in turn helps to control emotions.

 ## Stop and think

What is the difference between emotions and moods?
What are the emotions you typically see in your classroom?

When asked where motivation comes from, Peter, a Primary 7 pupil, got it right when he answered: 'Your feelings affect your motivation, they give you the energy to do things.'

Traditionally, emotions have been considered an individual phenome-non. However, when people identify with a group, the group becomes part of the self and group emotions can be triggered by group events.[4] People can experience strong group emotions in response to events that affect other group members, for example, anger in response to victimization of other group members. Group-level emotions contribute to shaping atti-tudes and behaviour, within and between groups. Teachers will know from experience that group anger, for example, is a powerful motivator of whole-class tendencies.

Draining emotions

 ## Stop and think

What do anger, fear and sadness motivate us to do?

Draining emotions are the warning lights that signal we are in difficulty. Fear, sadness and anger are our first line of defence against threats of danger, loss, injustice and trespass. The frustration of our 3A needs generates powerful negative emotions. Tightly controlling teaching, for example, might not seem harmful but pupils' perceptions of this teaching style arouse strong negative emotions.[5] They trigger a fight, flight or freeze response.

In a dangerous situation such tunnel vision allows us to focus on the threat and triggers decisive action. However, negative emotions also narrow our focus on the problem, stop us seeing the bigger picture and generate more negative emotions.[6] Expressing anger leads to more anger, hate and bitterness that amplify the negative impact of bad experiences. These negative emotions underpin the defensive reactions, in that:

- when angry, pupils invariably dwell on getting revenge (the opposing reaction)
- when anxious they focus on escaping (the hiding reaction)
- when sad they ruminate on what has been lost (the alarming and draining reaction).

Fatigue can have a similar draining effect to negative emotions. Fatigue, together with such draining emotions can have a devastating impact. Each of the above aspects of draining emotions contributes to some of our major social problems, such as knife crime.

Energizing emotions

In contrast, energizing emotions guide us to win-win situations in a way that broadens and builds a positive response.[7] For example,

- kindness generates loss of self-consciousness
- forgiveness reduces the negative hold of bad events
- gratitude amplifies our appreciation of good events.

Such positive emotions broaden our focus beyond specific action and create more flexible thinking.[8] They help us to keep things in perspective and nurture positive learning stances.

Positive emotions are not just reflections of well-being, they also help to produce it. They undo negative feelings and trigger spirals towards well-being. For every negative emotion we feel we need at least three positive emotions to flourish. A ratio of two positive to one negative emotion and below and we start to languish.[9]

Getting rid of draining emotions

For survival it makes sense for our brains to prioritize negative information. But we have to learn to keep our negative emotions in check and amplify any positive feelings we have. We can do this by, for example, learning to direct our attention to activities which provide 'flow', that is, activities that give positive feedback and strengthen our sense of purpose.[10]

The best way to get rid of negative emotions is through experiences that create positive emotions.[11] For example, feelings of rejection brought about by bullying can be ameliorated by spending more time with friends and having fun together. Positive emotions can be nurtured indirectly by:

- finding meaning within current circumstances
- finding benefits within adversity
- problem-solving effectively.

Elation creates the urge to be creative and push ourselves to the limits of our skills. Interest is triggered in contexts appraised as safe and offering novelty and a sense of challenge or mystery.[12] Interest creates the urge to explore new ideas and foster complexity, the ability to integrate complex relationships among concepts.[13] It has been argued that youth may have evolved to give complex organisms time to play and build resources during safe moments.[14]

The extent to which pupils generate energizing emotions can be enhanced. Programmes based on cognitive approaches to reducing depression and anxiety, for example, have been shown to produce 'learned optimism'.[15] Pupils' capacity to deal with draining emotions, caused, for example, by bereavement, can also be developed through support programmes such as Seasons for Growth.

The self-emotions: our personal compass

Self-development

> The self, Psychology's 'most puzzling puzzle'. (William James, 1930)

The self is thought to have evolved to prioritize all the demands made on our consciousness.[16] It represents the core of the person and brings coherence to experiences and directs people towards the discovery of their potential.[17] It looks, in particular, for areas where positive self-identity is possible and opts out of activities where it is not. It also compares itself to others in ways that reflect well on itself. The self is a social concept that develops through our relationships with others. A pupil's academic self-concept, for example, has been found to be more influenced by parents' perceptions of their abilities than by their actual grades.[18]

Very young pupils' thinking about themselves is based on concrete descriptive characteristics.[19] They tend to inflate their self-concept because they cannot yet accurately use social comparisons to self-evaluate and their parents usually give unrelentingly positive feedback. As a result young pupils' statements about themselves tend to focus on concrete characteristics that are often unrealistically positive.[20]

In early to middle childhood, the self-concept becomes better informed, although still characterized by unrealistic positivity and all-or-nothing thinking. At this stage, pupils focus on how they are performing now compared to when they were younger.[21]

By middle childhood, social comparison starts to rule out the fantasy-based ideas. Most pupils have by this stage adopted our preoccupation with who is the 'best' and can accurately rank every member of their class.[22] Around this age pupils develop specific evaluations of their competence in addition to a more global self-concept.

During middle to late childhood, trait labels that focus on abilities and interpersonal characteristics begin to appear and social comparisons are used. As a result more accurate evaluations emerge. At this age, pupils also begin to adopt the opinions and standards of others.[23]

Adolescents start to use trait labels to describe their personality characteristics[24] and they continue to develop their ideas about their scholastic abilities.[25]

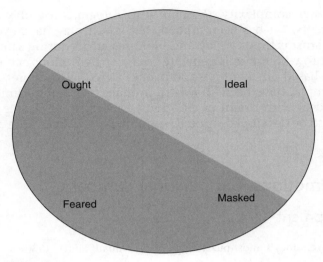

Figure 6.1   Possible selves

Our possible selves

The self-concept includes ideas about not only who we are but also who we might be, our future selves,[26] as displayed in Figure 6.1. These include:

- our 'ideal' self
- our 'ought' self
- our 'feared' self
- our 'masked' self.[27]

Any discrepancy between our actual and 'ideal' self triggers an approach towards our ideal goal.[28] If this is achieved we feel elated; if it is dashed we experience our 'feared' self and feel dejected.[29]

The 'ought' self reflects a sense of duty and is linked to acquiescent affiliation. Any mismatch between our actual and 'ought' self triggers a move away from the disapproved quality and towards the approved quality.[30] There are some things you just have to do, like forward planning! The main motives are to prevent the disapproval of others and escape from the 'unwanted self'. When this goal is achieved we feel relieved, for example, when we have produced the forward plan! If our 'ought' goal is not met we feel agitated.

When our affiliation is low, we often put on a 'masked' self to protect our self. While our masked self is maintained we can remain contained but as soon as it is threatened we feel anger, or antagonistic agency.

Some people lean more to the avoidance reaction and others to the approach stance, and these tendencies can lead to differences in well-being.[31] People who spend their lives avoiding things lead difficult lives as they have to prevent all the potential pitfalls that might occur.[32]

How our need satisfaction is expressed through the self-emotions

The concept of the self-emotions aims to replace the general feelings of well-being communicated by the popular but somewhat vague conception of self-esteem. The concept of the self-emotions is similar to the idea of global self-worth. More precisely, however, it identifies three elements that independently and collectively both reflect and impact on how we meet our 3A needs. These elements are:

- self-esteem that emerges through a sense of affiliation
- self-belief that comes from a sense of agency
- self-determination that is built on a positive exercising of autonomy.

Affiliation and self-esteem

Self-esteem has become the layperson's label for how people feel about themselves in general. Self-esteem has recently, however, been described more specifically as a gauge that monitors our affiliation levels. It tells us when our popularity is low to motivate us to do something about it.[33] Self-esteem drops in the face of public devaluation, such as bullying and teasing,[34] and is strengthened by peer acceptance.[35]

Agency and self-belief

If we see ourselves as competent in areas where we are keen to do well, the subsequent feelings of competence will nurture self-belief. The resulting sense of agency is closely tied to our status. And how we see our status within any group determines how we present ourselves. Those with high agency and status adopt risky self-enhancing strategies, where they call attention to their strengths. Those with low agency and status adopt a more restricted strategy where they deflect attention from themselves.

Autonomy and self-determination

Autonomy is the capacity for self-determination and the desire to contribute. It is linked to pupils' motivational resilience, that is, the realization that they are not powerless.

Types of self-emotions

Four different types of self-emotions are distinguished in this section and displayed in Figure 6.2, as another layer of the internal energizers matrix.

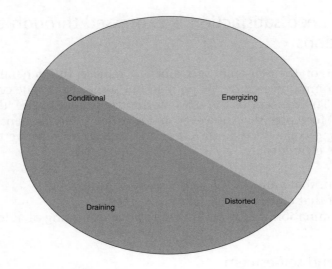

Figure 6.2   Types of self-emotions

Draining self-emotions

Pupils with draining self-emotions are more concerned with self-protection[36] as their fear of failure outweighs their desire for success. They are particularly concerned with protecting their 'private' self.

An understanding of self-emotions requires consideration of stability as well as of level. Some pupils lack a clear understanding of who they are and this leaves them at the mercy of events resulting in their self-emotions changing.[37] Change in the self-emotions is most likely during times of transition, given the new developmental tasks to be mastered and the new groups with whom one compares oneself. Pupils with the lowest motivational resilience are those with low and unstable self-emotions that lead to distress, anger and, ultimately, to self-harming. Normally pupils interpret events in biased ways that favour them[38] but those with draining self-emotions lack these self-serving biases. They may even prefer negative feedback to confirm their negative status. Most people seek verification of who they think they are, even if they do not think much of themselves. For such pupils, praise may trigger a conflict between a desire for approval and a reluctance to take the risks of a positive self-image. Such draining self-emotions can thus become self-perpetuating.

Conditional self-emotions

Although self-evaluation is a natural tendency, over-concern with the self may be triggered by conditional approval. As discussed earlier, one can seek affiliation by complying with others' values but sometimes the hunger for approval can create an acquiescent affiliation that restricts our growth.

Conditional self-emotions can lead to fulfilling your duties and becoming a *plastic perfect* kind of pupil. It is taking on board other people's motivational baggage.[39] If a mother, for example, praises her daughter for success, but shuns her following failure, then the child will subsequently treat herself as she has been treated.

Conditional self-emotions are seen in people who are constantly apologetic or who need to ingratiate themselves with others. This is depicted in children's fiction by, for example, the fat boy or the gawky girl who is the 'hanger on', desperately seeking the group's approval while being the butt of humour. This is in contrast to unconditional positive regard where we feel valued for who we are.[40]

A teacher with a psychologically controlling style, designed to ensure compliance, can engender such conditional self-emotions and acquiescent affiliation. Sometimes inexperienced or insecure teachers have cravings for approval themselves and when they come across insecure pupils they can fall into the trap of encouraging their dependency. While this is comforting for both needy parties it will be resented by the rest of the class.

Distorted self-emotions

> Some teachers think that some pupils are too confident and try to knock the confidence out of them. (Pupil support assistant)

It has been commonly assumed that antisocial behaviour, such as violence and bullying, is caused by negative self-esteem, but it can actually be a result of threatened esteem.[41] A bully, for example, often has an insecure but inflated view of his or her self. Feeling that he or she may lose esteem at any moment, the bully responds to combat any potential threat.

People with 'over-confidence' tend to think they are invulnerable, act with bravado and think rules are not for them. Such people are often insensitive to the feelings of others whom they may exploit for their own purposes.[42] They are hostile towards any feedback that criticizes them. Pupils who take the opposing reaction are likely to be driven by these distorted self-emotions.

Such distorted self-emotions echo antagonistic agency and both are linked to narcissism that involves high self-evaluations stoked by strategies such as fantasies of power, self-serving biases, admiration-seeking and social dominance.[43] They are maintained because aggressive people confuse status with popularity.[44] In one study, when teenagers were asked who they would invite to a party, those most likely to be invited were boys who were rated by their class peers as physically aggressive and girls who were rated as psychologically aggressive. It is clear that young people can achieve high status by bullying.[45]

Energizing self-emotions

Energizing self-emotions result from and reflect a focusing on our own values and needs as well as the demands of the situation. Such emotions allow us to be accepting of both self and others. High motivational resilience is most likely with such *non-conditional self-emotions*, characterized by pupils for whom success and failure do not implicate their view of the self. Such self-emotions are, like a robust argument, resilient enough to cope with attack from failure, criticism, rejection or competition.

While pupils with energizing self-emotions are interested in self-enhancement, particularly enhancing their 'public' self, the ego paradoxically becomes less dominant as we become more resilient. With stable energizing self-emotions, failure, rejection, disappointment and loss can all be experienced without the self being knocked. At the same time, when we succeed or are approved by others, we can feel pleased without our self becoming bloated.

One way to characterize such self-emotions is the concept of *mindfulness*,[46] that is, an open awareness where there is no fixed concept of self to protect or enhance. It is interesting that one of the characteristics of the 'flow' experience is feeling ecstatic, that is, standing outside the self (ek-stasis). The self can be thought of as a constructed image that can lead people to be overly attached to approval, achievements or possessions. In Buddhism, for example, well-being is described as the recognition that there is no fixed self.

How the self-emotions work together

Most models of the self are hierarchical and propose a general self-concept plus specific self-concepts related to different areas. Global and specific elements of the self mutually influence each other. An effort has been made here to delineate the three main elements of the self-emotions.

A pupil whose needs for affiliation, agency and autonomy are well met will have energizing self-emotions or, perhaps more accurately, *self-energizing emotions*. When any of these needs is thwarted, the *self-emotions* can become self-restricting, self-draining or self-distorting. For example, some people may develop distorted self-emotions when their affiliation needs are not met, perhaps because of their disagreeable personality or because of their role where they feel they need to remain detached.

Disengaged pupils have a complex bundle of self-draining emotions. They may have a cocktail of some or all of the following:

- a low need for achievement
- low self belief or low self-esteem or low self-determination
- a fear of failure
- a passive helplessness or self-protective attitude
- a competitive attitude to achievement
- pessimistic beliefs about the fixed nature of ability.

Pupils with self-energizing emotions will tend to be optimistic and enjoy mastery ratings of progress.[47] Beliefs about the reasons for taking part in learning combine with beliefs about their control over learning. It is the combination that seems to shape engagement.[48] A mastery attitude leads to optimism. If a pupil has a mastery attitude and is not progressing they can still have energizing self-emotions, unlike someone with a competitive attitude who will maintain positive self-emotions only as long as they are doing well. As it is not possible for all pupils to be the best, encouraging pupils to concentrate on achieving their personal best will be important for pupils' self-emotions.

Notice, for example, how the growth in popularity of marathon running in the past 20 years is all about running a 'personal best' rather than winning the race, a possibility open to only a small group of elite athletes. The finisher's medal is not a celebration of defeat, it is an endorsement of extraordinary endurance.

Fixed ideas about ability tend to lead to competitive goals because pupils become concerned with showing what ability they have. A competitive attitude to achievement in combination with fixed ability ideas leads to seeing low ability as the main cause of failure, which can make pupils avoid trying and leave them vulnerable to a fear of failure. Belief in their ability is precarious and they become pessimistic and preoccupied with their self-image.[49]

Summary of key points in Part II

- Our *needs* shape our *personality*, which in turn organizes how we meet our needs.
- Our need satisfaction in turn shapes our personality.
- Personality development is a process of emancipation towards increasing autonomy.
- A pupil's reputation within the peer group is a significant motivational catalyst.
- Personality can be characterized in terms of the two interacting processes of resilience and reactivity to form three personality types – resilient, cautious and impulsive.
- The reactivity and resilience model of personality type creates an arc of resilience.
- This is mirrored by an arc of autonomy that forms the outline of the learner needs matrix.
- Our emotions tell us how we are coping and motivate us to adapt.
- Draining emotions guide us to cope with threat, loss or injustice but they also narrow our focus and generate more negative emotions.
- In contrast, energizing emotions broaden our focus and leave pupils more open to learning.
- The self represents the core of the person that directs them towards the discovery of their potential.
- A pupil whose needs for affiliation, agency and autonomy are well met will have *self-energizing emotions.*
- When any of these needs is thwarted, *self-emotions* can become self-restricting, self-draining or self-distorting.

Part Three

What teachers do

7

What teachers do to motivate their pupils

The best teachers know you from the inside. (Jamie, 11-year-old pupil)

This chapter outlines what teachers do to motivate pupils using the *external (classroom) energizers*. These are the working tools with which teachers meet pupils' 3A needs.

Stop and think

What kind of teacher are you?

Some children are so highly self-motivated the teacher does not need to do anything to motivate them. Many others are sufficiently motivated that the teacher just needs to make sure they sustain their engagement. The challenge for teachers is to motivate all pupils, particularly the 'hard to reach'. When pupils are difficult to engage, the teacher's style becomes even more crucial. Their response can resolve any problems, or indeed transform them.

Teachers, however, can also aggravate a pupil's defensive reaction. The teacher can become part of the problem if they become exasperated, alarmed or threatened by pupils. All teachers are susceptible to being wound up by pupils who seek to take hold of the reins. Motivating teaching therefore requires insight into teachers' own reactions and how their reactions influence pupils. Teachers need to be able to identify their personal 'buttons' that pupils instinctively seem to know how to press.

We motivate others the way we motivate ourselves, just as we buy others the presents we would like for ourselves. So we need to be *in tune* with our own *self-motivation* before we can begin to understand how we can motivate others.

Stop and think

What is your motivation source that is driving you in your work?
Where did it come from?
How do you sustain it?
Is anything restricting, distorting or crushing your motivation?

The classroom energizers

Stop and think

Think about the key people who influenced you as you were growing up.
Who was the person who most positively influenced your motivation to
learn? How did they do it?

We can use learner need satisfaction to identify the conditions under which
the needs can be best met. All of the components of a classroom climate can
be categorized into four external (classroom) energizers, namely:

- engagement
- structure
- feedback
- stimulation.

These four energizers interact and reinforce each other to provide the ingredients
that are needed to meet pupils' 3A needs, as portrayed in Figure 7.1.

Engagement is the energizer through which teachers meet their pupils' need
for affiliation. Structure impacts upon pupils' sense of autonomy. Feedback is
the energizer that impacts most directly on pupils' sense of agency. Stimulation
influences equally each of the 3A needs.

How engagement nurtures affiliation

Engagement as process
Engagement is the main energizer through which teachers show they are
interested in and value pupils. In this sense, the term 'engagement' is a
process rather than an outcome. Pupils work hard for teachers who value
them as individuals. They need to know they count before they see any point
in trying to learn. Pupils feel valued when they feel understood and when
their teacher tries to find out who they are. The more engaged the teacher is
with their class, the more engaged their pupils will be with them. Teachers

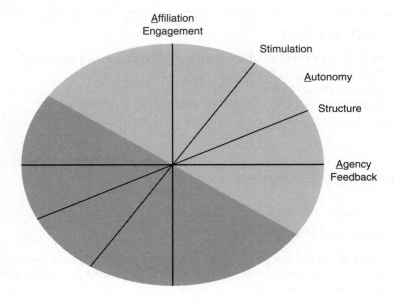

Figure 7.1   The classroom energizers and learner needs

nurture pupil affiliation by being approachable and creating a climate where pupils feel they belong. They encourage their pupils to be all they can be, while accepting them for who they are.

Some ways to show you care:

- Show respect for them.
- Be considerate and courteous.
- Attune to their individuality.
- Seek to understand them.
- Share high expectations.
- Nurture reciprocity.
- Stress self-improvement.
- Reassure pupils that it is OK to make mistakes.

Motivating teaching expresses itself through good working relationships with the whole class rather than relationships with individual pupils. The essence of motivating teaching is empathic communication with the group. Regularly asking questions about how pupils experience the classroom climate and your teaching style is an ideal way to develop a two-way attunement that will maximize engagement. Attunement is the sharing of affect.

Teachers can sometimes walk into a room and show self-defeating behaviour that gives pupils the upper hand and allows them to set the tone. Teachers need to be aware of the importance of this power dynamic and always be in control of the tone. The teacher builds affiliation and controls the tone through:

- the agreement and achievement of common goals
- getting to know the class

- letting the pupils get to know them
- helping the pupils get to know each other
- talking to them in small groups and in ways that let them share information about themselves, their interests and their experiences.

One primary school consulted its pupils about what encourages them and discovered that the traditional non-stop revision for the first two weeks of a new school session was a real drainer. The pupils suggested instead that the teachers' priority should be to organize learning activities in order to get to know the pupils and to establish class routines. The school readjusted and the teachers were delighted with the pupil response.

Stop and think

How do you show your interest in your pupils?

We all like to go back to places where people know us. Every pupil needs to be known well by at least one adult, and this can be achieved in a secondary school when every adult mentors a small group of pupils. Teachers staying with the same group for multiple years can also help promote affiliation through long-standing relationships.[1] Converting large schools into smaller units fosters personalized and continuous relationships between teachers and pupils.

Pupils' affiliation to school can be enhanced by extra-curricular activities that help build friendships. When pupils get involved in after-school clubs, where they can relax and show what they can do, they are more likely to develop a sense of affiliation with the school.

Schools can achieve higher levels of affiliation through greater community involvement by, for example, developing programmes that place pupils in community organizations to let them see that their learning is useful to others. These programmes are most effective when they offer close adult–pupil relationships, when they are linked to the curriculum and when they let pupils develop their own ideas.[2]

Pro-social classrooms
The impact of the peer group on individual pupils' engagement can be as positive as it can be negative. Some classrooms encourage peer exclusion more than others.[3] The teaching style affects how peers relate to each other. For example, pupils who want to please the teacher will gang up on someone if the teacher communicates that they do not like them, through, for example, their sarcastic comments. These pupils take this as a green light to harass the pupil in the playground. In this way teacher humiliation licenses peer rejection.

Pupils are more likely to act pro-socially when they are encouraged to behave pro-socially by, for example, being given dispositional praise, such as 'you're the kind of pupil who enjoys helping people'.[4] This nurtures a pro-social self-image and may be particularly effective with mid to late primary children who only have an emerging sense of their dispositions.

Participation in pro-social activities encourages further pro-social behaviour. For example, involvement with voluntary service is associated with higher levels of motivation to help others.[5] A teaching style that overuses rewards, threats and deadlines can undermine motivation by affecting learners' feelings of affiliation. In fact, pro-social behaviour is easily undermined by rewards, which shift the motives for behaving pro-socially from affiliation to extrinsic factors.[6] The reward should be in the activity itself, not in some 'prize' at the end which suggests, by definition, that the activity itself is a chore.

Collaborative group work
When pupils take a defensive reaction they will have particular difficulty sharing in active group learning. However, more active collaborative learning may, paradoxically, help combat or pre-empt some of their problems. The Social and Pedagogic Research into Group work programme (SPRinG) stresses collaboration and is designed to make class interaction as cohesive as possible by the teacher:

- monitoring and scaffolding group interactions
- creating the conditions where pupils are encouraged to get everyone to contribute
- encouraging energizing contributions rather than drainers such as criticizing others
- increasing peer dialogue about the task
- involving all participants
- encouraging higher-level task-related talk
- working towards a common goal.

SPRinG has been shown to reduce off-task peer interactions and increase engagement in group activities in comparison to teacher-led or individual work.[7]

How structure supports autonomy

Stop and think
What is the difference between accountability and blame?

Structure refers to the clarity of learning outcomes that let pupils know what is expected of them, together with the boundaries that give shape and direction to the class. Flexible or *rubber* boundaries that bend to the needs of pupils work best. Structure lets pupils know where they stand and how much autonomy they have. As such, together with stimulation, structure impacts most directly upon pupils' sense of autonomy. A motivating structure sets clear expectations and limits that communicate trust and hold pupils accountable. Accountability is a process for clarifying responsibility and spotting pupils who merit recognition rather than blame.

Clarifying accountability requires the power to grab, hold and focus pupils' attention.[8]

Some ways to show you trust learners:

- Negotiate rules.
- Seek commitment not compliance.
- Be firm but fair, give a way out through directed choice.
- Allow equal access to resources and equal opportunities.
- Give exclusive responsibility for planning.
- Allow pupils to express their opinions about their school experiences.

Holding the reins

 Stop and think

Considering the mother–newborn child relationship, who is in charge, the mother or the baby?

In thinking about motivating children, it is useful to reflect on nature's greatest learning laboratory, the mother–newborn child relationship. The baby comes pre-programmed to win his or her mother's commitment to meet his or her needs. The mother has to learn to meet the baby's needs while getting on with the rest of her life. She does this by negotiating a share of this power, via a combination of love and limits, through, in particular, routines that make the baby secure and therefore less demanding. By experiencing the mother's attunement, the baby learns that his or her needs will be met. The mother gradually gets hold of the reins through a mutual compromise based on reciprocity and trust.

Motivating teaching is a similar *power dynamic* but in the opposite direction. The teacher holds the reins. Holding the reins is an analogy for the shared experience of two-way communication where one person is in charge. Motivating teachers, however, know they have to move towards a more balanced relationship via reciprocity and agreement. When an authority figure provides autonomy to an individual for whom he or she is responsible, that individual's motivation will be enhanced.[9] This is the fundamental message of this book. The challenge is to find ways to support every pupil's autonomy.

The teacher is great but can be a bit bossy ... (pause) ... when she doesn't need to be. (Thomas, aged 10, invited to give feedback about his class teacher)

Teacher to new class at the start of term:	Whose classroom is this?
Class:	Yours miss.
Teacher:	It's not mine, it's yours, so you are responsible for organizing the seating to suit your learning. On you go.

Authority is an energizer but can also be a drainer if the teacher holds the reins so tightly that it discourages responsibility. Teachers can avoid this by embedding authority into the class processes and norms. This requires a more participative teaching style that shares responsibility with pupils.

The egg is another useful metaphor from nature to illustrate the role of structure. The eggshell needs to be strong enough to keep the yolk intact but not so strong that it strangles its development.

Teachers are often accused of being *control freaks.* They have to be! Pupils need guidance and boundaries, that is, they have to be controlled. As discussed in Chapter 1, what teachers need to control is the class atmosphere (as well as their own heart rate!). Teachers walk a tightrope every day, which involves controlling without coercing, colluding or crushing pupils. They can get it right by striking a balance between controlling and protecting pupils while releasing their potential for self-determination. This can be resolved by imposing authority then, in a staged approach, 'loosening the reins' to provide increasing opportunities for autonomy. In this way power assertion can be transformed into empowerment via power-sharing.[10]

Some teachers confuse this approach with being weak and giving in. However, giving autonomy does not mean you are 'going soft' and will not undermine your authority. The teacher never lets go of the reins. The teacher's role is to create a context in which learners can be as autonomous as possible. This requires teachers to loosen but never relinquish their responsibility. Teachers need to give up some of their power but still retain most of it, for example, through 'directed choice'. It's clear that such choices are limited and in one sense a bit of a 'con trick' but pupils go along with it, not because they are stupid but because they realize it gives everyone a respectful way out.

Teachers are sometimes reluctant to wean pupils away from teacher dependence. It is not easy for them to change their role from purveyor of information to manager of learning resources. Pupil autonomy is best achieved when the teacher acts as both a *facilitator* and a *resource.* Such a flexible teaching style creates engagement and builds achievement.[11,12,13]

Teachers cannot directly give pupils autonomy. Rather, they provide relationships that are rich in the 3As, out of which pupils begin to exercise their own sense of autonomy.[14,15]

Motivating teaching requires the teacher to:

- be *aware* of their teaching style and its impact on pupils' stances
- *attune* to the pupils' feelings, that is, their learning stances
- *adjust* their teaching style accordingly
- *affirm*, whenever viable, pupils' capacity for self-direction.

Stop and think

How much scope do you have to give pupils autonomy?

As shown in Figure 7.2, at one end the teacher has all the power and at the other end the class has the lion's share.[16] This continuum acts as a sliding scale and reflects the degree of delegation of authority. Teachers operate from different points of the continuum all the time.

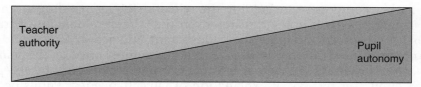

Figure 7.2   Teacher authority and pupil autonomy

Stop and think

Think of a particular class and locate your relationship with them in Figure 7.2.

When teachers think about responsibility, what comes to mind are often simple class tasks like running errands, cleaning the board and ringing the school bell. While even such basic responsibilities can bring out the best in many pupils, autonomy support involves finding more substantial ways to nurture pupils' own self-motivation. Fostering relevance and allowing criticism are particularly influential. Suppressing criticism is an important drainer; the opportunity to voice one's criticism is a fundamental aspect of autonomy.[17] Motivating teaching gradually builds pupils' capacity for 'personal power'. Sometimes there is too big a leap in the expected capacity for independent study from one level to the next in some education systems.

Bosses demand respect, leaders give it.[18]

Stop and think

Are you a boss or a leader?
What is the most important aspect of autonomy for you in your job?
What does management do typically when they are too tight, too loose and when they get it right?

Trust

Stop and think

What is trust?
Who do you trust most? Why?
How is your trust demonstrated?

Another key component in holding the reins flexibly is instilling a sense of trust in pupils. This is not surprising given that the development of trust is the first social process shaping the child–parent interaction[19] and builds the foundation of motivational resilience. Erikson defined trust as *the ability to accept what is given.*[19] For example, a teacher communicates trust by accepting what a pupil says by way of explanation of what happened. Pupils become very resentful when the teacher does not believe their side of the story. Participative decision-making also indicates the teacher has confidence in and trusts pupils. Trust occurs between people rather than within people.

Trust is illusory and more apparent in its breakdown than its development. Trust, like motivation itself, comes from within a relationship based on predictability, mutual obligations, respect and fairness. Motivating teaching ensures fairness through transparent systems that guarantee that everyone will get equal access to resources, for example, the computer, equal opportunities for their work to be displayed and equal chances to be class helpers and so on.

How feedback nurtures agency

 Stop and think

What are your main goals when you give feedback?

Feedback gives the teacher the opportunity to demonstrate how they manage themselves as a resource. Feedback provides information that lets pupils know how they are doing, guiding them from where they are to where they want to be. Good feedback also gives them some idea of their potential. Most young people are very interested in other people's opinions about them and how they are progressing. Feedback is the energizer that impacts most directly on pupils' sense of agency. Our own internal feedback is provided by our emotions, as discussed in Chapter 4.

Schools have changed in recent years from a control to a reward culture. The problem with this is 'reward inflation', that is rewards, like thrill rides, fireworks and special film effects, need to be constantly upgraded to continue to impact. Reward-based motivation is not sustainable or healthy. The reward culture is only a transition phase towards an ethos of self-determination and a culture of shared responsibility.

> I just want to retire from stickers. (9-year-old pupil.)

Teachers are often reluctant to praise for fear of making pupils big-headed or complacent. They misunderstand the function of feedback, which is to give information about progress in order to encourage continued effort and increase agency, not to massage pupils' egos. Of course, all the feedback does not need to come from the teacher. Peer assessment benefits pupils as well as making the whole thing more manageable.

Some ways to show you believe in your pupils:

- Give information about progress that stresses improvement.
- Recognize their achievements.
- Focus your praise on effort, participation and pro-social behaviour, to inform and encourage belief.
- Help them to repair mistakes, link failures with controllable causes and identify next steps.
- Give forward projection, for example, two stars and a wish.
- Replace criticism that drains energy with questions that invite answers and focus energy.
- Give recognition for teamwork and collaborative learning.

Motivating feedback
Motivating feedback:

- praises pupil effort and the way they tackle their work and so makes pupils feel responsible for and in charge of their success
- helps pupils become aware of 'how' they are smart rather than how smart they are
- stresses personal rather than relative progress
- avoids loading any messages with approval or disapproval
- downplays teacher evaluation by letting pupils rate themselves as much as possible.

Schools are increasingly developing a culture of celebration of achievement, both in and out of school. Peers acknowledging peers offers a good bridge between teacher reinforcement and self-motivation.

An important key to understanding pupil motivation is the degree to which pupils perceive their teachers' feedback style as informational and cementing relationships or controlling and souring relationships.[27] Rewarding pupils is unfortunately most often used in attempts to control pupil behaviour rather than to motivate their learning.

 Stop and think

What is the best feedback anyone has ever given you?
What made it so useful?
What is the difference between cementing and souring feedback?
Who is the person to whom you would go if you wanted feedback? Why?
What is the purpose of school award ceremonies?
What do you usually reward or praise pupils for?

Constructive criticism
Teachers struggle between giving pupils honest feedback and maintaining their confidence. When teachers give unsolicited help, indiscriminate praise

Table 7.1   Assessment as evaluation or feedback

Assessment as a form of evaluation

- Summative
- Assessment *of* learning
- Based on a fixed view of ability
- Focuses on the teacher with the aim of controlling
- Teacher led with little involvement of pupil
- The outcome does not lead to any adjustment in teaching
- Learning intentions and success criteria are not clear

Assessment as a form of feedback

- Formative
- Assessment *for* learning, or even *as* learning
- Based on an incremental view of ability
- Focuses on the pupil with the aim to inform, encourage, empower
- Joint venture between pupils and teacher with active involvement of pupil in self-assessment
- Outcome leads to adjustment in teaching
- Learning intentions and success criteria are explicit and up front

or sympathy, they soften the blow of failure to protect pupils but may unwittingly suggest to the student he or she has low ability, or that 'good enough' is acceptable. A well-chosen criticism on the other hand can communicate high expectations. As long as pupils feel their affiliation is secure, they will absorb critical feedback in relation to what they do. Comments about their personal qualities, however, are more threatening and hard to take. It is important that any criticism communicates feedback rather than failings to pupils.

 Stop and think

How would you respond to a pupil offering you feedback?
Do you ever invite feedback from your class or from individual pupils?

Nurturing confidence in pupils requires attention to be focused on specific aspects of their agency that are important to the student rather than vague attempts to make pupils feel good about themselves. Simply encouraging pupils to believe that anything is possible can lead to conceit or confidence without competence.[28] It creates a confidence bubble that will soon burst when a setback is met. Positive 'self-emotions' are more likely to be sustained through developing valued skills in real-life situations, rather than through praise.[29]

Assessment as evaluation or feedback
In Table 7.1, summative assessment as a form of evaluation is contrasted with formative assessment which, as a type of informative feedback, is much more

motivating. The transition from summative to formative assessment has involved a shift in the balance of power in the classroom. Not surprisingly some teachers are resistant to this and find it particularly difficult with challenging pupils.[30]

Praise

> ## Stop and think
>
> What is the difference between praise and encouragement?

Teachers have long embraced the praise culture but giving effective praise is a complex process. Praise can be rebuffed as patronizing or grudging. If the teacher is just going through the motions, praise will come across as hackneyed. Credibility and sincerity are a must or praise can be as offensive as empty compliments or ill-considered gifts, each of which signifies that the donor does not really know or care about the person.

Private forms of praise have the advantage that their value is not derived at the expense of others. Teachers need to use praise discriminately and filter out the habitual phatics such as 'good' and 'brilliant' that undermine its impact.

Flattery maybe gets you anywhere with colleagues. It does not, however, work with children who can detect plastic praise, that is, praise that just looks like the real thing, for example, when the teacher praises without even looking at the work.

The benefits of praise can be eroded in various ways. For example:

- *Contaminated* praise is telegraphed by qualifiers such as 'but' and 'why' in a way that distorts praise into criticism, for example, 'why can't you work as hard as that all the time?'
- *Grudged* praise is similar, for example, 'apparently you seem to have impressed some of your teachers.'
- *Sarcastic* praise is also draining, as in such comments as 'Don't tell me you're actually being nice to your neighbour!' or telling the truant 'Good of you to drop in'.

Praise is a common strategy used to try to boost self-esteem but some pupils cannot cope with it as it threatens their view of themselves as unworthy. Lethargy can be fostered by praise given, regardless of whether the child has actually done well. In this way unconditionality can undermine mastery. Love can be given unconditionally but praise must be graded to fit the effort and success.[31]

Common sense would suggest it is a good idea to praise pupils for being clever. Ability-related praise, however, can signal success is due to qualities pupils have rather than something they have done. It may lead children to concentrate on showing their ability rather than on learning. Even worse, it can unwittingly teach pupils to measure their ability from their performance.[32] Pupils may also come to see ability as something they cannot change. It can backfire by making children equate success with high ability and failure with low ability. This can make them put any failure down to their low ability which damages motivational resilience and leads them to give up in the face of setbacks.

Praise for effort encourages children to concentrate on learning as opposed to showing off their ability. It also helps them to put down their performance to effort that can be varied under their control. Pupils who are praised for effort will be more likely to think failure means they need to try harder. It is unfortunate that some schools give effort awards as the 'booby' prize.

Effective praise does not stop at 'well done' but goes on to say what was done well and why the pupil is being praised. The teacher says 'Good, you made a plan, so now you know what to do as you go along'. Praise is only as good as the information it imparts. Telling a pupil that he is working like a Trojan is only motivating if the pupil knows what a Trojan is!

There is a subtle but significant difference between *controlling* praise that gives approval and *encouraging* praise that recognizes effort. Too much controlling praise can teach children they have to please adults. Pupils do not need to earn encouragement. It can be given for nothing, something special, for effort or improvement, when the pupil is doing well or even making mistakes. Encouragement, like a well-chosen gift, will rarely be rejected. Teachers encourage pupils when they have faith in or notice pupils' efforts and their feelings.

How stimulation nurtures all 3A needs

Stop and think

How can you make homework engaging?

The classroom energizer, *stimulation*, impacts on each of the 3A needs. It comes from a curriculum that highlights the importance, relevance and fun of activities, and sets clear, achievable and specific goals. A motivating curriculum involves pupils and challenges their present capacity, while permitting some control. It also provides a sense of competence in relevant goals.

Relevance and meaning are key factors in a motivating curriculum. Homework, for example, will be more likely to engage when there is clarity of *purpose* of the intended learning and how it connects with and builds on ongoing work.[20] It is therefore worth spending a few moments explaining to the class why you are giving a particular piece of homework – how it fits in with what they have been learning and how you are going to link it in with your next lesson.

Motivating teaching feeds young people's natural curiosity by being enjoyable, interesting, surprising and eliciting fantasy that permits the use of pupils' growing abilities. Pupils are autonomously engaged when they actively construct their own knowledge via open-ended questioning, problem-solving, projects, experiments and debates.

Endings to lessons are crucial as they colour memories of the whole experience and leave pupils looking forward to coming back. It is important therefore to decide on a positive ending and work backwards in your lesson planning to make sure you get to the ending you want.

Teachers often think some lessons have to be boring, because of the repetition needed to consolidate skills. That, however, does not mean that pupils cannot be invited to try to make such routine work more interesting for themselves. For example, simulation and game-like elements can add meaning to what might otherwise be a boring activity. There is of course a lot of material available that makes learning fun such as alphabet mats, bingo with flash cards, quizzes, word searches and number fans.

Some ways to show you enjoy teaching your pupils:

- Promote the value and purpose of learning.
- Clarify the rationale, share learning intentions and outcomes and negotiate criteria of success.
- Enthuse, provide interest, relevance, purpose, pace and momentum.
- Capitalize on their interests, motivate by their goals.
- Recognize their potential to be smart in different areas.
- Look for talents and use them to benefit others.

Intrinsic versus extrinsic goals

Presenting the learning material as an extrinsic goal, for example, to win a prize, can undermine learning[21] because it shifts pupils' focus from learning to external indicators of success. Extrinsic goals, such as power and image, make pupils interested in comparisons and external signs of success.[22] Intrinsic goals, such as contributing to the community and self-development, lead to better learning because they connect with pupils' natural growth tendencies.

'Flow'

'Flow' happens when we become so absorbed in an activity that we lose ourselves.[23] It might be anything from painting to watching a film, to puzzling over a Sudoku or a Nintendo game. We are able to concentrate fully on the activity because it has clear goals and provides immediate feedback. We lose our normal sense of time – it either speeds up or slows down. Such flow experiences can only happen in an autonomy-supportive context. Scheduling some courses in longer blocks of at least 90 minutes to allow more sustained engagement and more individualized pacing can help to generate flow experiences.

Pupils become immersed when they get involved in their own creative sense-making, when pushed to understand, by having to wrestle with new concepts, explain their reasoning, defend their conclusions or explore alternative strategies and solutions.[24] In mathematics, for example, pupils with poor basic skills are likely to receive drill in basic concepts rather than challenging, open-ended problem-solving. But even pupils who have relatively poor skills can engage in deep analysis. There is also considerable evidence that mathematical concepts can be introduced at many levels and at almost any age.[25]

Stop and think

What is it about computer games that absorb children so effectively? What lessons can we learn from computer games for the activities we structure in class?

The expectancy X value model
Motivation will be determined by the extent to which pupils expect to do well and value the activity.[26] Only when both of these are present will motivation be positive. Pupils' expectations are based on probabilities of success, not necessarily that the pupils themselves are in control of the success, so it is different from agency. These three elements, expectancy, value and agency, determine the motivation level.

Stop and think

Try this out with your pupils. Ask each pupil to rate (a) how well they expect to do in and (b) how much they care about your subject, on a rating scale of 1 to 10. Then ask them to multiply rating (a) by rating (b). You can then rank order the class based on this score. It will be a quick way of measuring their motivation.

Firing on all four energizers

Stop and think

Which is the most important of the four energizers?
Which is the easiest and the most difficult to provide?

Geography lessons became unmissable when Mr Hill was firing on all four cylinders

Effective teachers do not just rely on a few motivational techniques but, rather, saturate the classroom with many aspects of the classroom energizers.[33] The energizers merge into one another as teachers use them in combination. For example, encouraging pupils to set their own intrinsic goals has the biggest impact within an autonomy supportive classroom.[34]

The self-motivated pupil can provide many aspects of these energizers for themselves, including:

- engagement through self-affirmation
- structure through self-discipline
- stimulation through imagination
- feedback from their emotional response.

Each of the energizers contributes important aspects of motivational resilience. For example;

- Engagement gives a sense of being valued.
- Structure offers a sense of security, trust and empowerment.
- Stimulation creates a sense of purpose.
- Feedback forms a sense of self-belief.

It is worth reflecting on what happens if one energizer is missing. As displayed in Table 7.2, if *engagement* is missing this creates a feeling of alienation that in turn leads to a loss of self-focus among pupils. Without *feedback* the pupils will feel an uncertainty that engenders insecurity. With no *structure* the class will deteriorate into chaos and fear will ensue that generates hopelessness among pupils. A lack of *stimulation* leads to boredom, which in turn causes anger and resentment.

Table 7.2   Impact of missing energizers

Energizer	Energizer	Energizer	Energizer	Outcome	Impact
....	Feedback	Structure	Stimulation	Alienation	Loss of self-awareness
Engagement	....	Structure	Stimulation	Uncertainty	Insecurity
Engagement	Feedback	....	Stimulation	Chaos	Fear, hopelessness
Engagement	Feedback	Structure	....	Boredom	Anger, resentment

Stop and think

Does this table give you any clues to help explain the engagement of any particular individual, group or class?
What is your signature strength in motivating pupils?
Which one change would improve your capacity to motivate?

How teachers use the classroom energizers

In motivation workshops, over 2,000 teachers have been asked to summarize, in one word, how they motivate their pupils.

Stop and think

In a word, how do you motivate pupils?

As can be seen from Table 7.3, teachers' responses have been categorized under the four headings of the classroom energizers. Their responses relate primarily to stimulation, then engagement, followed by feedback. Only a small minority mention structure energizers. While this is not presented as a scientifically robust piece of research, it does throw some light on how teachers prioritize their use of the classroom energizers. This suggests that teachers tend to be enthusing and caring and see the value of feedback. The lack of structural energizers suggests teachers have yet to grasp the fundamental importance of autonomy support. This pattern will probably be the same among teachers who become managers and in turn perpetuate this ethos.

What we have in our tool kit shapes how we see both our role and client group. These responses suggest that teachers tend to see pupils as children to be cared for and enthused, but not as responsible learners who need to be given autonomy to let them take control of their learning. In a sense, they see pupils as balloons to be inflated but not to be released to fly off.

Table 7.3   Teachers' use of the classroom energizers

Stimulation	41%
Engagement	34%
Feedback	21%
Structure	4%

The limited repertoire in relation to autonomy support is perhaps at the heart of the continuing discipline problems. Many pupil–teacher transactions remain one-way, reflecting both a restricted understanding of pupil needs and a limited flexibility in teaching style and a restricted range of energizing strategies. The challenge for teachers is to move beyond authority to share power through gradual autonomy support.

The four classroom energizers are summarized in Figure 7.3.

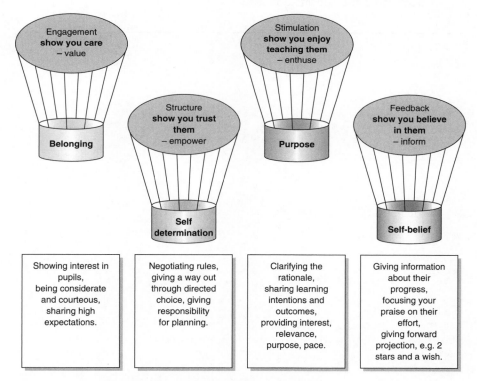

Figure 7.3   The classroom energizers with specific examples

Stop and think

Do some subject areas provide these energizers more readily than others? How would a visitor to your classroom know it was a motivating learning environment? Use the four energizers to answer.

Summary of key points

- Motivating teaching influences pupils' motivation through four classroom *energizers*, namely, engagement, structure, feedback and stimulation, that meet pupils' needs for affiliation, agency and autonomy.
- *Engagement* is the energizer through which teachers show they are interested in and value pupils, and so impact on their affiliation.
- *Structure* refers to the clarity of learning outcomes and boundaries that let pupils know where they stand and, as such, impacts most directly upon pupils' sense of autonomy.
- *Feedback* provides information that lets pupils know how they are doing and is the energizer that impacts most directly on pupils' sense of agency.
- *Stimulation* impacts on all 3A needs. It comes from a curriculum that highlights the importance, relevance and fun of activities, and sets clear, achievable and specific goals.

Teaching styles

This has changed the way I look at myself. One of the things that I always think about dealing with a challenging class is that they stop me being myself and I then adopt a different style or mask which I am not always comfortable in.

The teaching styles have made me aware of where I 'go to' when I am not in my default mode. I find this very interesting (and worrying as I become sarcastic and crushing!!). I have never considered this before and now have the ability to realize if this transition has happened and have the ability to change my style. (Feedback from a teacher after a motivation workshop.)

This chapter looks at teachers' mindsets, motivation and motives that influence their teaching style. First, it presents some principles of motivating teaching. The *teaching styles* are then presented. Next it considers the *classroom climates* that these different styles create. It concludes with a discussion of policy trends that may unwittingly undermine motivating teaching.

Motivating teaching

To motivate pupils, teachers need to adapt how they hold the reins. That is, they need to vary the level of autonomy they offer pupils, according to pupils' learning stances, in other words, pupils' way of exercising their autonomy.

Motivating teaching is more a question of being than doing, and is founded on:

- modelling the behaviour you are looking for from pupils
- eliciting the best from pupils by giving the best of yourself
- affirming, whenever viable, pupils' capacity for self-direction
- tuning into and adapting to pupils' feelings
- gaining influence by adjusting to the needs of pupils
- staying receptive to the full range of pupils' emotions
- providing opportunities that are in and of themselves motivating
- controlling without colluding, coercing or crushing pupils, *holding the reins* just right
- building a good working relationship with *the class*
- controlling the atmosphere
- asking questions about how pupils experience the classroom to develop a two-way attunement.

Great people make you feel that you, too, can somehow become great. (Mark Twain)

Stop and think

How do you embody motivation in your teaching?

Teacher perceptions

The world is a looking glass and gives back to everyman the reflection of his own face. (W.M. Thackeray)

Different teachers see the same children differently. Teachers can see some young people as difficult while others see the same young people as responsive. It is perhaps more accurate to say that teachers have *difficult relationships* with some pupils and *good relationships* with others.

Perspective is everything. Just as mountains can be challenging when seen from one perspective and gentle from another, so pupils can be seen differently from different perspectives. We need to be aware of the perspective we have and strive to see pupils from as many perspectives as possible. We can do this, for example, by seeing them in different contexts, or seeking the perspectives of pupils, classroom assistants, management, student teachers and parents.

Stop and think

Imagine your head teacher suggested that, because of your unreasonable way of dealing with people, brought about by your overblown ego, inadequate personality, chaotic lifestyle and dysfunctional marriage, you should see a life coach. Imagine further that your partner, family and colleagues are to be invited to a case conference to discuss your state of mind. How would you feel?

Once you had calmed down, chances are you would decide to ask your head teacher to explain exactly what he or she means. This is a nightmare scenario, but one in which young people can find themselves.

The most invisible, alarming, exasperating and threatening pupils are often the most poorly understood. Judgement is getting trapped in our own opinions about pupils in a way that renders us less able to understand them. And yet, ironically, the more we understand pupils the less distanced, alarmed, exasperated or threatened we are.

Motivating teaching requires hope; hope comes from understanding, and understanding comes from empathy. To be able to reason objectively about pupils, teachers need, first, to feel good about themselves as a teacher.

Busy teachers experience pupil misbehaviour as frustrating and undermining, and can view it as random actions that need to be suppressed. However, behaviour is always motivated, if not planned, and it usually has a purpose. A reflective analysis starts from the view that misbehaviour is a pupil's attempt to adapt to the classroom.

Teachers are not observers from some detached hatch but are a part of the action. Teaching is all about participating in collective emotions. Teachers create their own classroom reality through a series of potentially distorting illusions.[1] Perceptions also depend to some extent on what we expect to see.

Motivating teaching requires understanding pupils as holistically as possible. Teachers are bombarded by so much information in the classroom that they categorize pupils quickly, instinctively and subjectively. Subjectivity is inevitable, but can be flawed, and once the labels are in place they are hard to change. Erroneous information is collected via personal feelings that are often irrelevant but are treated as powerfully predictive. This is based on our misguided belief that our intuitions cannot be wrong.[2] We also mistake our familiarity with a situation for an understanding of how it works.[3]

Motivating teaching has to be both active and reflective, switching between participating and observing. Teachers need to get the chance to observe their class from the side, free from the demands of teaching, when they can watch whole-class dynamics and individual responses.

 Stop and think

What are the key signs you would advise a probationer teacher to look out for in their class during the first few weeks of a new term?

Teacher mindsets

In an early classic study,[4] managers were found to adopt one of two theories about human behaviour. They either took theory X, which believed people need to be coerced before they will work, or theory Y, which assumed that people can be self-directing. Similarly, some teachers have a belief in the need for coercion while others believe in self-direction.

Teachers' beliefs about their pupils' motivation have been found to make their teaching style supportive or suppressive of pupil autonomy. This, in turn, causes the pupils' behaviour to confirm the teachers' beliefs.[5,6] It is therefore important to understand how teachers develop their beliefs about pupils' motivation.

Some teachers believe that pupil personality is fluid and open to change, and so they do not jump to conclusions about pupils. Others believe that pupil personality is fixed and leap to conclusions on little evidence. It is as if they 'seize' on and then 'freeze' on their judgements.[7] They tend to apply a global label to pupils, assuming their personality consistently influences everything they do. They also believe personality can be assessed through a single piece of behaviour, just like some people believe a restaurant can be reviewed on the basis of one meal. Some medical professionals echo such beliefs when they apply labels such as autism to children on the basis of one-off, decontextualized, clinic-based assessments. This mindset leads to stereotyping pupils on the basis of slender evidence. Such closed mindsets are more likely to lead to a draining teaching reaction.

Teaching style is linked closely with teachers' personality, most clearly evident, for example, in how they use their authority or establish their classroom climate. Consequently, teachers struggling to control a difficult pupil or class can feel demoralized. If teachers construe disengagement in their class as a reflection of their teaching style and personality, it may lead to defensiveness and blame and, ultimately, to poorly thought out and ad hoc reactions. This can lead to seeing any opposition as a personal attack which, in turn, leads to a defensive teaching reaction. What has to be remembered is that 'disengaged' pupils are reacting defensively to protect themselves from threats. Yet, it can be hard to accept that threatening pupils are themselves threatened.

> The biggest challenge in my job is when the classroom terrorist meets the staffroom terrorist. The terrorist teacher applies the tight controls against which classroom terrorists love to rebel. (Deputy head of a secondary school during a motivation workshop)

The more threatening the pupils, the more disempowered teachers may feel and the more insensitive they can become to the impact of their behaviour. For example, they may use 'throw away' personal remarks which merely fuel the ' I'm being picked on' gripe'.

While some teachers think of themselves and pupils in the same terms and are interested in what pupils think about teaching and learning, other teachers see pupils as quite different from themselves – like lion trainers see lions. Consequently, they would not think pupils would have anything useful to say about their teaching and so they deprive themselves of useful feedback.

Teachers' motivation

Stop and think

What energizes you about your job?
Identify one change which would improve your motivation?

Teachers' own motivation predicts their teaching style. Teachers need to have their 3A needs met before they can engender them in their pupils. The less pressure they feel under and the more they see that their pupils are motivated, the more they will be motivated themselves and, in turn, the more autonomy supportive they will be.[8] Teachers tend to become tightly controlling when they feel pressured by management.[9,10] This happens:

- when authorities impose restrictions that leave teachers limited scope in determining the curriculum
- when they make teachers feel responsible for their pupils' behaviour and performance
- when teachers believe that their pupils are not motivated.

However, rather than there being a direct link between management pressure and teacher behaviour, the relationship seems to be among three factors, namely:

- pressure of work
- perception of pupil engagement
- teachers' own motivation.[11]

The chain of influence, outlined in Figure 8.1, starts from work pressure and goes through perception of pupils' motivation to teachers' own motivation.

As the process starts with teachers' perceptions of work pressures, any discussion about how we can improve pupil motivation must include the conditions that affect teachers' own motivation.[12] Changing the conditions from those that undermine to those that enhance teachers' support of pupil autonomy should be an important priority for any reforms.

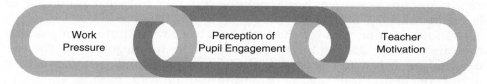

Figure 8.1   The motivation chain

Teaching styles

Stop and think

What do you understand by the term 'teaching style'?
How would you describe your teaching style?
Think of your best and worst ever bosses, and compare their styles.
What teacher behaviours towards pupils have you seen in yourself or others that you would describe as *the unacceptable face of teaching?*

Stop and think

Mr Brown is halfway through his first year of teaching. This morning he starts his first lesson in a foul mood and gets off on a bad footing when he reprimands the first pupil that annoys him by coming in a few minutes late. He then discovers this pupil does not have a pencil. He overreacts with agitation. His anger mixes with the pressure he is feeling as well as his fear for his fragile reputation. The pupil reacts by aggressively shouting back at him. Mr Brown insists that he has no right to shout at him. The pupil claims that he started it, he has been shouting at him for nothing.
What could Mr Brown do?

This section further develops the description in Chapter 7 of *holding the reins* into three *teaching styles*. The concept of teaching style covers a lot of facets including

- their attitude to pupils and their job
- their characteristic behaviour, actions and emotional expression
- their interactions and relationships with pupils
- the climate they create
- the impact on pupils
- how others perceive and respond to them.

Most significantly, teaching styles mediate a teacher's authority and communicate how much pupil autonomy they will support. The teaching styles matrix will be conceptualized as an arc that mirrors the autonomy arc. It contains the three overlapping teaching styles which are displayed in Figure 8.2.

The fundamental goal for the teacher is to communicate to pupils that they are on their side, and open to compromise and negotiation. The two dangers are being too protective, soft, easygoing and permissive with pupils or being too pushy or authoritarian and boxing them in. Inexperienced teachers can confuse their pupils by swinging between these hugging and squeezing styles. The trick is to get the balance right, to be flexible rather than too loose or too tight. Motivating teaching involves using each of the four classroom energizers and the full teaching styles arc flexibly. Teachers need to be able to loosen their grip and get control back very quickly, if necessary.

The style arc emphasizes relationships between the different styles, rather than their discrete differences. It is not a question of what is your discrete style, implying that you are either one or the other. It is more a case of a fluid movement between the styles. It is how one moves between the styles that makes each teacher's style unique. Many teachers, when asked to describe their style, will capture this by saying something like:

- structured yet informal
- friendly but not a friend
- funny but serious
- relaxed control
- open but authoritative.

This formulation can also be applied to a school ethos or indeed a national educational culture. Some government educational programmes are too vague, laissez-faire and open, while others can be too prescriptive and controlling.

Descriptions of the three teaching styles are detailed in Table 8.1, in terms of the four classroom energizers. As we are often not conscious of our own styles[21] it may be useful to use this checklist to get feedback from colleagues.

Only the shallow know themselves. (Oscar Wilde)

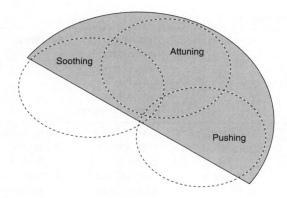

Figure 8.2 The teaching styles arc ii

You may also wish to get agreement among colleagues on this checklist. This is an oblique way to discuss the issue of teacher variation, to help achieve at least *a unity of purpose within a diversity of practice*, if not consistency.

Each of the two styles on either side of the attuning style will work with many pupils but can undermine some. As a result, they have been subdivided to indicate the risky aspects of these styles where caution is needed. These should be read across rather than down the columns.

 Stop and think

Which aspects of these styles did your own personal motivator have?
Do you have a dominant style?
Identify two aspects of your teaching style you like and one you dislike.
Where has it come from?

Motivating teaching involves being able to improvise your teaching style and take advantage of opportunities. This is the secret of the success of those computer programs that are customized to the user in such a way that the pacing is constantly being adapted to the individual.[13] Motivationally resilient teachers pivot around this style spectrum, adapting to the pupils they are teaching. They manage to communicate a sense of reciprocity and mutuality, that teaching and learning is a shared enterprise and this enables them to get their needs met through meeting their pupils' needs. The challenge to do this with 30 pupils in a class and 50 minutes to teach a lesson does not need to be stated.

Motivating teaching requires getting to know the class as well as possible and when necessary some pupils as individually as possible. The best way to get to know pupils is by trying to motivate them and observing how they respond to your teaching style and, in particular, to specific classroom energizers such as praise, deadlines or competition.

Motivating teaching uses words as its main tool and benefits from:

- an open style of questioning that promotes discussion and models and encourages self disclosure
- active listening

Table 8.1   The teaching styles

	Colluding, autonomy restricting, messes with pupils' motives	Soothing	Attuning, autonomy supportive, matches curriculum to pupils' motives	Pushing	Imposing, autonomy suppressing, bypasses pupils' motives
E N G A G E M E N T	1 tries too hard to be popular	1 aims to be popular	1 shows the class they're on its side	1 particularly values the successful	1 values only the successful
	2 over-protects pupils	2 protects pupils	2 works hard to create an 'improve yourself' climate	2 creates a 'prove yourself' climate	2 criticises judgementally to provoke
	3 encourages pupils to wallow in problems	3 encourages pupils to talk about problems	3 tunes into and acknowledges any negative feelings	3 downplays any pupil problems	3 suppresses negative feelings pupils may have
	4 is always apologising or mollifying	4 apologises readily	4 publicly apologises when appropriate	4 reluctant to apologise	4 would never apologise
	5 discourages high expectations	5 sets realistic expectations	5 shares challenging expectations	5 sets demanding expectations	5 sets unrealistic expectations
S T R U C T U R E	6 nags and pleads	6 fails to set limits	6 uses rules as a starting point in affirming pupils' capacity for self direction	6 boxes pupils in with tight rules and deadlines	6 uses threats and scare tactics to establish their authority
	7 gives too much freedom	7 dampens pupil initiative by their level of support	7 encourages initiative through a trusting, non-controlling style	7 blocks initiative	7 ignores or undermines pupils' ideas
	8 leaves pupils without a sense of direction	8 gives a lot of choice	8 seeks commitment through choice	8 doesn't encourage choice	8 seeks compliance
	9 reasons too much	9 conciliatory	9 flexible, compromises and gives second chance	9 takes a firm line	9 seeks revenge through punishment

Table 8.1   (Continued)

	Colluding, autonomy restricting, messes with pupils' motives	Soothing	Attuning, autonomy supportive, matches curriculum to pupils' motives	Pushing	Imposing autonomy suppressing, bypasses pupils' motives
S T I M U L A T I O N	10 bores pupils	10 spoon feeds pupils	10 capitalises on pupils' interests to promote learning as an intrinsic goal	10 promotes learning as an external goal	10 imposes learning on pupils
	11 lets pupils take a hit or miss approach	11 can be intrusive and interfering	11 nurtures reciprocity via fun, humour and banter	11 mono-polises the discussion	11 fixed on their own goals
	12 shows they don't see much point	12 apologises for uninteresting tasks	12 promotes value and purpose in the curriculum by reflecting on the relevance of outcomes	12 imposes while acknowledg-ing any limited interest	12 imposes the curricu-lum with lit-tle time for reflection
F E E D B A C K	13 gives plastic, insin-cere praise to conforming pupils	13 praises pupils, particularly for their ability	13 helps pupils recog-nise their effort and feel in charge of their progress	13 compares pupils openly through controlling praise	13 contami-nates success with sarcastic praise
	14 gives rewards inconsistently	14 gives rewards to control behaviour	14 offers occasional rewards to motivate learning	14 rarely gives rewards	14 reluctant to acknowl-edge signs of improvement
	15 makes pupils feel guilty for fail-ure	15 glosses over mistakes	15 treats mistakes as a pointer to ways to improve	15 meets failure with criticism	15 meets failure with disapproval and humiliat-ing criticism
	16 lets pupil opinion overrule	16 tries to accommodate	16 seeks feed-back from pupils about their class experiences	16 doesn't seek feedback	16 sees pupils as different from them and so discounts any feedback

- deriving meaning from what pupils say
- paraphrasing, that is, sending back the meaning you have taken from what was said
- being genuinely interested in what pupils say.

As with pupils and their stances, it is important for teachers to show the full range of styles and defensive reactions. Displaying defensive reactions shows that a teacher is human and allows them to model recovery, that is, resilience. Motivating teaching demands a huge amount of emotional labour. Being reasonable and positive while restraining any negative feelings, despite all the frustrations, can be exhausting. The more authentic and deeply felt their emotions are the better it is for a teacher's well-being.[14] Playing a role, where, for example, you try to display emotions that you do not feel, causes stress. To be able to stay receptive to the full range of pupils' emotions, teachers need to hold on to their sense of purpose.[15]

Defensive teaching reactions

> As a teacher I can be a tool of torture or an instrument of inspiration. I can humiliate or humour, hurt or heal. (Haim Ginott)

Teaching is a privileged position, touching the lives of children. However, teachers, like our emotions and our language, are never in neutral; they are either energizing or draining pupil motivation. The most motivating teachers manage to avoid getting locked into either extremes of the style arc. The knee-jerk reactions of teachers whose style is close to the edge can drag them into the dark side of motivation. Such 'off-key' reactions when teachers 'snap' are termed *defensive teaching reactions*. Figure 8.3 echoes the dark and light side of personality and portrays how soothing teachers can become overprotective and smothering, while on the other hand pushing teachers can become over-provocative and coercive. As with autonomy, these reactions can merge, *in extremis*, into a crushing reaction.

An over-soothing teacher may be popular with pupils but will not be a great teacher, as that needs both support and challenge. Similarly an over-pushy teacher may be respected and feared but will not be a great teacher because they will have casualties in their classes.

The soothing and pushing styles can slip into defensive reactions and thereby generate the *classroom drainers*. Even minor drainers can spoil the atmosphere and have a big impact on a class and individuals.

> ## Stop and think
>
> In the previous chapter you considered the person who most positively influenced your motivation to learn. Use the matrix in Figure 8.4 to rate how they treated you.
> First, rate how they valued you, gave you a sense of security and affiliation.
> Second, rate how they encouraged you, built up your confidence and nurtured your sense of agency.
> Third, rate how readily they allowed you to develop, how much they enthused and enabled you, how much autonomy support they gave you, that is, allowed you to be yourself. To select the most appropriate rating on the circle (you have a choice of two rating scales) you need to decide its location on either side of the circle, if the rating is less than 10 and more than 0. This will be determined by the priority they gave to either valuing you (which might have been protective and restricting) or encouraging you (which might have gone as far as provoking).

> ## Stop and think
>
> Identify the person who most negatively influenced your motivation to learn. Now consider how they did that and plot how they treated you in the chart above.
> Now compare and contrast the *motives* of your motivator and demotivator. Assuming you rated your motivator high on each of the three scales, that person's treatment of you will be somewhere in the *light side.* Their motive will have been to get the best out of you for your benefit. Compare your experiences with colleagues.
> Now consider the motives of your drainer.

This is more complex and will probably include one of the following three motives. The most clear-cut motive belongs to the person rated as low on the valuing and encouraging ratings, that is, blocking and trashing. Their motive was probably similar to the bully's motive to intentionally use their power over you to hurt or degrade you in order to enhance their status and esteem. The degree to which they crushed your motivation will depend on to what extent they provoked or blocked you, but also on your own motivational resilience to deal with it.

The motives of someone who had a more restricting or distorting impact are more complex. Let us take the restricting effect first. Such a person would value and care for you but in a way that held you back. This in fact is not uncommon and reflects the motives of parents and teachers who are overprotective of young people or who prefer compliance and conformity over growth. It could be described as being *warmly controlling*.

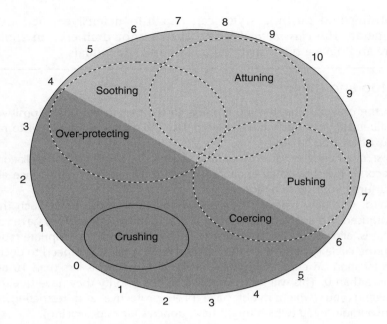

Figure 8.3   Teaching styles and defensive reactions i

Now we need to consider the motives of someone who pushes the other person but in a cold and coercive way. Their motive may be to provoke the person to try harder. This is being *coldly encouraging* while imposing their agenda. Or it may reflect a neglecting, could not care less attitude.

How you dealt personally with any negative experiences may have had a significant impact on your thinking about motivation. People who have had adverse experiences in how they have been treated and have overcome them can develop one of two beliefs about what people facing similar adversity should do. They may believe that people just need to toughen up, take responsibility for themselves and stop whining. Or they may believe that people need support while developing their resilience to deal with adversity. These beliefs will influence their teaching styles.

How teaching styles can slip into the dark side

 Stop and think

When does your teaching style get you into difficulties?

A teacher's style is constantly exposed to the full public glare of the classroom. When stressed we tend to revert to type, that is, to what we first or most strongly learned and what we feel protects ourselves. A teacher's default defensive reaction will be the dark side of their strength. It is difficult to change a knee-jerk reaction when under stress, so it is important to position ourselves from the start. In the same way, our starting position in any sport has to be right. If our default style is too close to either edge of the style arc, it does not leave us with much room to

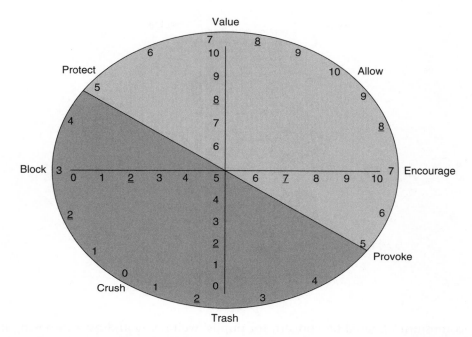

Figure 8.4   The styles and reactions matrix

manoeuvre and does not take much to push us into the defensive teaching reactions. Teachers engage in these reactions when they feel pressurized, threatened and out of control, or when their own needs crowd out their capacity to tune in to their pupils' needs.[16] A fuller picture of these reactions together with the teaching styles is portrayed in Figure 8.5.

The colluding reaction
The soothing teaching style has the danger of slipping into an overprotective, sentimental, colluding and *internally manipulating* reaction, perhaps created by acquiescent affiliation and restricted autonomy. The teacher is still trying to look after pupils but meddles with their motives. Some teachers can get carried away with caring and forget their teaching responsibility. This can manifest itself in a lenient, *wrapping-up-in-cotton-wool* reaction, motivated perhaps by fear or anxiety. It can also become an indulging or a manipulating reaction, involving guilt-induction, withdrawal of approval or bribing. The teacher will, for example, make deals with pupils while saying 'you owe me one' and casting it up sometime in the future. It can show itself by denying any responsibility for a task, claiming 'it's a waste of time but we have been told to do it'.

To avoid being too soothing, a teacher can reflect on how they use the four classroom energizers, especially structure.

The coercing reaction
The *pushing* style focuses on taking charge and setting the agenda in a way that effectively maintains order and gets through the course. However, if it

becomes unmitigated by concern for pupils' well-being and over-imposing it can bypass pupils' motives and suppress their autonomy. Such a directly controlling, high performance teaching style might not appear harmful but children's perceptions of this style arouse anger, anxiety or acquiescence[17] and these emotions trigger defensive reactions in pupils. Directly controlling teaching increases as pupils progress through school.[18,19] Children do not appear to become more resilient to such practices.[20]

In the coercing reaction, triggered perhaps by antagonistic agency, teachers can sometimes act like a robot and treat all pupils like a set of identical mini-robots. Such a rigid, impersonal style will fail to engage pupils, and the teacher will reap the behavioural backlash. Just think, for example, about how blanket reprimands are so demotivating and cause indignation among innocent pupils. Dictating pupil engagement merely galvanizes opposition. The only response teachers can *force* out of pupils is a defensive reaction.

The coercing reaction is marked by:

- *why questions* that suggest criticism and force pupils to justify themselves rather than look at alternatives, such as 'why can't you ever get your work in on time?'
- *closed statements* that suggest finality and preclude any hope of an open discussion, such as 'you are the most difficult pupil I have ever had to teach'
- *accusatory statements* that trigger defensiveness, such as 'you have to have the last word every time, don't you', 'your work is very shoddy'
- *condemning threats,* such as telling 8-year-olds 'you'll never get a job'.

Most teachers readily differentiate pupils in curricular terms. Some teachers are not so ready to differentiate pupils in motivational terms and do not see it as their responsibility to adapt to variable attitudes. If there are any problems

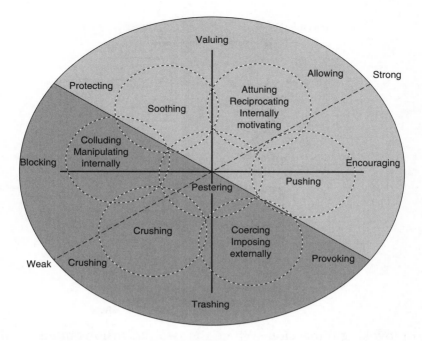

Figure 8.5   Teaching styles and defensive reactions ii

it is someone else's job to fix them. They have not recognized this as their responsibility, perhaps because they have not been trained in how to respond to different attitudes.

To avoid being too pushy, teachers can reflect on how they use the four classroom energizers and, for example, start paying more attention to pupils' feelings and perspectives via the Engagement Energiser.

The crushing reaction

Colluding and *coercing* reactions can merge into a crushing reaction, where the unacceptable face of teaching is evident, when, for example, the teacher publicly humiliates or frightens a pupil.

Once teachers have crossed into the dark side, some may struggle to stop and end up crushing pupils. Why might this be? The pupils react to the teacher's reaction and the changed atmosphere. Then the teacher has to react in turn, and so the tension escalates. Before they know it the teacher may have alienated the class against them, leaving them isolated and defensive. The blinkers then come down, the teacher loses self-focus and their negative emotions generate more negative emotions. They need to stop, reflect and to learn from the pupils.

The pestering reaction

A fourth defensive teaching reaction completes the picture to match the seven descriptions from the shower metaphor. People talk about *weak* versus *strong* teachers. As displayed in Figure 8.5, the weak and strong dimension can be considered as at right angles to and intersecting the protecting

versus provoking dimension. Where the two dimensions intersect in the middle of the matrix, lies the pestering reaction that is weak, pleading, ineffectual and nagging, that is characterized by inconsistency and a lack of fairness.

Stop and think

Remember the question posed earlier – What teacher behaviours towards pupils have you seen or done yourself that you would describe as *the unacceptable face of teaching?* Where would you locate your responses to this question, in the matrix in Figure 8.5?

Which defensive reactions do you most often fall into?

In what circumstances are you most likely to do this?

How can you recover from or limit the damage?

What could you do to avoid this reaction?

Are there any aspects of your style you would like to change?

Reflect upon each of the four classroom energizers to consider how you could change any aspects of your style.

Summary

The teaching styles can be summarized using the same format as the energy for learning matrix, and include five bipolar dimensions, namely:

- the affirmation support style, valuing versus trashing
- the agency support style, encouraging rather than blocking
- the autonomy support style, giving and taking as opposed to coercing and imposing
- the autonomy support style, asserting yourself rather than colluding with pupils
- the autonomy support style, facilitating in contrast to crushing pupils' autonomy.

This teaching style matrix is displayed in Figure 8.6.

Each of the teaching styles and defensive reactions are amalgams of where teachers are in relation to these five dimensions. Their style profile reflects the teacher's 3A need satisfaction as well as their likely capacity to meet their pupils' 3A needs.

What it feels like for pupils: classroom climates

> My ideal class is a place where I am not judged. (Primary 6 pupil)

Classroom climate is the collective perceptions of those aspects that impact on what it feels like to be a pupil in that classroom.[22] For example, when pupils put their hand up to answer questions, they are putting themselves on the line, and how the teacher responds influences the climate. Classroom climate is like a barometer that measures the impact of the teaching styles on the class. Reflecting on the classroom climate allows us to consider how our pupils feel about their learning.

Research has found that many teachers can only partially predict their pupils' perceptions of their climate, suggesting that teachers do not understand the climate in their classrooms as well as they might. [23] Teachers can use the classroom climate questionnaire (Appendix 2) to gain more insight into pupils' perceptions of their classroom and it can help them focus their efforts on those aspects that might need to be improved. Using such measures of desired change will also provide evidence on how the teacher is impacting on pupil motivation.

'Oh, don't worry Mrs Frost, I'm just emigrating to Mr. Smilie's classroom where I believe the climate will be more conducive to my psychological well-being.

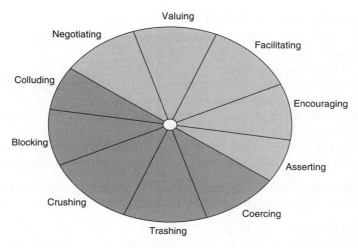

Figure 8.6   Teaching styles matrix

Stop and think

Do you think that what pupils think of your classroom climate is important?
How do classrooms differ in their climate?
How would you describe the climate you are trying to set?
Can you achieve a similar climate with each of your classes?
What are the main barriers to setting the climate you want?

Any classroom climate can be analysed using the lexicon provided by the four *energizers*, as displayed in Figure 8.7.

Stop and think

What would it be like in each of these classroom climates?

The affiliation and agency dimensions interact to form four types of climate. The *colluding* classroom is epitomized by:

- a climate that overprotects pupils from failure
- an undemanding pedestrian curriculum which encourages over-dependency
- pupils being 'spoon-fed', given lots of notes and encouraged to learn by rote
- pupils feeling safe but unchallenged, not feeling the need to produce their best work because 'good enough' work will be accepted, even praised
- the teacher doing most of the work and wanting success *through* their pupils.

This climate may be common in educational contexts where teaching is highly prescribed and qualifications driven. Here many pupils are externally motivated to get a particular qualification and teachers are held accountable, in an 'unintelligent' way, for the success rate of the class, that is, in a way that fails to take account of the full range of circumstances and of the achievements of individual pupils.

The *coercing* classroom is marked by:

- an over-competitive, insensitive and 'prove yourself' climate
- provocation
- unrealistic and unclear goals
- highly loaded teacher comments that voice comparison between pupils
- the teacher wanting success *from* their pupils
- learning is seen more as a means to an end
- pupils trying to show their superiority[24]
- pupils focusing on outcomes more outside their personal control, for example, beating others, attaining social approval and rewards.[25]

The *crushing* classroom is characterized by behaviours that most teachers would acknowledge are unacceptable, including:

- the use of sarcasm to humiliate
- setting unachievable or overwhelming goals
- shaming pupils and showing contempt
- oppressive discipline
- forced learning
- no choice or participation
- the teacher having low expectations and no interest in success.

Key characteristics of the *motivating* mastery classroom include:

- compromise and consideration
- autonomy support and encouragement
- efforts to share power with pupils as much as possible
- communicating and negotiating in a confident manner
- tuning in to the pupils' perspective
- helping pupils identify and follow their interests
- the teacher wanting success *for* the pupils

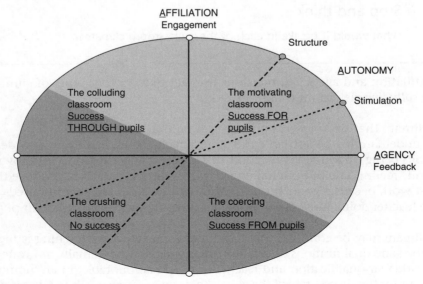

Figure 8.7   The classroom climates

- an emphasis on task mastery and improvement[26,27]
- effort and participation being more valued than success and end products
- achievement being seen to be within the individual's control[28]
- failure is used as feedback.

 Stop and think

What would be a good barometer of a motivated classroom?
Where in the framework would you generally place your classroom climate?
Can you identify any changes you would like to make to your climate?

Barriers to motivating teaching

While educational reforms aspire to improve pupil achievement, they also carry dangers that might damage pupil motivation. Two current policy trends are highlighted below that may unwittingly create barriers to motivating teaching:

- initiatives that dent teacher morale
- curricular reforms that highlight pupil responsibility while encouraging dependency.

Initiatives draining teacher morale

The plethora of initiatives designed to improve achievement is paradoxically in danger of undermining their own aims by denting teacher morale. The open-ended nature of trying to enable children to achieve their potential in combination with the quest for continuous improvement is a recipe for stress. Every new initiative is a potential burden, particularly if it does not take into account the culture of schools or connect with their central mission.[29]

A preoccupation with outcomes can also be counterproductive. There is a danger of losing sight of learning for its own sake. The purpose of educational initiatives is always to unlock potential but this can get crushed in the overemphasis on targets. As discussed above, the more teachers feel under the control of stringent targets, performance appraisal and monitoring, the more they may download this pressure to pupils through a coercive teaching style.

While teachers are doing more and more to and for pupils, they cannot actually motivate them in this way.

> The will to learn is an intrinsic motive ... that becomes a 'problem' only under specialized circumstances like those of a school, where a curriculum is set, pupils confined, and a path fixed.[30]

The richest motivation is self-motivation and that is a door that is unlocked from within. Teachers, however, have a huge role in influencing how pupils motivate themselves, by providing opportunities that are in and of themselves motivating. Children acquire the values that help them thrive in school through a process of internalizing these values. Schools should therefore support young people's natural tendency to internalize values rather than force them.

Motivating others is like making a fire. You prepare the ground with some kind of motivational kindling and provide the spark but the fire has to take hold itself. Thereafter the fire only requires fuel and occasional stoking.

Curricular reforms highlight responsibility while encouraging dependency

Progressive curricula in most countries highlight pupil responsibility, yet practice may be actually encouraging dependency in children. To raise attainment, teachers increasingly spoon-feed children who consequently fail to assume responsibility for their own learning.

Stop and think

Who is responsible for success and failure in your class?

Your answer is probably that everyone is responsible. Yet why is it that most teachers feel responsible for everything? Teachers taking responsibility for everything was possibly feasible and appropriate 30 years ago, but not today. Teachers need to share responsibility with their pupils. Too many pupils come to school with the assumption that the teacher will control, entertain and teach them. They will taunt newly qualified teachers coming to terms with this multi-faceted challenge.

One head teacher summed it up when he suggested to me – 'schools are places where young people go to watch old people work'.

The curriculum is crucial but there are other, equally if not more, crucial components of the educational experience. Teachers affect pupils more through their teaching style than their curriculum. Pupils internalize a school's values through identification with teachers. Reform focused exclusively on the curriculum gives the high moral ground to those teachers who think they have little responsibility for creating the climate that engages pupils and reinforces a teacher identity based on discrete subject teaching. It is time to move on to a broader teacher identity that incorporates teaching style and classroom climate. Delivering the outcomes expected of modern curricula will require teachers to give more of themselves.

Summary of key points

- Teachers' own motivation predicts their teaching style. The less pressure they feel, the more they will be motivated and, in turn, the more autonomy supportive they will be.
- Any discussion about improving pupil motivation must include the conditions that affect teachers' motivation.
- The teaching styles arc mirrors the arc of autonomy.
- Motivationally resilient teachers pivot around this style arc, adapting to pupils as appropriate.
- Knee-jerk reactions of teachers close to either extreme edge can take them into the dark side of motivation. Such reactions are termed *defensive teaching reactions* which generate the *classroom drainers*.
- Any classroom climate can be analysed using the lexicon provided by the four *Energizers* that interact to meet the '3A' needs.
- Initiatives designed to improve achievement are paradoxically in danger of denting teacher morale.
- Progressive curricula highlight pupil responsibility, yet in practice may encourage pupil dependency.

Part Four

How pupils adapt

9

The learning stances

Comments on the learning stances

Class teachers

The learning stances are a great way to think about what is going on in my class.

The learning stances are so much better because the pupils can see they are not trapped in labels like the 'bad' boy.

I didn't realize that emotions were so important in my pupils' motivation to learn.

I'm confident in dealing with different stances now and I have more strategies for dealing with problems.

It has made me look at my class and the pupils in a different way. I now make assessments at a different level – not just at the National Curriculum level. I look at where the pupils are coming from.

The learning stances give me more information that is useful in getting to know a new class.

Pupils

I used to think pupils were good and bad but now I know there is a whole range of stances, it's given me a bigger picture. (Keith, Primary 7)

Since this happened we have seen a big difference in the class:

- We understand each other better.
- Boys don't hate each other now.
- I'm more confident now.
- I play with everyone now.
- Everybody now gets along better.
- We're more together as a class.

I know a lot of stroppy people and it's helped me deal with them.

The stances really made me think about what kind of person I am.

The stances teach you about yourself and help you describe yourself better.

I feel stronger now and name-calling doesn't affect me the way it used to. I can deal with it better.

The stance diary stops you going into denial about your behaviour. It helps you face up to your behaviour.

Before these classes I just thought I was happy or sad but now I know my stances and I can stance myself.

I can stance other people now and deal with them better.

There are parts of yourself that the teacher knows but you don't and this helps you find out about it.

Parents

The learning stances have helped me take off the blinkers. When you see where they are on the stances, you see the issue right away.

It helped me consider my children's feelings about school. When I was at school, children didn't have feelings.

My eyes were opened. I used to be pessimistic but now I'm more optimistic.

Others

The learning stances are a means of generating positive change, not just a static descriptor. (Educational psychologist)

This is the best example of applied educational psychology I have ever come across. (Educational psychologist)

I use the stances as my personal frame of reference. (Further education trainer)

Most of the classroom energizers engage most pupils. There are some specific energizers that work particularly well for some pupils but can in fact drain others. For example, encouragement is, by definition, an energizer that works with most pupils, but praise does not work for every pupil and can backfire. There are also some drainers that are particularly off-putting for some pupils but can, in fact, motivate others. For example, humiliation demoralizes most people, but not all – think about diet clubs. Provocation similarly will have varying effects. The same approach can be an energizer and a drainer.

 Stop and think

Which factors in the list below energize or drain you? Compare your response with colleagues.

- public praise
- deadlines
- authority
- tight limits
- sarcasm

(Continued)

(Continued)

- failure
- uncertainty
- competition
- provocation
- challenge
- gambling
- high-profile responsibility
- tests
- being put on the spot
- teamwork
- high expectations
- choice
- criticism
- money
- pressure

What makes any of these an energizer? How can something be a drainer when used by one teacher with a particular child and an energizer in the hands of another teacher with the same pupil? Answering these questions will require a consideration of teaching style. A matrix is presented near the end of this chapter to help work out what makes each of the list above an energizer or a drainer.

There is nothing that does not have the potential to motivate someone, in some way, and there is nothing that does not demotivate someone. There can often be a gap between a teacher's intention and impact. Pupils can take a teacher's intended energizer, for example, banter, and experience it as sarcasm. In the same way, there are potential drainers, such as provocation, that work as energizers for some pupils. The key factor is the teaching style, how the teacher is holding the reins. If too tight, banter becomes sarcasm, that is when it is hurtful and the child cannot reciprocate. If too loose, praise is experienced as plastic and insincere, and therefore ineffectual. The impact also depends crucially on how pupils adapt to the situation. How can teachers anticipate the pupil response? The answer is through the learning stances.

This chapter builds the learning stances matrix as another layer of the motivation matrix. It presents the distinguishing features of the learning stances. It explains what the stances are, how we can identify them and where they come from. The chapter highlights the dynamism of the learning stances. It shows how teaching styles can be in or out of step with learning stances. Finally, it looks at how the stances can be used to find the right buttons to press for different pupils.

The learning stances

Man is not the creature of circumstances. Circumstances are the creatures of men.
(Benjamin Disraeli)

Danny's learning stance during French lacked a little 'joie de vivre' ...

The learning stances portray how pupils interact with the learning climate. They are a way of looking at '*engage-ability*' in learning. The learning stances are the ways pupils engage positively and the defensive reactions are used to describe how they disengage. For brevity we will use the term *stances* as the generic term for both. The stances are classroom expressions of pupils' personalities and emotions. They reflect an orientation towards a specific context or activity rather than an enduring disposition. They mirror the teaching styles and reactions, and both styles and stances are founded upon the 3A needs matrix.

The stances are learned attitudes that reflect both how pupils feel about themselves and their current intentions about learning. They are shaped by the beliefs they hold about themselves as learners. The stances are defined from the perspective of the observer. From the teacher's angle, they are a reflection of how the teacher feels about the pupils. Most people will see pupils in the engaged stances similarly, but there will be less agreement between teachers on those pupils who are seen as taking up defensive reactions.

> I find this pupil exasperating; he takes the initiative without asking permission. (Class teacher 1)

> I think this pupil is a real asset to the class; he uses his own initiative and is very helpful. (Class teacher 2)

From the pupils' perspective their stances reflect their identity as a learner, how they feel about their role in the class. Pupils can readily grasp and use the stance matrix to reflect on their own behaviour.

The learning stances matrix

The purpose of this matrix is to develop our capacity to adapt to pupils. It offers a common language with which teachers can discuss and make sense of their pupils' motivation. It can help them get to know their pupils better and find ways to engage all of them. It crystallizes our current knowledge about learner psychology.

It is a dynamic matrix that stresses the fluid and expansive nature of personality. It profiles how individuals change in response to the different classroom situations and as a result of how they feel.

These pupil comments highlight this dynamism:

> You can look back at your earlier stances and see how you've changed.
>
> Throughout the day our stances change.
>
> I realize that people can change all the time.

Personality type as the basis of the stances

Each pupil has a unique personality that interprets their needs and shapes how they try to meet them. Personality shapes how we think, feel and adapt to our environment.[1] In particular it influences how we think and feel about ourselves. Pupils show their personalities in expressive behaviour, particularly through the expression of their emotions. It is appropriate, therefore, to model the stances matrix on personality type.

As discussed in Chapter 3, there is nothing problematic about being *cautious* or *impulsive* and each has its advantages. *Resilience* is being as impulsive as possible and as cautious as necessary.[2] This lets you express emotions and impulses when you can but contain them when you need to. People low in resilience lack this flexibility and tend to become chaotic or rigid in response to stress.[3]

The three-way formulation from the personality types is mirrored to create the learning stances, as displayed in Figure 9.1. They also mirror the teaching styles.

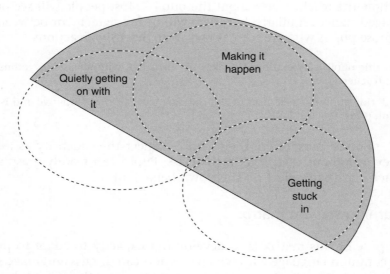

Figure 9.1   The learning stances

The stances as autonomy indicators

As discussed in Chapter 3, *autonomy* is an arc whose two ends become increasingly discrete relative to each other. As you move from the midpoint of full autonomy there is an increasing tendency to react and show *restricted* or *distorted autonomy*.

Each of the three positive learning stances reflects variants of high levels of autonomy, the capacity to be in charge of your own learning. The higher the levels of agency and affiliation, the greater the autonomy and the more engaged the pupil will be. Such pupils are consistently engaged in most aspects of school. Autonomy comes from taking on board external controls and values. For example, the discipline teachers and parents provide helps young people to gradually develop their own self-discipline.

We saw earlier that if external controls are not internalized, the young person develops distorted or restricted autonomy. In addition, some learners have a more enduring disengagement from learning that is shaped by both low agency and low affiliation. This leads to a third low autonomy reaction that combines aspects of restricted and distorted autonomy, reflected in a sense of being overwhelmed and pressurized by internal or external forces. This small minority of pupils can get locked into this reaction and become particularly hard to engage.

Such overwhelmed autonomy is partly caused by and reflected in emotional instability, the tendency to experience disruptive negative emotions that lead to passive forms of coping. Emotional instability makes pupils vulnerable to negative mood and causes them to overreact to problems. A cocktail of impulsiveness, negative emotionality and an avoidant style of coping (anger + alienation + anxiety + apathy) underlie disengagement in adolescence.[4]

Emotional instability is seen in young children's anger and anxiety. Very early in childhood, fear triggers shyness while anger triggers aggression. Children who show irritable distress present both anger and anxiety.

> Johnny is 4 years old and attends his local early years centre. He has a chaotic home life, being brought up by a single mother who is alcohol dependent. He is timid and withdrawn most of the time. However he can be unpredictable and, without warning, explode with rage.

These forms of low autonomy are displayed in Figure 9.2. The arc of autonomy and its shadow form a circle around the two-dimensional space located by affiliation and agency. Individuals have a point on each of these dimensions and on the autonomy circle. Joining up these points will outline the space which that individual is most likely to occupy at any particular time.

Low agency can lead to anxiety, apathy or acquiescence, depending on the affiliation level and the nature of the pupil's capacity to exercise autonomy. Similarly low affiliation can lead to anxiety, alienation or anger, depending on level of agency and the pupil's autonomy reaction. Low autonomy can be expressed in acquiescence, anxiety or anger, depending on the level and nature of affiliation and agency.

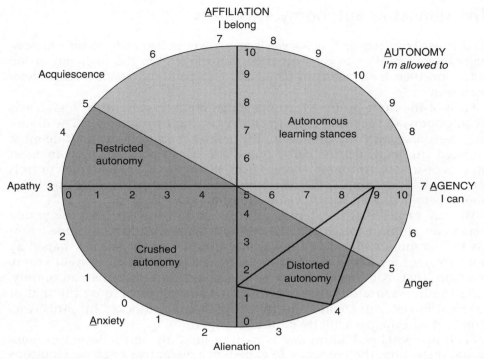

Figure 9.2   The low autonomy reactions

 Stop and think

Consider where you are right now in your job on each of the rating scales and join up your three points to find your current space. Is this linked to and reflected in your teaching style?

The defensive reactions

If all of our 3A needs are met, our personality flourishes and expresses itself through the learning stances. If our needs are not met, our personality is compromised and we react defensively. These reactions are given descriptive labels in Figure 9.3. They echo the basic fight, flight or freeze response to threat. They reflect how people have varying thresholds to threat and are primed in different ways. The *acting up* reaction is located in the centre of the matrix as it combines a mixture of defensive and positive elements. These seven descriptors mirror the labels from the shower metaphor.

The learning stances and reactions can now be circularly arranged within the 3A needs matrix, as displayed in Figure 9.4. The stances and reactions are defined by locating them within this matrix, each overlapping its neighbour.

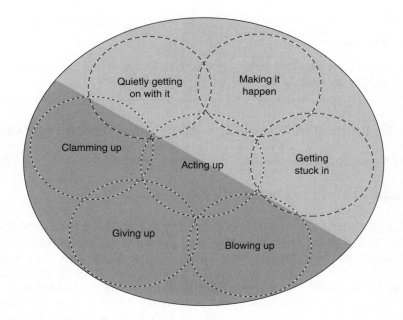

Figure 9.3   The stances & reactions

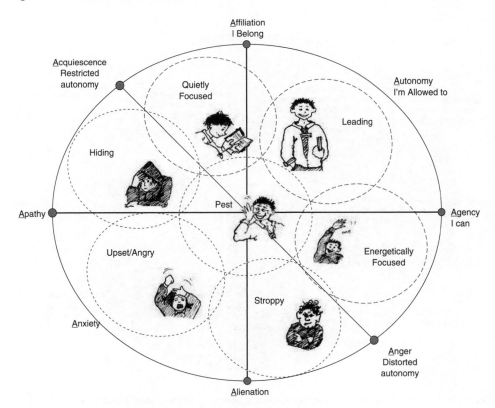

Figure 9.4   The learning stances & reactions ii

Stop and think

Do you see pupils' defensive reactions as feedback on your teaching style or their problem?

The distinguishing features of the learning stances and reactions

The distinguishing features of the stances are summarized in Figure 9.5.

How pupils are spread across the stances

Table 9.1 presents the distribution across the stances and reactions that was found when a group of teachers allocated pupils into the stances they most often occupied. These pupils were aged 10 and 11 in the later stages of primary schooling in approximately 50 schools in a large urban education authority in Scotland. These data help illuminate the scale of the different stances. The gender differential is not surprising. What is perhaps surprising is the relatively small number of pupils allocated to the opposing reaction.

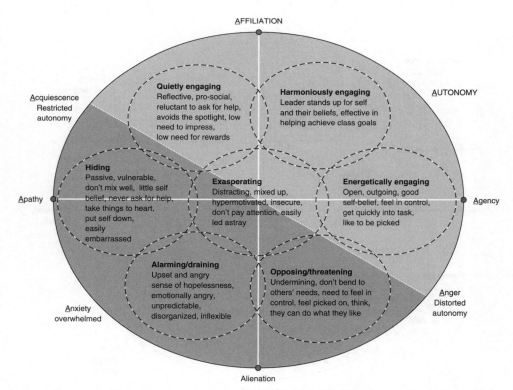

Figure 9.5   The distinguishing features of the learning stances and reactions

Table 9.1   Spread of pupils across the stances

	All	Girls	Boys
Harmoniously engaging	15	19	11
Quietly engaging	38	42	33
Energetically engaging	21	21	20
Positively engaged	73	82	65
Exasperating	12	7	17
Hiding	10	9	11
Opposing	3	1	4
Alarming and draining	2	1	3
Defensive reactions	27	18	35

n = 1760

Stance dynamics

> I'm in and out of these stances all day. (Craig, 11-year-old pupil)

> I realize I can have more than one stance and I can change every day. (Linda, 10-year-old pupil)

The strength of the stance matrix is its fluidity. Stances are like blood pressure, changeable depending on the situation we are in. Fluctuations in the 3A need satisfaction predict fluctuations in well-being[5] and stances. Pupils move from one stance to another. Because all the stances are to some extent available within individuals, the classroom can trigger each of them.

The dynamism of the stances underscores the need for teachers to be flexible in their response and adaptable to the changing stances. It is important for the teacher to understand their role in creating a classroom climate conducive to helping pupils 'move around' the stances. Even small changes in the classroom atmosphere make a difference.

 Stop and think

Consider a personal experience where your stance changed in the course of an event, a staff meeting or training course, for example.
How did your stance change and what made it change?
Consider this: show pupils the stance matrix presented at the end of this chapter. Ask them to put their finger on the stance they tend to be in one situation, for example, mathematics. Then give another situation, for example, Physical education, then the playground and so on. Ask what their finger is doing. Moving will be the answer.

How can you tell what stance someone is in?

Fortunately, we do not need to be mind-readers. We can read a pupil's stance through such factors as:

- their attitude, manner and behaviour
- where they choose to sit in the class
- what they say, how they say it and what they do not say
- their posture, demeanour and body language, especially their facial expressions.

The face is a particularly rich source of information and a good guide to our emotions.[6] Happiness, however, is the only positive emotion we show facially.

Where do learning stances come from?

The learning stances reflect, in part, pupils' personalities. Thinking about personality will help us to better understand pupils' stances and generate ideas about what suits pupils best. These insights are applicable to both the transient and more enduring stances as they are both underpinned to some extent by personality.

Motivation operates at three levels, namely:

- the global (personality)
- broad contextual (school)
- situational levels[7] (the classroom).

The global level is stable. Motivation becomes more malleable as we move down the hierarchy. Motivation also has a top-down and bottom-up effect, for example, how pupils get on in school affects their global motivation, and vice versa. An individual's motivation to learn gradually becomes an enduring disposition but pupils' stances are very malleable. A learning stance is not a lifestyle. Not only do pupils' learning stances vary between different contexts but also, with their mood, within the same context.

Each pupil's personality organizes their own set of internal energizers, including their motives and self-emotions. These energizers, along with attitudes picked up from parents and peers, also influence their stances.

A pupil's stance at any one time, however, is also related to their 'standing' in the group. A pupil's stance cannot therefore be considered independently of the class dynamics. The hierarchy in any group is not a property of the individuals, but of the group and is a description of the relationship between people.[8] Hierarchies are dynamic and change as people jockey for position. Teachers may unwittingly socialize their pupils into particular stances. Teachers can, for example, isolate a pupil by saying 'You're not allowed to go to the toilet yourself'. Other pupils can latch onto such nominations and reinforce them in order to seek teacher approval.

Stop and think

Compare the impact on pupils' learning stances of traditional questioning and the more inclusive 'no hands up' technique.

Personal diversity

It may be necessary to experience all the stances to be a well-rounded person. Our inner landscape is fluid and shifting, reflected in this model of healthy multiplicity. Just as it is good to have a range of different types of friend, we need to be able to express ourselves through a range of stances. In fact the correlations between children's behaviour in different contexts is very low. All pupils vary across classes, roles and relationships and some pupils vary more than others. Such variability is not necessarily problematic.[9]

There will be times and situations when each of the stances, even the defensive reactions, will be appropriate. For example:

- Some *opposition* helps establish our independence and it is helpful to be combative at times. The opposing reaction is highly adaptive if you are being abused in your home. Conflict is not always bad and can prick a suffocating conformity or prompt a group to address issues that might otherwise be overlooked. Controlled, verbal aggression can be used to win arguments and achieve high status.
- It makes sense to keep your head down and *hide* in staff meetings with a new boss, when you do not yet have the measure of them.
- The capacity to give voice to our distress, evident when *alarming and draining*, far from being undesirable, may be a precious skill.[10] We need to help pupils to make sense of and voice their distress as a first step towards improving their situation.
- Being *exasperating* is one way to communicate the need for clarity and certainty.

Although the stances can be separated, it is important to emphasize that we are all able to take up each of them. Just as we celebrate cultural diversity, we should also celebrate *personal diversity*. The matrix gives a greater understanding of how our stances can create a more unified self. We know intuitively about personal diversity and often see pupils in a different light when in different situations. Problems occur when a pupil becomes entrenched in a self-defeating reaction and they discover the 'power' these defensive reactions can give them.

The stance matrix encourages teachers to try to see any pupil's weakness as a strength, for example, stubborn defiance in the oppositional reaction could be seen as a strength of character. It might not help in the face of that stubborn defiance *there and then*, but it might prove helpful in dealing with that pupil in the future. Key strengths and weaknesses of each of the stances are highlighted in Table 9.2, together with their key features.

Questioning techniques for the different stances

To offer a practical example of how the stances can be used to plan your approach in the classroom, typical examples of how pupils in each stance would respond to a 'question and answer session' are outlined in Table 9.3, together with helpful and unhelpful ways of dealing with them.

Implications

While every pupil is different, teachers do not need to take a different tack for every individual! Fortunately, pupils are more similar than they are different.[11] To motivate every pupil, teachers need to personalize their style to pupils' stances. At the same time, a key factor in motivating teaching is having a good working relationship with *the class* as a whole, as opposed to separate relationships with individual pupils. The optimal teaching style engages most of the class and adapts to individual pupils when they show defensive reactions.

Each stance is best dealt with by a subtle style adaptation using the energizers rather than an individualized approach. Teachers therefore should use the energizers to establish their learning climate then supplement as appropriate with stance-specific adaptations.

The characteristics of each stance together with the internal energizers underpinning them provide the clues needed to work out how to adapt the energizers. Support interventions should not aim to push children into a particular direction but, rather, to guide the pupil's propensities for change in the direction that is optimal for them.

Styles over stances

Motivating teachers manage to adapt their styles to resonate with most of the stances in their classroom. They also manage to control their own knee-jerk reactivity to pupils' defensive reactions. Teachers adopt a teaching style that communicates their authority. The way they make requests of pupils, for example, signals their understanding of the relationship between themselves

Table 9.2   Strength and weakness of each stance

Stance	Energetically engaging	Quietly engaging	Harmoniously engaging	Hiding	Exasperating	Opposing	Alarming and draining
Key features	Keen to impress, competitive, attention-grabbing	Focused in their own heads, co-operative, stay in the background	handle power and pressure well, attention holding, collaborative	Deal with anxiety by avoiding, good at putting teachers off trying to get them to work	Deal with insecurity and confusion by distracting, attention-seeking	Lacking empathy, deal with threat by being threatening, tension seeking	Deal with their draining feelings to draining others
Strengths	High energy, impulsive, sociable, enjoy praise, show initiative, determined to succeed, optimistic, open, competitive	Empathic, independent, reflective, methodical, self-motivated, mastery attitude to achievement	High self-belief, innovative, able to deal with peer pressure, principled, assertive, think critically, handle power well	Sensitive and compliant	High energy, endearing	Self-sufficient, questioning, challenging, stubborn defiance	cautious, articulating their distress is a first step towards improving their situation
Weaknesses	Can be intolerant of others who hold the group back, may show off, can take over in a group situation	Can be deferential, indecisive, self-effacing, lack spontaneity, over-compliant and over-trusting	None	Easily embarrassed, shy, little self-belief, apathetic, self-protective, submissive, hard to read	Insecure and confused, dependent, 'hyper-motivated', over-impulsive	Feels aggrieved, own needs outweigh other's needs, denies own feelings while manipulating everyone else's, dismissive of others yet driven by reputation	Apathy and alienation, aggressive and withdrawn, learned helplessness, difficult temperament low self-control, self-destructive behaviour

Table 9.3   Questioning techniques for the different stances

	Energetically engaging	Quietly engaging	Harmoniously engaging	Hiding	Exasperating	Opposing	Alarming and draining
Pupil response	Their hands are up every time, they give full answers	They will know the answer but prefer to let others answer it; answers are to the point	Answer confidently and question respectfully; will ask questions to clarify meaning	Make themselves invisible	First with their hands up but do not know the answer; give silly answerws	Give cheeky answers while smirking	Sniggering, blushing
What they do not need	Do not allow them to answer all the questions	Do not jump in too soon with the answer. Do not make them the centre of attention. Do not force them to give an opinion	Do not allow them to answer all the questions	Do not ask too many questions that put them on the spot	Do not ask too many questions. Do not respond to distracting questions	Do not question aggressively. Do not give questioning commands – 'would you like to …'	Do not ask too many questions
What they need	Challenge a correct answer to condition them against the expectation that a challenge automatically means they're wrong. A 'correct' challenge might be: 'Yes, that's right. How did you know that should be the answer?'	Increase wait time after questions. Allow thinking and preparation time. Encourage them to expand on one-word answers. Suggest they can ask you after class, if they need to check things	Allow them to ask difficult questions about the school and the curriculum. Give them a list of questions and ask them to select the most useful ones to answer. Give them responsibility for questioning each other. Ask why questions	Ask questions you know they will be able to answer	Ask brief, snappy questions to check comprehension and keep them 'on their toes'	Use questions to communicate critical feedback rather than direct criticism	Get them to ask their own questions. Increase 'wait time' and give preparation. If they say they do not know, ask what would they say if they did. Get them to ask their own questions to which they will know the answers, to let them discover they know more than they think

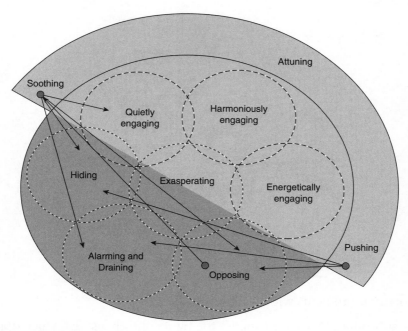

Figure 9.6   Dancing out of step

and pupils. Pupils take a stance that reflects how they see the relationship and how they intend to respond.

Dancing out of step

Outlined below and displayed in Figure 9.6, are some examples of when the style is out of step with the stance.

The potential problems with the over-soothing style:

- Pupils in the quietly engaging stance can become resistant if they feel they are being intruded upon or manipulated.
- For some pupils, the *pleading* aspect of the soothing style is like a red rag to a bull. Weakness is provocative, perhaps because it is too good an opportunity for them to show their superiority. A weak teaching style may also provoke an opposing reaction, perhaps because pupils intuitively know that they need a firmer structure and it is their way of demanding it. A style that fails to enforce authority may also provoke contempt. This style can also push some pupils from the exasperating reaction into more defensive reactions.
- Lethargy develops when praise is given regardless of whether the child has actually done well. Pupils with restricted autonomy react to the *colluding* aspect of the soothing teaching style by paying lip-service.
- Teachers who take a pitying reaction to pupils in the alarming and draining reaction can unwittingly encourage them to wallow in their problems.
- Some pupils see a caring style as a result of their manipulation of the teacher rather than a genuine caring.

The potential problems with the over-pushing style

- The authoritarian reaction applies the tight controls against which opposing pupils like to rebel. Such strict discipline is interpreted as rejection and further proof that adults are not to be trusted. When an imposing teacher reaction meets an opposing pupil reaction, both motivated by a distorted autonomy, the outcome is inevitably confrontation. Both are knee-jerk reactions that are trying to protect their egos. Pupils with distorted autonomy have had to learn the hard way to survive by looking after themselves. They come to resent a change of the rules when someone tries to impose their will on them. Perhaps both of these could be described as posturing reactions, like rival state presidents, who need each other to posture to their electorates.
- Hiding pupils do not try, as trying and still failing drains their self-emotions. A provoking teaching style that pressurizes them to try harder causes further avoidance. Pupils with restricted autonomy have been getting away with having a quiet life for a long time. If someone tries to change that, they withdraw even further.
- A similar, though less extreme reaction can be triggered in quietly engaging pupils by such a pressurizing style.
- This provoking style can have a crushing impact on pupils in the alarming and draining reaction as it aggravates their feelings of being out of control.

The least helpful approach for each stance is summarized in Table 9.4.

Dancing in step

Displayed in Figure 9.7 are some examples of when the teaching style *dances in step* with the learning stance and engages the defensive reactions.

The art of the dance is in being aware of the space in between the dancing partners. Motivating teaching is all about negotiating the space in between

Table 9.4 The least helpful approach for each stance

Stance	Energetically engaging	Quietly Engaging	Harmoniously engaging	Hiding	Exasperating	Opposing	Alarming and Draining
Worst teaching reaction	Suppressing their energy	Over-intruding, taking them for granted	Setting them up by holding them up as stars	Exposing, compelling to take active part	Confusing with responsibilities, over stimulating, further distracting	Imposing, revenge seeking, directly criticizing or ridiculing, personalizing	Overwhelming, pitying, personalizing, getting sucked in

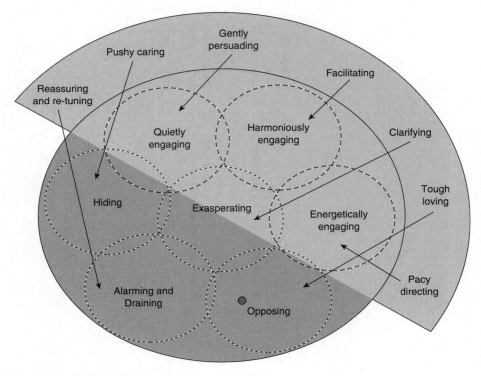

Figure 9.7   Dancing in step

the teacher and the class. The teacher and the class must collaborate to enable each others' movement.

The most helpful style for each stance is summarized in Table 9.5. These sub-styles will be further detailed in Part V.

Energizer or drainer?

At the start of this chapter the question was posed, what makes something an energizer or a drainer? The same technique can be an energizer or a drainer depending on how it is used, that is, the style. The classroom energizers can be used in different ways, depending on the teaching style, with variable impact on learners. The impact of any given intervention will be determined by its place on the style matrix. Some examples are illustrated in the matrix in Figure 9.8.

Praise can be draining within a colluding reaction, when it is experienced as plastic praise, or within a coercive reaction, when it can come across as contaminated praise. It can be experienced as encouraging if used genuinely within an autonomy supportive style. Sarcasm can be humiliating when used within a crushing style, when it is used to hurt and communicate contempt, but it can be used as a bonding tool within a flexible style, when it is two-way, clever and humorous.

Table 9.5 The most helpful teaching style for each stance

Stance	Energetically engaging	Quietly engaging	Harmoniously engaging	Hiding	Exasperating	Opposing	Alarming and draining
Best teaching style	Pacy directing to encourage their initiative while keeping them focused, promoting their enterprise, stimulating, surprising	Gently persuading, Inviting, non-intruding, quietly acknowledging; gently probing, finding the balance between letting them get on with it and pushing them enough	Facilitating, challenging, complexifying, giving discretion, maximizing trust, finding the balance between maximizing their influence and not setting them up as stars	Pushy caring, protecting through clarity of expectations, and supported participation; providing escape routes, finding sources of satisfaction beyond the curriculum	Clarifying, providing certainty and focus, helping them to find their place in the group, being patient, improving their status	Tough Loving and attuning, motivating them by their goals rather than your control minimizing what is threatening them	Reassuring and re-tuning to give a sense of control

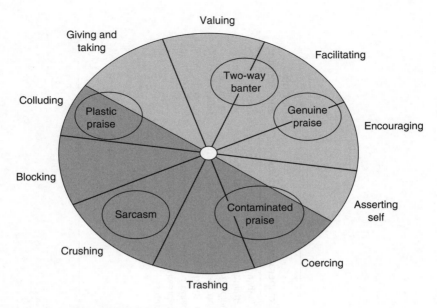

Figure 9.8   Energizer or drainer?

The stance-specific energizers and drainers

The main purpose of the stances is to help teachers adapt their style to different pupils, to find the right 'buttons' to press. For example, what Tony Blair spotted in Ian Paisley was not the intransigent priest others saw but his vast ego. Consequently he made him a Privy Counsellor and got the best out of him.

Outlined in Table 9.6 are some examples of the energizers that work well with particular stances and drainers that make them worse. Further illustrations will be detailed in Part V.

Further uses of the stance matrix

In addition to the main purpose of the stance matrix to help teachers to find the right 'buttons' to press for particular pupils, the matrix also for *everyone*:

- offers a common language about engagement in learning
- helps understand why teachers need to treat different pupils differently.

For *young people*, the matrix:

- allows them to label their feelings and lets them communicate their motivation to their teachers
- puts them in charge of their motivation
- develops an optimistic growth mindset that helps them see a way to improve

Table 9.6 Stance-specific energizers and drainers

Energetically engaging	Quietly engaging	Harmoniously engaging	Hiding	Exasperating	Opposing	Alarming and Draining
Energizer	Energizer	Energizer	Energizer	Energizer	Energizer	Energizer
Make them responsible for generating interest if they find the work boring, by seeking ways to make it more challenging and worthwhile. Promote their organizational skills	Respect their need for privacy and distance	Make the responsibilities real by agreeing them on the pupils' terms. Allow them to ask difficult questions about the school and to give real feedback to teachers. Offer opportunities for public speaking and for innovation and creativity	Negotiate private challenges and safe responsibilities. Provide activities where they can display their strengths and get recognition from peers. Prepare them and give a head start to let them contribute to the class. Use small group activities more than whole class activities	Track progress by positives, e.g. how many times they answered questions rather than how many times they shouted out. Give clear signals that prepare them to attend to instructions, particularly at transitions. Give a limited number of 'ration' cards for target behaviours	Encourage participation in positive coalitions such as competitive team sports. Give high-profile responsibilities. Share your perspective with them on their behaviour in a way that describes rather than judges	Maintain familiar and important routines and other means of reassurance. Help them replace self-defeating language with more positive self-talk. Use planning time and summary time to emphasize. predictability and self-control. If they respond badly to praise, ask them what they think of their performance and then comment on their evaluation

(Continued)

Table 9.6 (Continued)

Energetically engaging	Quietly engaging	Harmoniously engaging	Hiding	Exasperating	Opposing	Alarming and Draining
Drainer	**Drainer**	**Drainer**	**Drainer**	**Drainer**	**Drainer**	**Drainer**
Do not allow them to be too competitive and bossy. Do not suppress their enterprise and organizational skills	Do not intrude in their work	Do not hold them up as stars. Do not undermine their pro-social behavior by giving unnecessary rewards	Do not give long periods of individual work. Do not use a 'blank sheet' approach to writing	Do not distract them by over emphasizing rewards beforehand. Do not oppress any self-initiated secondary activities that help their concentration. Do not create an over-stimulating classroom	Do not encourage them to vent their anger. Do not take it personally and so make yourself the issue. Do not box them into a corner	Do not let them spend too much time in passive entertainment. Do not pity and encourage them to wallow

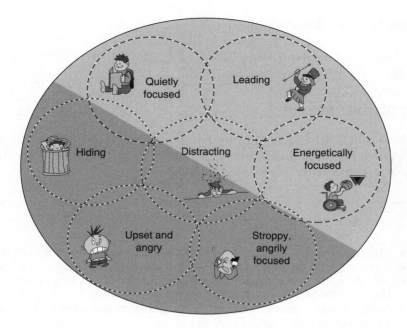

Figure 9.9   The learning stances – young person's version

- provides opportunities for teachers to reflect with them about their own learning stance, which helps identify their level of self-awareness, willingness to change and capacity to respond to support.

For parents, the matrix:

- helps them share information about their children's progress and support their children's engagement in learning
- helps them to find out directly from their children how they see the social dynamic of their class and their place in it.

For *teachers*, the matrix:

- helps to 'cut to the chase' in meetings about individual pupils and classes and gives a structure for a focused discussion
- assists them in making sense of the huge amount of information they take in about pupils and avoids 'typing' pupils quickly and subjectively
- helps them to understand the class dynamics. The matrix can be likened to a weather satellite: while it cannot prevent problems, it can anticipate them. It could be used to engineer a balanced group composition that allows the pupils in the 'dark' stances to be distributed rather than congregated together
- enables teachers to articulate to parents their concerns in as objective and supportive a way as possible.

For *support agencies*, the matrix:

- helps them understand the pupil in the context of the class and peer group.

Young person's version

Figure 9.9 depicts the version of the stances developed and used with pupils. Young people from age 9 can understand and use it. Children as young as 7 can grasp a matrix with three or four stances.

Summary of key points

- The stance matrix portrays how pupils interact with the learning climate.
- The stances are circularly arranged within the matrix created by the 3A needs.
- The strength of the matrix is its fluidity and dynamism that underscores the need for teachers to be flexible in their responses.
- Support interventions should guide the pupils' propensities for change in the direction that is optimal for them.
- The main purpose of the stance matrix is to help teachers differentiate how they treat pupils. Teachers should use the energizers through their teaching style to establish their relationship with the whole class, then adapt their style to the individual defensive reactions.

10

The layers of the matrix

This chapter recaps on the main components of the motivation matrix to highlight how the internal energizers, classroom energizers, stances and styles are all mirrors of the same basic template, formed by the 3A needs within the arc of resilience. It includes a discussion about the implications for the classroom of the way the self-emotions underpin achievement. The chapter concludes with a checklist covering the important motivational milestones in the process of the development of stances.

Personality types, traits and learner needs

The 3A needs fit into the circular matrix formed by the arc of resilience and its shadow. Personality can be characterized in terms of the twin qualities of reactivity and resilience that interact to determine how we adapt to our circumstances. Resilience is shaped by how we react to stress. As one moves away from optimal resilience around the arc of resilience the individual becomes either increasingly cautious and rigid or impulsive and chaotic. The impulsive/cautious dichotomy becomes increasingly discrete until the lowest levels of resilience when the two strands merge again in the dark side of reactivity. As we have seen, the path teachers and pupils take and the length of that path shapes the defensive reactions they adopt.

Some of the layers of the matrix are presented in Figure 10.1, highlighting the personality types, personality traits and learner needs.

The stances

The stances are located within this circle and displayed in Figure 10.2.

The stances can also be located within the five bipolar dimensions, used to form the energy for learning matrix in Chapter 5, namely, the affiliation and agency dimensions plus the three elements of autonomy, as displayed in Figure 10.3. The stances are an amalgam of where pupils are on each of the five dimensions, which reflects their 3A need satisfaction.

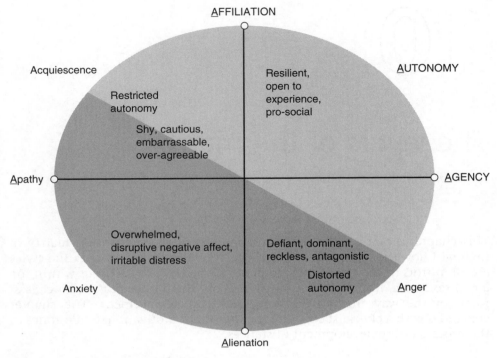

Figure 10.1   Personality types, traits and learner needs

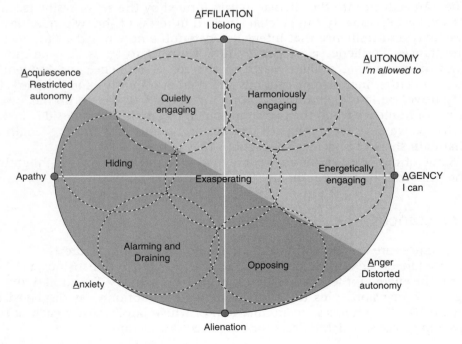

Figure 10.2   The learning stances and reactions iii

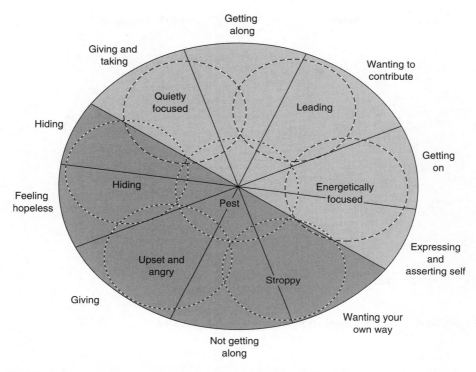

Figure 10.3   The stances within the energy for learning matrix

The internal energizers

The emotional underlay of the stances

The emotions underpinning the stances are presented in Figure 10.4.

Left to their own devices, our emotions are likely to push us towards self-indulgence, anger or self-destruction. Aristotle believed that human behaviour, if left unexamined, typically errs towards extremes and he outlined a *golden mean*. Aristotle's idea of the golden mean mirrors the arc of resilience and is illustrated in Figure 10.5.

The self-emotions

The stances reflect and are shaped by our emotions, especially the self-emotions. These form another layer, as displayed in Figure 10.6.

Further layers of the internal energizers matrix can be added, including the personality traits and attachment patterns as profiled in Figures 10.7 and 10.8.

These layers are like skin. The learning stances are the surface while the internal energizers are the layers underneath.

The dynamic between teaching styles and learning stances is similar to that between parenting styles and early attachment patterns.

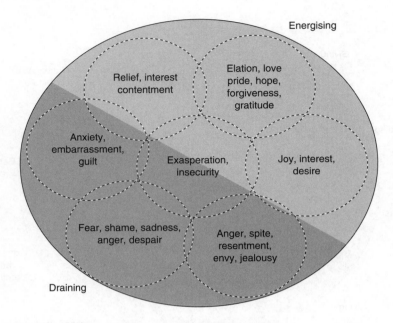

Figure 10.4   The emotional underlay of the learning stances

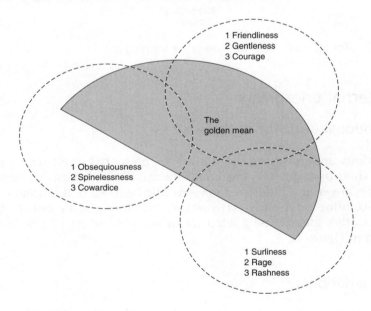

Figure 10.5   The golden mean

Considering the different layers of personality and attachment patterns together, we can see how the over-agreeable trait, cautious personality type and false positive affect attachment pattern together with low agency creates acquiescent affiliation and restricts autonomy. In stark contrast, the disagreeable trait, impulsive type and distorted affect attachment pattern with low affiliation creates antagonistic agency and distorts autonomy.

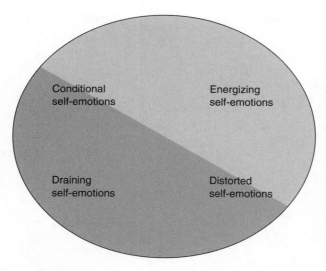

Figure 10.6   The self-emotions

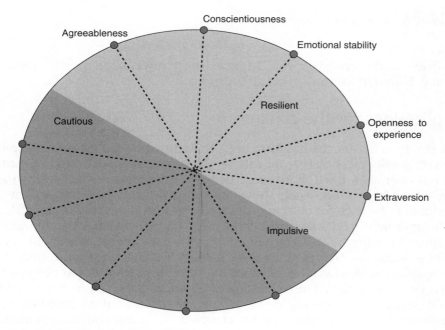

Figure 10.7   Personality types and the big 5

The classroom climate

The learning climate will reflect how the different teaching styles use the class-room energizers. It is presented in another parallel matrix in Figure 10.9.

Engagement is the energizer through which teachers mainly meet their pupils' need for affiliation. Structure impacts upon pupils' sense of autonomy.

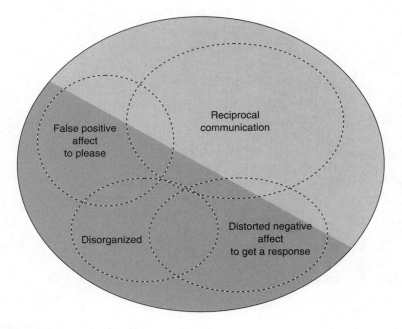

Figure 10.8   Attachment patterns

Feedback is the energizer that impacts most directly on pupils' sense of agency. Stimulation impacts on all 3A needs.

Implications for the classroom

The key to achievement has long been thought to be self-esteem. There has been little evidence however for this.[1] Positive self-esteem does not guarantee, nor is it essential for, self-motivation. Girls, for example, have less positive self-esteem than boys but generally show more positive motivation.[2] Yet self-esteem continues to be thought of as important for teachers to nurture in pupils.[3]

The argument developed here is that it is the *self-emotions* that should be nurtured by schools. It is the self-emotions – how pupils feel about themselves as learners – that mediate between ability and achievement, providing an explanation of why some children fail to achieve what might be expected based on their ability. The achievement chain is displayed in Figure 10.10. Pupils' sense of self-esteem, self-belief and self-determination together act as intervening variables between the classroom climate and achievement.[4,5] Teachers impact on achievement obliquely via their teaching styles and classroom climates that impact on their pupils' self-emotions.

Stop and think

In terms of the three self-emotions, what do you think is the main purpose, priority and potential of schools?

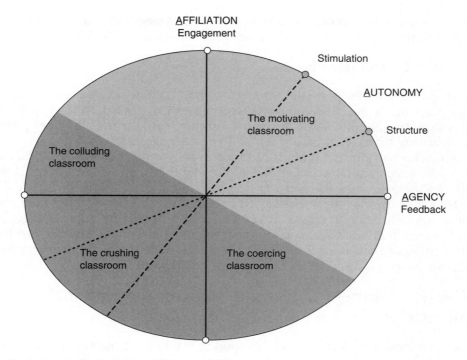

Figure 10.9   Classroom climates ii

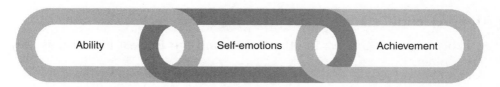

Figure 10.10   The achievement chain i

The self-emotions are under the influence of a range of factors, including, for example, pupil appearance, parental approval and peer influences. Teachers also exert powerful influences on pupils, who more often than not place great trust in them. Teachers are perceived as expert authority figures and significant sources of feedback.[6]

Self-esteem is only one of three self-emotions. Rather than think in a paternalistic way of schools *giving* children self-esteem, schools should be places where children are given the autonomy support to develop their energizing self-emotions. That is, the purpose of schools should be pupil self-determination.

Teachers readily impact on pupils' sense of affiliation through the way they treat them. They also nurture their sense of autonomy and, in particular, a mastery attitude to achievement by how they organize *stimulation* and learning activities. Teachers try to engage their pupils by modelling enthusiasm for learning and caring for pupils in order to build self-esteem. But they may miss opportunities to impact on their pupils' autonomy through an autonomy-supportive teaching style. The traditional approach is perhaps based on a limited notion of how motivation works and of the role of self-esteem in particular.

What more can teachers do?

Perhaps the greatest potential teachers have to enhance their pupils' motivational resilience lies, first, in how their feedback can impact on the key mindsets that shape pupils' sense of agency. Teachers can nurture confident pupils by teaching them to think of their ability as changeable.

The self-emotion that schools can most readily impact on is Self-Efficacy in Goal Achievement – *the 'SEGA' factor*.[7] Developing a competency of any kind strengthens our sense of agency.[8]

However, these agency beliefs need to be accompanied by a sense of autonomy[9] and affiliation to create the optimal motivational resilience. The second area where there may be scope for improvement is in how teachers can further enhance their impact on their pupils' autonomy through an autonomy-supportive teaching style, as highlighted in Chapter 8.

The development of learning stances: motivational milestones

We now look at how the stances develop in the light of the key motivational milestones detailed throughout the previous chapters. These milestones may help to guide early intervention strategies. The learning stances emerge as children become increasingly aware of status and conditionality in the classroom.

The pre-school stage

- Babies show an interest in other babies and this interest increases as they get older.[10]
- Children become wary of strangers at 6 months old.
- By the end of a child's first year, low emotional stability shows itself through anger and fear.[11] Fear is related to later shyness while anger is linked to reactive aggression in the early school years.
- Frequent and intense expression of negative emotions is an early precursor of low agreeableness.
- Children begin to challenge parental authority, but they still perceive parents as all-powerful.
- Children become aware of pecking orders around 3 years, when competitiveness starts.

Start of primary

- Theory of mind, i.e. the capacity to understand others' intentions emerges around 4/5 years of age
- Children learn to deceive others about their intentions and emotions
- Around the age of 5 children are working out what makes someone good or bad and are developing a view of goodness and badness as fixed or changeable qualities

- Children see their teachers as all powerful
- Most children feel positive about themselves, based on parents' positive feedback
- Rough and tumble play increases to help sort out the pecking order.[12]

Early to mid-primary

- Pupils start to focus on how they're performing now compared to when younger.
- Verbal aggression gradually replaces physical aggression.
- Aggression becomes less directed towards possessing objects and territory and more towards hostility to others.
- Planned aggression emerges later than reactive aggression, around age 7 years.
- There is an increase in self-talk.
- Self-control becomes established around the age of 7 years.

Mid-primary

- Children start to use comparison and become preoccupied with who is the best.
- Concerns about acceptance increase sharply, reflected in an increase in gossip.
- Cliques become important.
- Pupils develop specific evaluations of their competence.
- Pupils begin to take on board the opinions of others about their competences.
- The self-emotions start to emerge.
- Explanations of progress stabilize into a style by about age 9 years.
- Pupils begin to realize that they can have different feelings at the same time and so become open to the concept of dynamic stances.
- Children first start the process of detachment from their parents by seeking alternative attachment figures among peers who are similar to them in status.
- Pupils learn that parents are not all-knowing and that they can even be deceived.
- Pupils are still forming a clear perception of their dispositions.
- The alarming and draining reaction is the last stance to emerge as the separate emotional tendencies of fear and anger merge into emotional instability.

Late primary

- The Machiavellian personality starts to emerge around 9 years of age.
- Pupils' conception of intelligence may change so that needing to try hard comes to signify lesser ability. As pupils grow older, their beliefs about the nature of ability sometimes change from a view of ability as malleable to a view of ability as fixed.
- Ideas about ability consolidate around age 10/12 years.[13]
- Most underachievers do not give up until around 10, after which they become motivated to deliberately work below their potential.[14]

- Girls' participation in sport drops around 10 years.
- Pupils become increasingly aware of the difference in supportiveness between friends and non-friends.
- The number of close friends increases up to about age 11 after which it starts to drop.

Adolescence

- There is a decreased investment in academic activities and increased investment in non-academic activities, particularly during the middle grades of secondary education.[15]
- There is a loosening of cliques and a process of de-grouping, followed by an increase in cohesiveness among senior pupils.
- There is an increase in capacity for abstract reasoning and perspective-taking.
- Parents are increasingly seen as imperfect and vulnerable.
- The best friend becomes someone for whom adolescents develop sexual desire.
- Adolescents can work out both self-deception and the deception of others.
- Hypocrisy is a cardinal sin in adolescence: working out truth is very difficult but very important.
- The central task is physical, emotional, and intellectual integration that requires the ability to think abstractly about the reasons for one's own and others' behaviour.
- Late adolescence offers potential for self-transformation and the first real opportunity for individuals to take charge of their lives.[16]

Summary of key points

- The self-emotions mediate between ability and engagement. Teachers impact on achievement obliquely via their style and the classroom climate that shape pupils' self-emotions.
- Schools should be places where children are given the autonomy support to develop their energizing self-emotions. The purpose of schools is pupil self-realization.
- Teachers readily impact on pupils' sense of affiliation through their *engagement*. They also nurture their pupils' sense of autonomy by the way in which they organize learning activities and provide *stimulation*.
- The greatest potential teachers have to further impact on their pupils' motivational resilience lies in how they can influence pupils' sense of agency through feedback and sense of autonomy through an autonomy supportive teaching style.
- Key stages in the development of motivation include:
  - mid-primary where self-control becomes established around the age of 7
  - late primary when underachievers start to want to fail
  - late adolescence, which offers the first real opportunity for individuals to take charge of their lives.

Part Five

The stance-specific teaching styles and energizers

What makes pupils tick and how can you keep them ticking without winding them up?

In Part V each of the pupil defensive reactions is presented in a separate chapter. First, each reaction is profiled with reference to the 3A needs. Second, some ideas about what lies behind the reactions are offered. Finally, after a quick recap of the key internal drainers, the *stance-specific* dos and don'ts are then itemized, in terms of each of the four classroom energizers. These suggestions will be more readily achieved in some learning contexts than in others. If agreement can be reached on the dos and don'ts by everyone working with the same pupils it will help to develop a consistent approach.

The stance matrix has been designed to help teachers generate their own solutions to their motivational challenges. It can help teachers reflect on and analyse their classes, and forward plan ways to adapt their teaching styles. This section offers examples that try to go with the grain of pupils' strengths and to accommodate their flaws.

Remember that the stances are fluid in nature: pupils move in and out of them. Most, however, have a default stance and a default reaction. Some pupils' stance profiles are difficult to categorize, probably because they fall in between two stances or reactions, for example, they may be hiding and alarming and draining, or opposing and alarming and draining.

As you read these descriptions, you may wish to focus on particular pupils with whom you are working, in order to bring the profiles to life. You may also wish to consider what reaction these particular young people trigger in you.

The full set of learning stances and defensive reactions

Although three stances and four defensive reactions have been presented so far, the full set actually consists of nine stances and reactions. The *threatening* reaction is an extension of the opposing reaction and is outlined in Chapter 11. The *mutedly engaging* stance falls inside the overlap between hiding and quietly engaging and is presented in Chapter 15.

Both additions, because of their location in the matrix, can be considered a hybrid learning stance/reaction. Some pupils can adopt proactive threatening stances while others can be reactively threatening. Similarly some pupils can decide to be mutedly engaged, while others react this way defensively. The full set is displayed in Figure V.1.

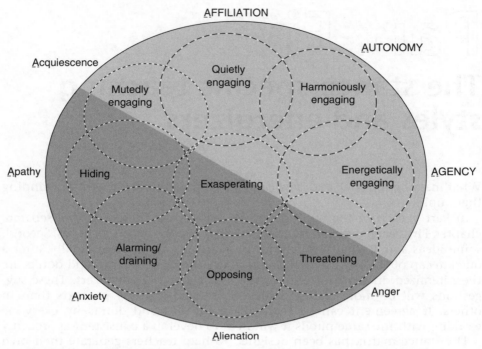

Figure V.1   The complete learning stances and reactions

11

The opposing reaction

Billy, a 14-year-old, entered the senior management corridor. Mr Macgregor, the Deputy Head [DHT] called to him to get out – 'You know you're not allowed in here'. Billy didn't respond. The DHT repeated the demand, each repeat becoming louder. Billy eventually decided to leave but the DHT had become so furious with him that he wanted Billy to stay and so blocked his way. Billy claimed he was doing what he was told. The DHT continued to block his way, saying 'you're in big trouble, you're going nowhere'. Billy kicked Mr MacGregor in the shin and ran off.

The opposing reaction is all about trying to change the environment. Pupils who are most at risk of getting stuck here experience school as impersonal and uncaring.[1] They do not see how working hard in school will help them to attain their goals. They feel that schools are not connected to their community or to the job opportunities they consider to be open to them and teaching does not draw on their pre-existing understanding. They perceive the way they are treated as unjust. They are particularly sensitive to any threat to their 'tough' status among their peers.

Distinguishing characteristics

The opposing reaction is presented in Figure 11.1.

3A profile

Affiliation
They feel rejected by adults and retaliate by showing little interest in pleasing them. They may be overtly oppositional, or they may keep the teacher happy but manipulate the peer group behind the teacher's back. They may think they are popular because their behaviour can give them high status, which they confuse with popularity. In reality, they tend to become unpopular because of their aggression and unpredictability. The most problematic classes, however, typically have one or two pupils who react this way but are genuinely popular with their peers and therefore particularly undermining of the teacher.

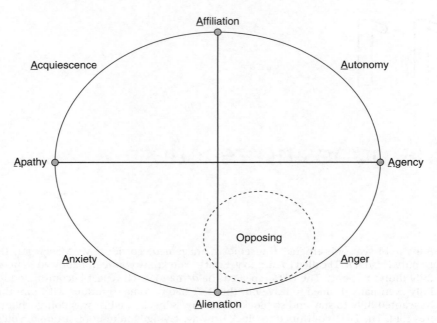

Figure 11.1   The opposing reaction

Agency
The opposing reaction reflects a variable self-belief in pupils' capacity to cope with school. They can be focused, if interested. Often there is no shortage of ability but they are not fulfilling their potential. They do not bring the right books or equipment.

Autonomy
Pupils will go along with things until their distorted autonomy is threatened, when they're not getting their own way or compare badly with peers.

This opposing reaction is marked by:

- a defiant, rebellious posture
- an 'I'm here on sufferance' attitude
- a refusal to accept reasonable boundaries
- having an answer for everything
- a need to have the last word
- a feeling of defeat if they have to do as they are told
- making gestures of forced compliance or inappropriate laughter.

Pupils in the opposing reaction can be opinionated and find it hard to compromise. They deflect criticism. They have closed chauvinistic attitudes, feeling they know it all. They make out they do not care, thinking they would be successful if they tried. They may see learning as a test of their worth and sabotage it rather than be found out. They prefer competitive goals and measure success in terms of being better than others. So when self-assessing they may cheat.

But Craig, we agreed you'd hand in your essay 6 weeks ago....

Frankie was an extraverted pupil who struggled with the work but had an exceptional talent in humour. She had extreme temper tantrums, where she vented her anger on the classroom furniture. This provided harmless entertainment to the other pupils. Her popularity made her feel she could do what she liked, and she did.

Why do they oppose?

Outlined below are some of the factors that underpin this defensive reaction. Pupils who react in this way have the most to lose from the class's success. For some pupils locked in this reaction, change requires huge effort and significant costs, in terms, for example, of disloyalty to their background and damage to their reputation. The factors include:

- rebelling against authority
- coercive parenting
- boredom proneness
- attempts at satire
- maintaining a tough reputation.

Rebelling against authority

Some pupils, especially boys, find structure oppressive and want to challenge it. Girls are socialized to be more accommodating than boys.[2] Rebelliousness involves wanting to do something contrary to that required by authority. It is not driven solely from 'within the individual' as it needs some external pressure, like an authority figure. Tight controls can paradoxically provide the challenge against which some pupils will want to rebel. Rebelliousness can often just be a form of fun to heighten excitement.[3]

> Since the community support officers have been introduced, graffiti has gone up 300%. This service needs to be maintained with its high profile in problem areas. *(A local council's Standing up to Antisocial Behaviour annual review, Spring 2006 – with no apparent awareness of the paradox)*

Rebelliousness can also have a performance aspect and a sense of theatre can increase opposing pupils' bravado. Such pupils, sometimes referred to as *'Limelight junkies'*, cannot get enough exposure.

Coercive parenting

A particular pattern of parenting is likely to encourage pupils to react negatively, namely, the excessive use of harsh punishment, with little encouragement or praise. Responsiveness involves mutuality and understanding, when the parent is in tune with the child.[4] Parental coercion and rejection trigger oppositional behaviour.[5] Most pupils look to authority figures for direction but some are ambivalent about granting that power, because of their earlier harsh treatment from their parents.

Boredom proneness

> Boredom is the root of all evil – the despairing refusal to be oneself. (Kierkegaard)

Boredom usually stems from a situation where none of the things that a person can do appeal to them. When you are bored you do not put much energy into your behaviour. The solution is to try to put meaning into what you are doing. Meaning energizes, while boredom drains our motivation. Some pupils, for example, are bored by lots of unnecessary warming up and decontextualized drill practice in PE and they only become fully engaged in the game itself.

Individual difference in boredom proneness is an important factor in understanding the opposing reaction. Boredom relates to a high need for excitement.[6] An aggressive reaction to boredom is more likely in pupils of a sensation-seeking and impulsive disposition.[7] Because of this, boredom has been thought to be the cause of much serious crime.[8]

Stop and think

Do you see boredom reactions at staff meetings?
Do you ever detect this reaction in your own behaviour?
Are you ever aware, as a teacher, that you are boring the class?

Attempts at satire

Pupils can use humour to get back at a teacher, like the satirist or mimic. Jokes are a way of complaining about oppression, making a point in a funny way that would be too risky to say directly. This is illustrated in the court jester who was the one person who could make silly but risky and pointed comments to the monarchy.[9]

Maintaining a tough reputation

> Being seen as tough is important to get a big reputation in this school. (George, 11 years old)

Some pupils will go to great lengths to protect their tough image by non-conforming, as expressed through a range of behaviours. Smirking, for example, can be a way of conveying bravado and disrespect. Some boys indulge in *recreational* violence to maintain their image.

It is important for many boys to be accepted by other boys[10] and this is often dependent on negotiating an acceptable reputation, incorporating aspects of 'laddish' behaviour and risk-taking.[11] Such 'laddishness' often runs counter to the expectations of the school but is seen as a reasonable cost to be paid.[12] Pupils need to balance academic demands and popularity, and some will pretend not to work, while catching up privately. Tall, good looking, athletically gifted and stylish boys earn lots of points on the 'cool' ladder, which they can use to off-set any points lost from working hard.[13]

Boys like to show off recklessly to girls because they seem to know intuitively that girls prefer risk-prone males to risk-averse males.[14] Such recklessness can be motivated by this desire as it can make you stand out as independent and assertive.

The threatening reaction/stance

> ### Stop and think
>
> Do you have any opposing pupils whom you have experienced as threatening?
> What was it about them that created this impact?
> What reactions did it bring out in you?

The threatening reaction is an extension of the opposing reaction and is marked by open dissent and a refusal to conform. This can also be, as suggested earlier, construed as a learning stance because pupils may be putting on a performance and are *in control of being out of control*. They like to be *in command and out of control*. Their level of self-control can be detected by the rapid change in their attitude when set a firm consequence or reward. Their aggression can also be well planned and driven by expectation of reward.

Others who take up such a defensive reaction are smarting from injustice, tend to communicate in the form of argument and in the teeth of reason, and get under your skin. These are the pupils who cause teachers to heave a sigh of relief when they are absent or to feel their heart sink when they come in late. They find their place by being feared. Both educational and social failure has led them to give up trying to gain status via acceptable methods. Unfortunately, they can become hardened and find some form of distorted satisfaction in being hostile.

> The intoxification of anger, like that of the grape, shows us to others, but hides us from ourselves. (John Dryden)

Some pupils who take this defensive reaction deny their own feelings, while imposing them on others. Ironically, they know how to manipulate teachers' emotions and can leave them feeling threatened and drained. The longer they stay locked into this reaction the more their intuitive interpretation of human motivations becomes hard-boiled and cold.

> The most dangerous creation of any society is the man who has nothing to lose. (James Baldwin)

3A Profile for the threatening reaction

The threatening reaction is displayed in Figure 11.2.

Affiliation
They look to other non-conforming peers for acceptance and they are often attracted to older peers. They may become the ringleader. They may feel estranged, a feeling epitomized by victims of miscarriage of justice. Adolescents joining a gang are typically low achievers in low-status crowds.[15] They sense

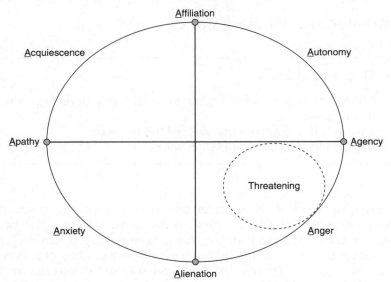

Figure 11.2   The threatening reaction

and exploit others' vulnerabilities ruthlessly. They often instigate problems that get others into trouble.

Agency

They show antagonistic agency, unrestrained by any affiliation needs. They are highly competitive and enjoy situations that let them show their superiority. They can become over-competitive, even with friends, and put down anyone who threatens to outdo them. They have a high need to impress and look for status from antisocial activities.

Autonomy

They are touchy and aggrieved, and have negative expectations of how others will deal with them. They resent and taunt authority. They feel they are always picked on and struggle to let go of any sense of unfairness. They think attack is the best form of defence. They relish power struggles and are compelled to win them. They avoid reciprocal fun and engagement or turn them into battles because they can't control them. Small incidents become major events as they are easily aroused by anger. They are *tension-seeking* and spoiling for a fight. They get involved in feuds even in situations that have nothing to do with them. They think their anger is something that happens to them rather than something for which they are responsible. Their aggression, however, can be controlled and they may have a quiet aura of power. They may act older than their years, having had little opportunity to be a child, and think they have outgrown school. They may feel they have to prove themselves, having learned to survive rather than have their needs met. They bottle up their feelings and have developed a mask of invulnerability. They are 'unembarrassable' and will behave in public as if they are in private. They are keen to let others know that they know their rights.

Why do they feel so aggrieved?

Stop and think

Pupils would not stay stroppy if they were not enjoying it. Do you agree? Consider the last time you were angry. Looking back, do you feel you had a right to be angry?

The answer to the second question is likely to be yes. Most people feel their anger is legitimate, a righteous rage. We get angry when we experience a threat that is seen as unjust interference with our attempts to realize our goals.[16]

> Justice has two beautiful daughters, anger and courage. Anger at what injustices remain and courage to ensure they don't remain. (St Augustine of Hippo)

Some of the factors underpinning the threatening reaction are outlined below and include:

- expectations of hostility
- proactive aggression
- low empathy
- the need to dominate
- the disagreeable personality
- narcissism
- distorted negative affect
- peer rejection.

Expectations of hostility

How a person anticipates what others are going to do is shaped by their expectations. Hostile expectations, for example, inflame aggression.[17,18] It is not so much that they hold these assumptions as these assumptions *hold them*.[19] They encourage the tendency to retaliate when provoked. Pupils in this reaction judge aggression positively, feel confident about it and come to think it's quite legitimate.

Proactive aggression

The threatening element comes from a proactive aggression that is well planned and driven by expectation of reward. Proactive aggression starts later than reactive aggression, around 7 years of age.[20] It is associated with social learning and positive evaluations of the consequences of aggression. These pupils feel confident in using aggression to achieve their social goals.[21] This source of antagonistic agency is in stark contrast to that of the harmoniously engaging stance, where agency is based on the capacity to resist peer pressure to get involved in risky behaviour.

Aggression can result in a feeling of pleasure which reinforces the behaviour. Young people can confuse this enjoyable release of aggression with their anger.[22] Aggressive behaviours may sometimes be intelligent and help the individual to achieve their goals. Indeed, controlled, verbal aggression, used in winning arguments, can earn high status.

Low empathy

Aggression can only happen if there is a lack of empathy.[23] A deficiency in empathy is a key characteristic of this reaction. Empathy involves both an emotional and a cognitive response, via perspective taking.[24] Generally, young people who react this way do not lack emotionality, but their self-focused emotions compete with empathy.[25] They are too caught up in how *they* feel.

For some pupils, other people's weakness seems to provoke a desire to attack their vulnerability. So a weak and pleading teaching style is like a red rag to a bull. Aggressive pupils ignore their victims' distress and may in fact claim it is the victims who are being hostile. Such young people often know their power is false and might like to give it up, but they have no alternative to fall back on. Anonymity, a situation where no one knows who someone is or recognizes their individuality, also promotes aggressive and destructive behaviour.[26]

The need to dominate

Nothing is more difficult than to acquire self-confidence without arrogance. (Theodore Zeldin)

All of us are motivated to exercise control over our lives and some people are also keen to control others. The default reaction of pupils with a strong need for control will be a function of how this need has developed. People who have had positive experiences of exercising control over important life events develop *autonomous control-seeking*, which is satisfied through leadership positions.

For others, however, exercising control may be a way of combating feelings of chaos or frustration. They fight these feelings by striving to exercise control over other aspects of their lives. This could be called *chaos-avoidance control-seeking*. Those whose desire is driven by a chaotic background can become manipulative and dominate their peers. Difficulty trusting people combined with a high desire for control may not be that uncommon. A link has been found between desire for control and suspiciousness.[27] An excessive need for power over others has been found to have the same effect as being highly stressed.[28] People with darker personalities have been found to have relatively higher levels of non-verbal ability. Perhaps the frustration from their inability to communicate their ideas triggers manipulative behaviour.[29]

Dominance allows control but it is not autonomy. The behaviour of threatening pupils is not autonomous but impulsive and results from exposure to an over-controlling and cold parenting style.[30]

Unstable high self-esteem has been found to be associated with aggression.[31] Students with high but unstable self-esteem are touchy. A bully, for example, often has an insecure but inflated view of himself or herself. Feeling that he or she may lose status at any time, the bully dominates anyone who is seen as a potential threat. People whose self-esteem is inflated may respond to negative feedback with hostility, often in a way that is out of proportion with the threat. On the other hand, an overly inflated esteem can unwittingly invite attack or rejection, without the person realizing why this is happening.[32]

Their hostility to feedback and inability to learn from experience or ask for help are linked with a self-protective, avoidant information processing.[33] Their over-confidence makes them think that they are invulnerable and that rules are not for them. Such people exploit others for their own purposes.[34] They use aggression self-protectively, to deny the legitimacy of any criticism.

Stop and think

What is the difference between the *confidence* shown in this reaction and that shown in a positive stance?

The disagreeable personality

Personality traits have implications for pupils' behaviour. Low agreeableness, for example, is linked to aggression.[35] The profile of antisocial young people includes manipulative behaviour, captured by the antagonistic pole of the agreeableness trait and linked to impulsiveness.[36]

Low agreeableness involves a preoccupation with one's own goals and a lack of sympathy for others.[37] Bullies tend to use aggression for solving interpersonal problems and have a Machiavellian tendency to perceive others as targets for manipulation, driven by a high need for social success.[38] Their calculating behaviour reflects an underlying personality trait that involves manipulation for personal gain.[39] The Machiavellian personality, in short the manipulative personality, involves low empathy and self-interest.[40] Pupils as young as 9 years old can show this trait.[41]

Narcissism

Nearly all people can stand adversity, but if you want to test people's character, give them power. (Unknown)

Narcissism has helpful aspects such as self-sufficiency, but it also has less desirable aspects such as self-importance and selfishness.[42] It is linked to thought distortions that maintain self-enhancement at the expense of social relationships.[43] Narcissists are prone to self-enhancement by taking credit from others. Narcissism is the opposite of agreeableness. Narcissists are people who:

- think they are better than others
- want to be admired
- are hypersensitive to criticism
- tend to have poor relationships because of their dislike of intimacy
- seek scapegoats for their self-made problems
- misuse relationships to enhance their self-image.

Narcissists are characterized by

- a façade that hides a fear of inadequacy
- an excessive need for attention
- a concern with how well they are doing relative to others
- a chronic need to prove themselves.

Consequently they like evaluative contexts that let them show their superiority.[44] They need to be recognized for their ability and want to contribute at an important level. They tend to be moody in response to any threat to their image. They are over-competitive and derogate people who outperform them. Other people exist for them and they prefer the company of people who admire them.[45]

They expect special treatment because of their uniqueness and are preoccupied with defending their rights. This leads to being easily offended, to less forgiveness and more revenge.[46] They seem unable to let go of any bitter feelings and demand justice before forgiveness. All these factors keep them trapped in these negative emotions.

Antagonistic agency and low affiliation are the locus of narcissism.[47] Narcissists tend to be disagreeable extraverts[48] who have positive views of themselves but negative views of others. Narcissism is being emotionally invested in one's superiority.[49] It involves high positive self-evaluations maintained by fantasies of power, self-serving biases, admiration-seeking and social dominance.[50] Their inflated sense of self-importance encourages a blinkered self-deception.

Distorted negative affect

Typically, parents of a bully encourage this reaction and deny that their child might be a bully. While exasperating pupils have exasperated parents, threatening pupils tend to have threatening parents.

Parents of pupils presenting this reaction tend to be rejecting and controlling. The young child feels unloved and anxious about strong feelings, in themselves or in others. This leads to self-containment and wariness about getting involved in close relationships. Security is achieved at the cost of an over-reliance on the self and a distrust of authority.

Their problems often start with an overactive and irritable temperament. They may have anxious mothers who lack nurturing skills. Such insecure babies develop hostile relationships with their parents by the end of their first year. Family living conditions can make things worse. They are often exposed to harsh discipline and are trained, albeit unwittingly, to be antisocial by

parents, who ignore their social overtures and reward aggression with attention or let them get their own way when they create a fuss.[51]

As young pupils they will have learned to control their emotions by
denying them and so they appear somewhat detached. They have learned
how to avoid rejection but not how to elicit caring. Although they become
good at manipulating other people's emotions, they are poor at recognizing
their own. Ironically they become skilled at pressing teachers' 'emotionality
buttons'.

Those with a history of rejection and abuse, attempt to control the dis-
tressing relationship by copying their parent's aggression. These pupils
become bossy and make derogatory remarks to parents. They are particularly vulnerable in the face of their own and other people's distress. They
are dismissive of intimacy and become *'counter-dependent'*.[52] If you cannot
express hurt, you repress it and this is the first step to cultivating paranoia.[53] It starts with the parent demanding that the child suppress his or
her anger at the parent who is causing the anger. To shield his or her parents, the child avoids blaming them for the feelings they have caused.
Anticipating hostility, the child prepares to counter it by meeting his or
her peers with a cold aggression. His or her suspiciousness creates what it
predicted and a vicious cycle is begun. Designed initially to protect
against recurrences of the painful past, this defensive reaction becomes
entrenched and grows with the child.

Peer rejection

The most common reason for peer rejection is aggression.[54] Aggressive pupils,
however, often do not see themselves as having poor relationships.[55]
Aggressive pupils are more likely to stay friendless, which leads to risks of internalizing problems and further rejection. Verbal aggression gradually replaces
physical aggression as pupils move from pre-school to primary. Aggression
becomes less directed towards possessing objects and more towards taking out
anger on others.

Some pupils, even as early as the pre-school years, start to target their
aggression on peers and this triggers peer rejection that, in turn, precludes
them from the activities needed to develop their social competence. Peer
rejection and early signs of aggression predict long-term behaviour problems.[56] Aggression combined with academic difficulties is especially predictive
of future difficulties.[57] The only source of affiliation they will find is with
other aggressive peers. Pupils who drop out of school tend to be rejected by
their peers and associate with others who do not see school as useful[58].

It is interesting to compare the 'classroom terrorist' with the real terrorist.
The typical profile of terrorists includes personal dissatisfaction with life
and belonging to an aggrieved group that feels a perceived injustice. They
are recruited from oppressed communities, swept up in a collective defiance. Their new group gives them status and protection. They feel absolved
of any responsibility and can justify their actions. In seeking vengeance
there is an irrational and destructive willingness to sacrifice the self as well
as the target.[59]

Stop and think

How closely does this description fit the 'classroom terrorist'?

The classroom terrorist can, in extreme cases, become the real terrorist where students wreak vengeance on their former teachers and classmates.

What works and what makes it worse?

Stop and think

What is the worst thing you can do with pupils in this reaction?
What is the best thing you can do with pupils in this reaction?

Points to note

As pupils who get locked into this reaction tend to be both difficult to relate to and unreceptive to critical feedback, the most applicable energizers will be structure and stimulation. It will be important to avoid confrontation and the response needs to be positive. Key challenges will be to find ways to reduce what might be threatening them and to identify alternative sources of status. Important points to note include:

- Individuals high in *distorted autonomy* are tuned in to external influences and so are responsive to external rewards[60] and easily flattered.
- While teachers instinctively quell any opposition, we need to take advantage of their creative deviance[61] and listen to those dissident voices that raise difficult questions, offer the chance to see through our blind spots and push us to clarify our values. Theirs is a raw version of the discontent that might not otherwise appear on the surface.
- Some pupils come across as 'know it alls'. Try to affirm them by at least accepting that they think they do, and challenge them to demonstrate their knowledge, as opposed to dismissing or patronizing them.

The key internal drainers

- They lack empathy.
- They will go along with things until their distorted autonomy is threatened.
- They deal with threat by being threatening.
- They are tension-seeking.
- They deny their feelings while manipulating others' feelings.

Their strengths

- They are self-sufficient, stubborn, questioning and challenging.
- They offer a creative deviance that raises difficult questions.

The best teaching styles

- Tough loving and attuning.
- Motivating them by their goals rather than your control.
- Finding strategies for reducing what might be threatening them.
- Trying to help them find solutions to their grievances.
- Providing appropriate sources of status.
- Affiliation-building through understanding.
- Offering them a share of the reins.

The worst teaching styles

- Imposing.
- Damaging what little empathy they have by seeking revenge.
- Directly criticizing or ridiculing.
- Personalizing.

Stance–specific energizers

Engagement – to show you care – what they need

Recap of their affiliation profile:
- They do not feel any allegiance to school and feel rejected
- they find their place by being disliked or feared
- they look to other non-conforming peers for acceptance.

Controlling the atmosphere rather than their behaviour.
Trying to see their opposition as a strength to marshal.
Trying to find something you like about them.
Tuning in to rather than opposing them.
Ignoring the image they may be trying to project.
Interacting with them in a setting that is more rewarding than the usual showdowns.
Making a point of attending events in which they are taking part, such as sport or music events.
Taking turns in communication and making your turns short.
Receiving any initiative they put forward by repeating what they said.
Reinforcing any pro-social behaviour by developing an exclusive low key allegiance with them, through non-verbal cues.
Combating any sense of anonymity by, for example, displaying lots of pictures of every pupil.
Setting up befriending schemes with mentors who are high status and able to establish rapport.
Encouraging participation in positive coalitions such as competitive sports teams.
Putting them together with high-status models with whom they might identify.

Considering bringing them into the class later, once the class has settled.
If they are angry:

- getting them seated
- approaching them based on their feeling, not yours
- calming them down by validating how they feel. 'I can see how you'd be upset about that'
- asking what is wrong and repeating back what they say to clarify their views
- asking 'what do you want me to do?'

Accepting your own anger and responsibility for it.

Engagement – what they do not need – avoid

Letting them set the tone.
Being intimidated by their reputation.
Taking their behaviour personally and making you the issue.
Personalizing any reprimand and emphasizing their personal features as opposed to their unacceptable behaviour.
Letting them sit in a prominent position.
Letting them bully you.
If they are angry – avoid at all costs:

- getting drawn into their anger
- encouraging them to vent their anger
- telling them they are wrong
- trying to make them take responsibility for their anger
- trying to reason and talk them out of it.

Feedback – to show you believe in them – what they need

Recap on agency profile.

- They have a high need to impress
- like to be in command and out of control
- are sensitive to any threat to their 'tough' status.

Turning any potential criticism you have into questions. For example, 'You seem to be having trouble, what can we do about it?'
Sharing your perspective on their behaviour in a way that describes rather than judges.
Keeping feedback to brief descriptions of their behaviour. 'Come on, you're messing about' is easier to accept than 'You're such a pain'.
Delaying discussing difficult issues about recent events until the next day.
Showing forgiveness and giving them the opportunity for a fresh start.
Inviting them to express remorse and repair the harm they have caused.
Encouraging them to reflect on and acknowledge the effect of their attitude and behaviour.
Making sure any consequences are related to their misbehaviour, respectful and revealed in advance.
Encouraging recovery by recognizing any misbehaviour as a mistake and looking for some kind of reconciliation.
Stressing the bad choices and behaviour – not their badness.

Allowing some choice about making amends, to give them a measure of control.
Recognizing the slightest contribution to the common good.
Using public praise and private punishments.
Giving competitive rewards.
Trying to give immediate rewards and feedback, no matter how incidental, using, for example, self-correcting materials, answer keys or by organizing pupils to give feedback to each other.
Finding a significant reward, for example, daily gym.
Finding something you admire about them and telling them.

Feedback – what they do not need – avoid

Making personal comments that will fuel the 'I'm being picked on' gripe, especially personalized judgemental criticism and angry insults.
Trying to out-argue them or shout to make a point.
Using mediation in restorative justice when there is a wide power imbalance between the parties and when they are not ready to accept responsibility.

Structure – to show you trust them – what they need

Recap of autonomy profile.

- They are easily aroused by anger and provoked by weakness
- feel they have to prove themselves and respond to any threat to their image
- enjoy situations that let them show their superiority
- interested only if they see the point or when they're setting the agenda
- boredom prone and 'unembarrassable'.

Ensuring fairness and clarity.
Keeping them close to you.
Denying them an audience, if they are being confrontational.
Using 'time out' to help them reflect.
Letting them come back when they feel ready, under 'their own steam'.
Dissipating their tension by letting them walk it off.
Recapping on advice, individually, as they are leaving the class.
Having them solve the problem later, in their own time.
Flexibly negotiating deadlines.
Picking your battles, prioritizing the things you want them to do.
Focusing on their learning to tackle their discipline issues.
Contracting with them. That is, offering incentives in exchange for specific negotiated outcomes. These are rewards for levels of improvement that are reasonable to the pupil. Specify a few levels of progress with equivalent levels of rewards so that pupils can earn small rewards, even if they do not get the top reward. They earn credits that can be spent on a menu of rewards, the prices depending on their appeal.
Negotiating a contract that imposes agreed costs as a consequence for failing to achieve negotiated goals.
Using a motivation contract with the class. Referring to the contract whenever a dispute or conflict arises and discussing the issues in terms of the contract not the person.

Exploiting their potential for positive leadership.

Giving them, whenever possible, high-profile responsibilities.

Trying to deal as soon as possible with any sense of injustice or grievance.

Using private reprimands. Speaking quietly, staying logical and affirming any positives.

Counting backwards from 20 to help you calm down.

Structure – what they do not need – avoid

Focusing exclusively on discipline, at the expense of their learning.

Letting them direct the conversation or manipulating you into responding to questions, designed to distract you.

Getting sucked into pointless arguments about, for example, any 'secondary non-verbals', tutts, sighs and so on.

Banning them from enjoyable activities and insisting that they watch from the side.

Stimulation – to show you enjoy teaching them – what they need

Making the activities relevant.

Making the point of activities clear.

Finding activities where they can do well in comparison to their peers.

Challenging them to demonstrate their knowledge

Reducing the difficulty level, if required, to show they can cope with the subject.

Setting goals in terms of learning accomplishments rather than tasks completed.

Finding an alternative direction for their energy.

Creating lots of challenge and novelty.

Providing high profile competitive activities.

Setting a challenging context, including multiple task demands, high arousal, speed tasks, rapid action, high pressure situations such as competitive sports or public speaking.

Getting them to solve a problem for themselves, for example, making a forward movement in basketball in three moves, by challenging them to do it in under 5 seconds.

Helping them develop strategies for coping with boredom. Helping them manage their boredom by letting them decide when to take a break or how to organize their work schedules.

Being spontaneous, by changing how you do things, surprising them, keeping them guessing, to minimize their potential for boredom.

Involving them in enterprise education that has an immediate attraction because of its real-life connections.

Offering directed choices (no matter how seemingly trivial) where the alternatives are pre-arranged. 'You can do this or that, it's your choice.' Ask them to tell you their choice to make sure they understand the consequences. If their language limits their capacity to formulate options, ask other pupils to come up with sensible choices.

Stimulation – what they do not need – avoid

Relegating them into lower achieving groups because of their defensive reaction.
Forgetting about the importance of the curriculum to hook them into positive behaviour.
Giving lots of unnecessary warming up and decontextualized drill practice.

The value of humour

Stop and think

What is the opposite of having a sense of humour?
Do you need a sense of humour to be a motivating teacher?
Do you find it easy to laugh at yourself in the classroom?

Humour is a key energizer in creating an engaging climate generally but there is also no better way to handle opposition. Laughter releases endorphins – the feel-good chemicals – and is our way of communicating that we are not a threat. It promotes a shared sense of purpose and a feeling that we are all in the same boat.

Humour allows the expression of anger in socially acceptable ways. Joking is a good way of anchoring criticism and making the point while being funny. It is a good way of cajoling people into changing their behaviour, while still respecting them.

Personalized jokes are good ways of communicating to pupils that the teacher knows them well. Respectful banter, to which pupils can give as good as they get, works well, though there is a fine line between this and the cruel comedy of sarcasm that is at the expense of pupils. It is all about laughing with, not at, pupils. The teacher also needs to be able to laugh at themselves. Humour creates reciprocity between teacher and pupils and so builds warmth and trust. It signals that the teacher does not take himself or herself too seriously and so avoids any sense of superiority.

Teachers do not need to be humorous. They do, however, need to be able to appreciate the value of humour. Not every teacher can 'do humour' but everyone can spot the pupils who can and feed off the humour they create.

Stop and think

Have you ever been in this opposing reaction yourself?
What were the circumstances?
What was done that you found supportive?
Think of a pupil or pupils in your class who take on an opposing reaction.
To what extent do they conform to the description above?
What techniques have you used to support them?
Select the strategies from the list above that might work for these partic-ular pupils.

12

The alarming and draining reaction

If you are upset and angry you concentrate on what is making you upset and angry, not your work. (Alison, aged 10)

Laura was a looked after and accommodated 10-year-old. One minute she was angry and the next minute tearful. Laura was scared and outrageous in equal measure, a victim and a bully. She constantly complained about the other pupils in order to seek physical contact with the support assistants. Friendships never lasted as she rejected other people before they could reject her. Although desperate for attention, she spoiled her work if the teacher tried to correct it and ripped it up if she was praised. She appeared to be carrying the weight of the world on her shoulders. Events came to a head when cutting her arm started her on a self-demolition course.

This reaction is rooted in 'self-draining' emotions, reflecting a sense of apathy, anxiety and alienation. Any pupil can react in this way, when their feelings overwhelm and bewilder them.

Some of them can get 'locked' into this reaction when they become unable to act on any of their strengths. Any low achievement resulting from limited ability can become underachievement due to low motivational resilience. Pupils who become trapped in this reaction tend to have significant needs due to the cumulative effect of all the 'risk factors' in their lives and their vulnerability to resilience ratio. They are both upset and angry and they really bother their teachers. Anger and fear are separable in early infancy. Later they merge gradually into the broad trait of emotional instability.[1] These pupils are at the bottom of the class pecking order and they know it. They are the last to access resources and the first to get pushed around. Consequently their self-emotions are like a leaking air balloon, vulnerable to the smallest prick of criticism or failure and constantly needing to be blown up by reassurance.

Distinguishing characteristics

The alarming and draining reaction is presented in Figure 12.1.

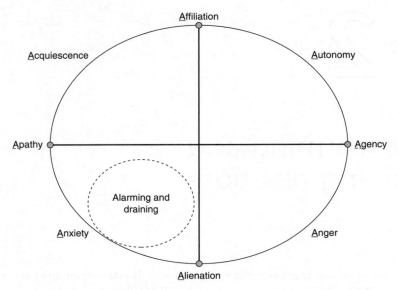

Figure 12.1   The alarming and draining reaction

3A profile

Affiliation
Pupils react in this way when they find it hard to mix with their peer group. Their poor social and communication skills make them particularly vulnerable in unstructured situations. They may be seen as sneaky by peers and are easily bullied. They may play 'kick me' games. They are attracted to a younger age group or prefer to be around adults. They are difficult to get close enough to to help, taking a long time to develop trust. While desperate for praise, they often fail to handle it. Their self-respect hangs by a thread. They expect to be rejected and will reject others before others reject them. They often seek physical contact for reassurance.

Agency
Pupils in this reaction lack self-belief. Their passive learned helplessness makes them slaves to self-doubt. They become increasingly unwilling to take risks. They may even give up before they start. They do not believe effort will make any difference, as they tend to hold a fixed and global idea of their ability and make pessimistic explanations of their progress.

Autonomy
These pupils feel overwhelmed and drained of ambition. Their feeling of powerlessness is shown in small ways such as berating parents or criticizing peers. If it persists pupils can become defeated or defeatist, seeing everything as pointless. Pupils who find it hard to get out of this reaction tend to 'catastrophize' and see any setback as a disaster. They focus on what is wrong with them and dwell on their negative emotions rather than try to solve the actual problem. They may feel nobody cares about them, put themselves down and

may end up self-harming. Triggers are difficult to identify and pre-empt. They are unable to self-soothe. Their bad-tempered mood swings make them emotionally volatile and quick to anger. They can be hostile even to those close to them. They can swing rapidly between being pleasant and hostile. They may defiantly enact their own agenda because of the problems they have controlling events. They can be reckless and unpredictable and their behaviour can become dangerous when their mood darkens.

Why do they feel overwhelmed?

The pupils who fall into this reaction most often come into school carrying a great deal of emotional baggage. This reaction is involuntary rather than based on any deliberate attempt to oppose their teachers. They have limited flexibility and show a tendency to keep making the same mistakes or become disorganized in response to stress or change.[2] Some of the main factors underpinning this reaction are outlined below, including:

- early development
- disorganized attachment pattern
- self-draining emotions
- depression and anxiety
- emotional detachment
- negative identity
- perfectionist parents
- problematic personality traits
- peer rejection
- multiple and chronic risk factors.

Early development

Pupils take on board important aspects of their earliest care giving experiences that influence how they relate to others.[3] These experiences shape how they mix with others by triggering emotional reactions. Some young people approach new situations anxiously or angrily. This hyper-vigilance has helped them survive their unpredictable homes, but leads to interpreting other situations rigidly. They see their environment as exploitative and so their relationships are characterized by conflict.[4] Maintaining such high vigilance is also tiring and we noted in Chapter 6 the effect of fatigue combined with negative emotions.

The problems of pupils with long-standing difficulties start early. Their parents see them as irritable, distressed and overactive babies. They often have anxious, aggressive and unresponsive mothers. When these insecure babies reach pre-school age, they turn their aggression towards their peers. The only source of affiliation they can get will be from other aggressive peers.

We generally seek events that are good for the self. Early attachments provide the basis for this positive bias in thinking of the self as good. However, the effect of maltreatment, harsh discipline and abuse is to switch this tendency to a negative bias.[5]

This reaction also arises out of social conditions. Single parents and parents living in poverty are more likely to have a harsh and chaotic parenting style.[6] Pupils who experience neglect and harsh discipline become primed to explode and do not have to look far to see examples of aggression being used to get what you want. Some pupils attempt to cope with this uncontrollability by exercising control over other aspects of their lives and will, for example, refuse to attend school. This could be called *chaos-driven* control.

Disorganized attachment pattern

Many of the pupils caught up in this reaction will have had carers who were frightening. The parents' unpredictable or violent behaviour may have led them to be afraid of or for them. This fear of their parent triggers attachment behaviour but the parent is the source of the distress. This causes a sense of helplessness. They are overwhelmed by turbulent emotions and future distress may trigger an upset and angry reaction. Ways of trying to deal with these feelings include:

- becoming aggressive with others
- becoming compulsively obsessed with minor activities as a way of stopping thinking about strong feelings.
- identifying with the source of the fear (seeing the self as bad)
- becoming absorbed in behaviours under their control (for example, rhythmic rocking, head-banging or self-biting)
- projecting past events into new situations, especially where there is some ambiguity in other people's intentions.

Most behaviour that appears bizarre has served some self-protective function in the past.[7] Achieving safety and comfort are basic motives underpinning our behaviour. Exposure to danger leads to the most distorted forms of behaviour. The key is finding ways to reduce the threat. The disorganized attachment pattern is a powerful predictor of aggressive behaviour towards peers. In addition, if during the first couple of years mothers perceive their children to be difficult, the risk of the pupils becoming aggressive increases.

Self-draining emotions

The least socially competent pupils are those who are both aggressive and withdrawn. They typically attack whatever or whoever causes them distress. Isolated and inhibited pupils show emotional withdrawal and a 'careless' style of self-management. Others may show promiscuous affection with strangers.

Pupils who have intense and confusing emotions tend to be drained by these experiences and often use avoidance strategies to cope.[8] They lack emotional clarity, the ability to identify and describe specific emotions and understand what they mean. Depressed mothers spend more time with their pupils in 'negative states' and this lack of 'emotional scaffolding' means that it is hard for the pupils to understand and control their emotions.

Shame-prone pupils with low status are particularly vulnerable to rumination, focusing on damage to the self and feeling a lack of control.[9] Losing self-esteem creates hostility. Among students with low self-esteem those with the greatest emotional difficulties are those with unstable self-esteem.[10]

Students can become trapped by their draining emotions when they are unable to minimize the importance of their weaknesses and lack self-serving distortions,[11] that is, ways in which we sometimes reinterpret negative events to prevent ourselves from agonizing over them. They may even prefer negative feedback to confirm how they feel about themselves and so will reject praise. Negative self-draining emotions can thus become self-perpetuating.

Depression and anxiety

Symptoms of depression fall into:

- low mood
- listlessness
- sadness
- feelings of worthlessness
- catastrophic thinking.

The last point is thought to be the root cause of the others.[12] Depression is caused by a feeling of a lack of control. We can experience feelings similar to depression, albeit fleetingly, for example, after important failures. One of our main goals is concerned with moving towards our ideal self.[13] Achieving a goal with an ideal self-focus (for example, the lead role in the school show) makes us feel elated. Failing to achieve such a goal leaves us feeling dejected.

Depression has been thought to help people accept their position and signal submission, and so avoid any further antagonistic behaviour from others.[14] It is a way of communicating that they do not pose any threat and should be left alone.

Depression is caused, in part, by anxiety that reflects exaggerated threats and feelings of vulnerability.[15] The line between depression and low mood is blurred; just thinking negative thoughts or being pessimistic are associated with changes in the brain areas responsible for planning.[16]

Depression is sadness that is out of proportion to the situation and as such drains motivation. It can be masked in childhood by overactivity or aggression. In adolescence, it is marked by negativity, by a feeling of being misunderstood or by antisocial behaviour. Staying focused on learning is a huge challenge when you are depressed.

There is a close link between anxiety and depression in young people.[17] Some anxious pupils can get themselves worked up about what's going on in the classroom, for example, the way some teachers shout at other pupils.

Emotional detachment

Most pupils readily turn to others for support. For some, however, sharing emotional concerns can be difficult. This can happen when pupils feel their parents are rejecting and they become less willing to rely on them.[18] While autonomy is healthy separation from parents, *detachment* is far from healthy and increases the likelihood of young people underachieving and getting involved in risky behaviours.[19,20] Conformity to the peer group has also been found to be stronger among adolescents who feel alienated from their parents.

Emotional reliance, the capacity to garner emotional support, is associated with well-being.[21] If you can rely on others, you are more likely to be feel self-reliant. Young people show more willingness to rely on parents who have an autonomy-supportive rather than controlling style, that is, parents who encourage them to use their initiative, take decisions and follow their interests and inclinations. Most resilient individuals rely on mothers who are responsive. Those who are unwilling to rely on mothers who are unresponsive[22] are also resilient. Some students may feel compelled to turn to their mother for support regardless of her actual responsiveness. However, relying on someone who is not supportive may be counterproductive. Although greater emotional reliance has been found among women, the benefits for well-being are similar across genders.[23]

Negative identity

A negative identity comes from negative beliefs about one's:

- affiliation, 'nobody cares about me'
- agency, 'I'm doomed to fail'
- autonomy, 'nobody trusts me'.

It is perpetuated by inferring negative beliefs about the whole self from a specific incident.[24] This overgeneralizing is caused by a dysfunctional self-concept, triggered by experiences of loss or failure. Young people who lost their mothers before the age of 11 years, for example, have a slightly increased risk of depression, creating a mindset about loss that is permanent and pervasive.[25] Similarly, people who have been abused can develop pessimistic explanatory styles and blame themselves for their abuse.[26]

Although self-evaluation is a 'natural' tendency, preoccupation with the self is a by-product of need deprivation.[27] Faulty self-knowledge is exacerbated by prolonged worrying about personal problems and the belief that worrying is a useful strategy. Anxiety results from appraisals of personal threat and aggression results from appraisals of hostile intent in other people.[28]

Anxious individuals focus on threatening information and are driven to examine their thoughts.[29] This perpetuates negative emotions. Such self-focus tends to bog you down in the details and render you unable to see the big picture.

Sensitivity about the self is linked with shyness in evaluative settings.[30] This is especially problematic when pupils face a threat to their self-worth in social settings, such as classrooms.[31]

Self-focused goals have been linked to low well-being and depression[32] and predict negative adjustment and risky behaviour.[33] It is actually better to have 'other focused' goals that are for the common good.

Pessimism can further damage your identity. It involves negative expectations that result in a lack of persistence. This personality trait is thought to be influenced by parental attitudes and appears to be relatively enduring.[34]

Perfectionist parents

The manipulating parenting style has been found to cause depression and low self-esteem.[35] Here parents intrude upon pupils' feelings and use manipulative techniques such as guilt-induction and love withdrawal.[36] They make harsh evaluations, which leave the young people feeling a failure.[37] They demand that they and their children meet their unrealistic standards and project their wishes onto their children.[38] Perfectionist fathers tend to be dominant and hostile, while perfectionist mothers have been found to be more submissive.[39]

Young people exposed to this parenting style can start to adopt perfectionist tendencies, leading to:

- setting excessively high standards
- rigidly adhering to these standards
- pursuing almost unattainable goals
- being overly critical of themselves
- defining their self-worth in terms of achieving these self-imposed standards.[40]

Problematic personality traits

We become increasingly good at adapting to our environment in ways that suit our personality.[41] A mixture of impulsivity and sensation-seeking, low self-control and negative emotions have been found to underlie disengagement in adolescence.[42] Impulsivity mixes with negative emotions and an avoidant style of coping to produce problem behaviour.[43] If you avoid things you do not learn and so you become stuck.

Both low agreeableness and emotional instability are linked to 'reactive aggression'. Low conscientiousness, agreeableness and openness to experience have been found to be associated with poor behaviour.[44] Internalizing problems, such as anxiety and withdrawal, are associated with emotional instability and low conscientiousness.[45]

Emotional instability, the tendency to experience disruptive negative affect, has been found to drain goal-setting behaviour, leading to passive, emotion–focused forms of coping.[46] Emotional instability confers a vulnerability to negative mood, poor peer relationships and overreactions to problems.

Pupils high in emotional instability are especially vulnerable to the alarming and draining reaction because they:

- pay more attention to their worries
- focus on threatening information rather than the task
- make more negative judgements about themselves
- are highly attuned to threats, self-blame and negative self-belief
- perpetuate negative emotions by worrying about their worries
- are vulnerable to self-consciousness
- are sensitive to criticism.

Teachers rate victims of bullying as low on agreeableness and conscientiousness and high on emotional instability, suggesting these victims are more interested in their emotional than learning needs and have difficulty regulating their emotions.[47] This can make teachers impatient with and unsupportive of the bullied child.

Peer rejection

Aggressive pupils are likely to stay friendless, which in turn leads to risks of internalizing problems and further peer rejection. Peer group adversity has great consequences on how pupils come to see themselves. Some pupils end up blaming themselves for being ridiculed and this may lead to negative views of themselves as socially incompetent and so they experience school as threatening.[48]

Pupils who are not accepted by peers in the early stages of schooling are at greater risk of chronic bullying which predicts later disengagement.[49] The peer group's dislike of an individual triggers further rejection, especially when these feelings are collectively shared in a way that somehow justifies the rejection. Pupils who drop out of school tend to be rejected by the peer group and associate with the minority group who do not see school as useful.

Multiple and chronic risk factors

It is the number of risk factors rather than any particular influence that best predicts the alarming and draining reaction.[50] Three particular factors together put a child at risk of developing this pattern, namely:

- a difficult temperament
- parents with limited skills at disciplining and nurturing
- parents who are under excessive stress.

Mothers of children who have a difficult temperament are at increased risk of marital stress. The lower the mother's marital satisfaction, the more likely she is to dislike her children and to have an ineffectual and inconsistent parenting style. Unhappy and unmarried mothers of challenging children may face particular difficulties in being positive towards them.[51]

Once a child develops a pattern of opposition, their emotional response to frustration then comes into the equation. As they are unable to get their needs met through positive behaviour, they become frustrated, which leads to aggression, and this aggression often works for them. Pupils who do not have social skills learn, for example, to bully their way into the peer group.

The propensity towards aggression is one of our most long-lasting traits, second only to intelligence.[52] Children who display irritable distress during their first months elicit, by the age of 2, more negative interactions from their mothers. Pre-school children who display restlessness and volatile emotions show antisocial behaviour by mid-primary. Difficulty getting along with pre-school peers is the single best predictor of antisocial behaviour at age 11.[53] And having a conduct disorder during adolescence is the best predictor of criminality as an adult.[54] Well-established patterns of aggression do not go away.

A key to whether oppositional behaviour will become a long-standing problem is the presence of attention deficit hyperactivity disorder (ADHD). Any child who is both oppositional and has ADHD is at particular risk of developing a long-term pattern of aggression.

The successful management of risk is a powerful resilience-promoting factor in itself.[55] However, risk factors are cumulative. Pupils may often be able to overcome single risks, but when they accumulate, their capacity to thrive diminishes. Multiple risk factors also appear to aggravate each other rather than simply having a cumulative effect. Transitions are periods of heightened risk, illustrated by the frequent decline in academic performance of vulnerable pupils on transfer from junior to senior schools.[56,57]

The most common sources of stress for pupils tend to be chronic events, such as bullying, having no friends, extended parental conflict or multiple changes of school, rather than acute experiences, such as bereavement. Ongoing 'hassles', rather than major life events, have the biggest impact.[58,59] Adults tend to think of acute and major life events as stressful, whereas pupils are more concerned about daily 'hassles'.[60] Professionals can, for example, dwell so much on a pupil's history of abuse that they miss the point that their new school placement will break down if they do not address the issue of the child being snubbed in the playground. Thus, while acute life events *may* result in adverse impacts, chronic adversities are more strongly associated with risk.[61] Pupils showing continuities of difficulties into adulthood are likely to have been exposed to continually adverse circumstances throughout childhood.[62] This is perhaps why serious parental conflict is potentially more damaging than parental death.[63]

Risk prediction summary

Outlined below is a summary of the main risk factors as pupils grow up.

By the end of Year 1

- Fear is linked to later internalizing problems, such as shyness and sadness.
- Anger is linked to later aggression.
- Irritable distress is linked with both internalizing and externalizing problems.

By the end of Year 2

- A disorganized attachment pattern predicts aggressive behaviour towards peers.
- The mother perceiving the child to be difficult increases the risk of the child becoming aggressive.

Pre-school

- A difficult temperament predicts antisocial behaviour by mid-primary.
- Difficult peer relationships is the single best predictor of antisocial behaviour at 11.
- Anxious solitude is linked to peer exclusion.

Key factors in whether opposition in pre-school becomes long term include:

- ADHD
- parents' limited skills at disciplining and nurturing
- parental stress
- mothers of defiant pupils are at an increased risk of marital stress
- low marital satisfaction leads to harsh and inconsistent discipline
- it is worse if the mother is unmarried
- unavailable fathers, who are inconsistent and rejecting, have adverse effects on engagement.

Start of primary

- Anxious, solitary and aggressive pupils with low social competence and low ability are at high risk of peer rejection.
- *Planned aggression* is associated with exposure to aggressive models rather than physical abuse. It starts around age 7 years.
- Aggression combined with academic difficulties predict later disengagement.
- Shame-prone pupils with low status are particularly vulnerable to rumination.

Adolescence

- Rejected pupils who associate with the minority peer group that does not see school as useful are more likely to drop out, especially girls.
- Withdrawn pupils become increasingly disliked by peers.
- Shyness with sociability can make young people vulnerable to mis-using drugs and alcohol, to cope with their social difficulties.
- A conduct disorder is the best predictor of adult criminality.
- Adolescents' engagement is predictive of whether they will join a gang.

What works and what makes it worse?

 Stop and think

What's the worst thing you can do with pupils in this reaction?
What's the best thing you can do with pupils in this reaction?

Points to note

As the alarming and draining reaction is an amalgamation of the other three defensive reactions, the list of specific energizers for these reactions should also be considered.

The motivational resilience of pupils in this reaction will be shaped, in part, by the extent to which they are enabled to mix with the class in a way that reduces their feelings of helplessness and promotes a sense of control. This requires hope. Hope comes from understanding, and understanding comes from empathy. They need intensive care. They also need help to make sense of and give voice to their distress. We need to try to respond to their emotional stage rather than their chronological age.

The best way to remove self-draining emotions is through experiences that induce self-energizing emotions. This can be done by helping them to, for example:

- find benefits within adversity
- keep things in perspective
- infuse ordinary events with positive meaning
- develop more effective problem-solving.

The key internal drainers

- 'Self-draining' emotions and self-destructive behaviour.
- A sense of apathy, alienation, anxiety and crushed autonomy.
- Dealing with draining feelings by draining self and others.
- A difficult temperament and faulty mindsets.

Their strengths

- Sensitivity and caution.

The best teaching styles

- Finding what reassures them and gives a sense of control.
- Affirming, attuning and re-tuning.
- Helping them to make sense of and give voice to their distress.
- Taking a detached businesslike approach, not complicating with concern until they can handle it.

The worst teaching style

- Damaging what empathy they might have.
- Exposing or overwhelming them.
- Pitying them.
- Personalizing.

Stance-specific energizers

Engagement – to show you care – what they need

Recap of the affiliation profile:

- They are vulnerable in unstructured situations
- are difficult to get close to and expect to be rejected and so reject others
- have poor social and communication skills
- are easily bullied and ostracized.

Approaching them based on their feelings, not yours.
Trying to understand, see the situation the way they see it.
Communicating that you are interested in them by, for example, getting them to talk about something that really interests them.
Interacting with them in a setting that is more rewarding than the usual confrontations.
Tuning in to rather than opposing them.
Listening to their views, recognizing their issues and appreciating their perspective.
Providing a close relationship from at least one unconditionally supportive adult.
Setting up befriending schemes with mentors who are credible, model non-stereotyping attitudes, who are able to establish rapport and use persuasion.

Using self-identified mentors to whom they are naturally drawn rather than assigned mentors.

Helping them to learn that there are better ways than fighting to get what they want, for example, joining in the game and sharing with others.

Helping them to articulate their fears in terms of the worst thing that can happen, to help them recognize how improbable their fears are.

Putting them together in collaborative learning groups with supportive high-status peers.

Providing a support group where they can share experiences with others in similar situations.

Giving them roles which are valued and let them contribute to the class's success.

Keeping a sense of humour.

Keeping them physically close.

Helping them notice the signs of building inner tension.

Giving them techniques and tools (such as cards) to let them communicate that they are getting upset.

Pointing out how their angry thinking leads to unhelpful ideas such as hating others.

Always separating from them amicably.

Engagement – what they do not need – avoid

Thinking of their emotional outbursts as attempts to manipulate you.

Getting drawn into their anger, taking it personally and then personalizing any reprimand.

Grouping them with other vulnerable or argumentative peers.

Trying to make them take responsibility for their anger.

Trying to reason and talk them out of their anger.

Alienating the class against them.

Treating them as a victim.

Feedback – to show you believe in them – what they need

Recap on the agency profile:

- They have low self-belief, hold a fixed idea of ability and make pessimistic explanations of progress
- see themselves at the bottom of the pecking order
- give up quickly or before they start.

Using lots of rewards and certificates to celebrate success, however small.

Giving tangible and non-competitive rewards, immediately whenever possible.

Praising publicly for any exceptions to their problematic behaviour and the slightest contribution to the common good.

Re-tuning them by, for example:

- tracking progress by positives, for example, how many times they answered questions rather than shouted out.

If they respond badly to praise,

- ask them what they think of their performance and then comment on their evaluation

- use adult to adult dialogue to praise them indirectly
- keep praise brief with little emotion and attention
- nurture their capacity to praise themselves, by keeping a daily diary of sucesses
- give *coded* praise via an agreed private code, for example, using the weather or conditions in the room to communicate approval.

Teaching them to recognize their own achievements.
Helping them to generalize any strengths to other areas, by seeing the connections between skills.
Encouraging an explanation style that lets them take credit for good events and not automatically accept responsibility for bad ones.
Encouraging them to put down progress to their effort and failure to insufficient effort or inappropriate strategies.
Conveying the belief that their ability is not fixed.
Helping them to think of themselves from their strengths rather than their weaknesses.
Helping them to replace self-defeating language with more positive self-talk.
Suggesting they dispute their pessimistic thoughts by treating them as if they were written by people out to annoy them.
Encouraging them to focus on trying to better their previous performance.

Feedback – what they do not need – avoid

Pushing them into 'blame traps' that condemn them.
Using public reprimands and punishments.
Applying severe punishments that damage any empathy they might have.
Keeping them permanently on behaviour-monitoring programmes.

Structure – to show you trust them – what they need

Recap on the autonomy profile:

- They may see their environment as punitive and project the past into new situations
- poor understanding of their emotions
- too much self-reflection and self-focused goals
- shame-prone
- irritable distress, impulsive and sensation-seeking.

Providing fairness and clarity.
Maintaining familiar and important routines.
Preparing them for any unfamiliar situations or tasks by pre-visits, photos and name cards for new people.
Setting predictable rules and limits.
Use planning time and summary time to emphasize predictability and self-control.
Making a plan with them that tries to anticipate any problems and suggests ways to deal with setbacks.
Encouraging them to set 'other focused' goals that are for the common good.
Being patient, counting back from 20, being the broken record.
Helping them to develop their own goals.

Motivating them by their goals rather than your control.

Focusing on the primary issue.

Using calm assertion and slow pace to change the atmosphere and help them to think.

Giving a limited number of cards that allow them some leeway with problematic behaviour, such as wandering round the room. They have to spend these in a specified time period. The period can be gradually extended or the rationing decreased in the same time period.

Organizing a time-out system. Using discrete time out such as sending them on an errand. Teaching them how to use self-directed time out.

Structure – what they do not need – avoid

Providing an audience.

Trying to fix them or force them to be what you want them to be.

Moving to the consequences too quickly.

Getting sucked into arguments about any secondary tutts or sighs.

Stimulation – to show you enjoy teaching them

Helping them develop strategies for coping with boredom.

If they have a problem with stopping an activity, giving them a warning before ending the activity, or restricting it to a period towards the end of a natural break.

Setting goals in terms of learning accomplishments rather than tasks to be completed.

Giving time and repetition to process instructions.

Giving secondary activities to help them focus, for example, a relaxation ball or doodling.

Letting them demonstrate what they know or have learned.

Using strategies to develop listening skills and attention control, for example, random use of tape-recorded message to encourage listening skills.

Giving manual manipulative activities to build a sense of control.

Setting small achievable steps that grade the challenge, starting with a level they can easily control.

Teaching them motor sequences, such as folding their arms and taking a deep breath to help them stop and calm down when frustrated.

Using step by step instructions with symbols or photographs.

Getting them to ask their own questions, to which they will usually know the answers, to let them discover they know more than they think.

Putting their particular fears and worries into a story where they get resolved.

Encouraging them to write regularly about their feelings, to help them deal with their difficult circumstances. Focus them on what has been happening, how they feel about it and why they feel that way.

Telling historic stories and ancient myths that can create a sense of roots.

Giving them opportunities to 'make a difference' by, for example, helping others through volunteering.

Discussing trigger points privately in a solution-focused way.
Teaching relaxation techniques they can use at times of high distress.
Giving them alternative words to use to express their anger.
Helping them to anticipate positive outcomes through the use of imagery.
Computers can provide particularly helpful energizers. They:

- offer a competitive but private therefore low threat climate where engagement is unconditional
- allow pupils to be self-taught and less reliant on teachers
- provide stimulation through play-orientated small achievable targets
- provide a high level of multitasking complexity, decision-making and risk-taking
- offer feedback that is consistent, objective and, crucially, non-judgemental
- are customized to the user in that the pacing is constantly being adapted to the individual.

Stimulation – what they do not need – avoid

Forgetting about the importance of the curriculum to energize them.
Giving complex tasks such as vague project work.
Giving too much choice, too many instructions, too many transitions, using too much group work.
Asking questions in a way that sounds like they are being tested all the time.
Oppressing any self-initiated secondary activities that help their concentration.
Over-intruding with support, for example, allocating a one to one support assistant all the time.
Letting them spend too much time in 'passive' entertainment, for example, watching television.

Dealing with their anger

The biggest challenge in managing this reaction is dealing with emotional anger. Unlike pupils who veer towards the threatening stance, this group are too upset to *enjoy* their anger. Their aggression is perhaps their way of avoiding having to deal with difficult emotions.

The causes of anger
What triggers anger is usually an unwanted interference from another person that is blocking our goal. Angry outbursts are caused by rapidly escalating arousal. The arousal is the problem. The speed at which anger develops creates the illusion that these explosions appear out of nowhere. Understanding requires the ability to slow our perception of events to see the chain of cause and effect more clearly.

Angry pupils think that their outbursts are something that happens to them rather than something they do. Nothing angers angry pupils more than attempts to make them take responsibility for their unconscious intentions. One of the best ways to take the sting out of a raging pupil is to ask, 'What do you want me to do?'

Angry behaviour can become addictive because it makes complex situations easy. It is futile to try to convince an angry person that he or she is wrong.

Slow the pace and take any opportunity to break the rhythm. The key is to get them to think.

Angry people are not afraid of their anger and in fact it may make them feel focused and energized. Instead of worrying about the strange sensations in their bodies, they pay more attention to external events which they think are the source of their anger. Anger is a cathartic process that dissipates their agitation, leaving them relaxed and calm.

Anger starts small and grows. Getting angry is ritualistic but if you disrupt the pattern, you can nip it in the bud. The trick is getting them to notice the signs and to use them as cues to do something to avert an explosion. Often, the first sign is the inability to sit still. People who are getting angry usually feel tense, which shows up as clenching and unclenching muscles, as if warming up for a fight.

Dealing with people when they are angry
Anger is a form of communication which aims to evoke the same feelings in the person you are angry with. If you can let them know that you see their point of view, you can sometimes prevent them from having to demonstrate. It may feel like you are being manipulated but thinking in these terms is unhelpful. Our own emotions make us view what are really just frightened and confused people as dangerous. Try to look at events from the angry pupil's point of view. Explosive pupils are thinking of themselves, not us. They are displaying their distress so that we will make them feel better.

Pupils explode into anger because they believe it will get them something they want. The trick is to get them to realize that their anger is getting them the opposite of what they want. The key is our reaction. Anger stimulates anger.

There are times when it is best to listen to what people have to say about what they are feeling, but not when they are angry. Our first goal is to calm them down. We are more effective in dealing with the explosions of pre-verbal pupils because of our expectations about them and confidence in handling them. With older pupils, we tend to try to talk people out of their emotions. Reasoning, however, just adds fuel to the fire.

Ask for time: 'Give me a minute to think about this'. This will prevent you from saying the first thing that comes into your head. Breathe deeply to calm yourself. Speak softly. Step away to get something like a file or your glasses.

Validate how they feel. Listen and answer, 'Yes, you have a right to feel the way you do'. This is not saying that they are right, only that they have a right to feel that way. You can validate their emotions by saying 'I can see how you'd be upset about that'.

Negotiate. The opposite of fighting is negotiating. It is important that angry people believe in the inevitability of consequences enough to want to avoid them. Never threaten anything unless you're sure you can make it happen.

Stop and think

Do you have a school policy on anger, for example, regarding its expression and management?

Stop and think

Have you ever been in this alarming and draining reaction yourself?
What were the circumstances?
What was done that you found supportive?
Think of a pupil or pupils in your class who take on this reaction.
To what extent do they conform to the description above?
What techniques have you used to support them?
Select the strategies from the list above that might work for these particular pupils.

13

The hiding reaction

Robert was like a Christmas present waiting to be opened. (How one child described the change in Robert following lessons on the Learning stances)

Johnnie had never really liked school, and had perfected the art of doing just enough to keep his teachers 'off his back'. He much preferred spending his days in his bedroom, on his computer. Recently he was more often there than at school. Johnnie turned up in class on Monday morning. 'Nice of you to drop in' his teacher stated, loudly and sarcastically. The rest of the class looked at each other and sniggered. Johnnie's face went bright red. He just wanted a big hole to swallow him up. He slipped out of the school during the morning break and was never seen in the school again.

This reaction is taken by pupils who become skilled at 'staying out of the way'. They are easily embarrassed and particularly fearful of exposing and making a fool of themselves in front of their peers.[1] With some pupils, an element of passive aggression may underlie their reaction where they turn their back on the class or the teacher. Hiding pupils experience the classroom from a detachment zone where they are merely observers.[2] If they hold on to this reaction they can become skilled at putting teachers off trying to get them to work. They are difficult to get to know and set teachers the biggest challenge when writing end-of-term reports.

These problems do not take care of themselves when they leave school, get a job or find an interest. This invisible form of disengagement increasingly impairs some young people's engage-ability and their employability. If their hiding becomes chronic at school it can persist through long-term employment instability.[3]

The pupils who are vulnerable to hiding will make up a significant proportion of the underachievement in any school. They are also potentially the underachievers who will be the most responsive to support as:

- they are often aware of their problems
- they are open to supportive feedback
- the values in their family background are more likely to be similar to the school's values
- they experience a high level of self-conscious emotions such as embarrassment but also have the potential for pride

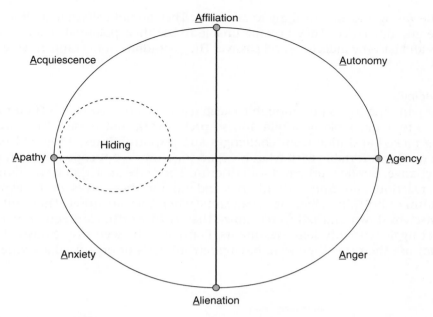

Figure 13.1   The hiding reaction

- they may well be motivated to learn but their social and emotional problems have become a barrier to their engagement.[4] Were these difficulties to
be alleviated, they may re-engage with learning.

Distinguishing characteristics

The hiding reaction is presented in Figure 13.1.

3A profile

Affiliation
When pupils react this way it is difficult to know what they are thinking.
They make themselves almost invisible by, for example, sitting still or avoiding eye contact. They rarely disclose much about themselves and are reluctant
to talk to teachers. They are timid, lack social potency and find it hard to
make demands on others or take any initiative in a social situation, reflecting
an acquiescent affiliation. They tend to be shy and verbally inhibited, and
prefer solitary activities even among familiar peers. They may be threatened
by peers and are likely to be bullied. They find groups difficult, being easily
embarrassed. They will, for example, blush when praised or teased. They have
often missed out on a lot of school and so are not really part of the class.

Agency
Pupils are more likely to react this way when they have little self-belief. They
experience school as unpredictable and out of their control. They assume they

will be wrong and are unwilling to take risks. They do not believe that effort will make any difference. They become unable to see their potential. They cannot focus and become indecisive and passive. They withdraw from competitive situations.

Autonomy

Their participation is just enough to keep teachers 'off their back'. Their main goal is to avoid looking stupid and so prefer work that is easy. They avoid being picked and hide from challenges and responsibilities. They will hang back until comfortable with what is expected. They do not cope well with failure, change, public reprimands or criticism. They take an acquiescent 'punch-bag' reaction and find it hard to stand up for themselves or to express criticism or hostility. They may even smile when they are upset. They will put themselves down and fail to recognize their own worth. Consequently, they will struggle with any self-assessments. Praise may be seen suspiciously. They do not use their free time well, having few interests or organized activities.

Why do they hide?

The variables behind the hiding reaction are numerous. Pupils may be, for example:

- hiding from the fast pace and demands of the curriculum
- struggling with low ability in a particular skill
- suffering from bereavement or loss

- embarrassed by the state of their clothes
- ignored by the teacher
- bored by school
- isolated from the peer group
- feeling that their contributions to the group are clearly dispensable.

> I'm chosen for nothing, in fact you could call me 'the unchosen'. (David, aged 10)

This section explores some of the factors underlying the hiding reaction, including the following:

- low motivational resilience
- anxiety
- living in violent areas
- conditional love
- self-protection
- shame-proneness
- peer rejection
- shyness.

Low motivational resilience

This reaction reflects a sense of apathy, restricted autonomy and/or acquiescent affiliation rather than alienation. They are usually escaping *from* something as opposed to escaping *to* something. They can become committed underachievers, set low goals and fail to persist in the face of difficulties. They resist taking responsibility for their progress as they do not want to be burdened with continuing expectations. They may in fact be motivated to perform poorly, to avoid success as they are afraid of achievement.[5] So they keep expectations low through vague responses. Any low achievement that may have initially resulted from limited ability can become underachievement due to their low motivational resilience. The majority of rewards and satisfaction in school come from achievement in the curriculum. Low-achieving hiding pupils do not experience much of this.

Anxiety

 Stop and think

What do you get anxious about?
What's the difference between anxiety and fear?

Anxiety disorders are the most common form of stress in childhood. Anxiety is not the same as fear, which occurs in a situation of real danger. It is a more general response, usually focused on future events, that is out of proportion to the actual threat.[6] It is aroused by a threat that is imminent but difficult to anticipate and gauge, and is experienced as having negative, yet uncertain and diffuse, personal implications.[7] Some pupils use up most of their energy worrying about what might happen, rather than what is happening. The most common sources of anxiety for pupils tend to be chronic events.

Anxious pupils, who have social difficulties can show high empathy in a conflict situation. So the *nice* pupil may hide in a difficult class, because they are sensitive to class tensions.

Blushing is a sign of anxiety or embarrassment. Some pupils, however, think that others will notice their blushing and so they become extremely embarrassed, which in turn leads to more blushing. This 'hang-up' probably reflects that they think others are judging them. Their fear of showing how anxious they are is probably their biggest problem. The vicious cycle starts with the pupils being anxious in class, making it more likely that they will think that they are making a fool of themselves, which in turn causes them to blush more (www.phobics-society.org.uk).

Living in violent areas

Pupils exposed to violence in their community may be particularly likely to fall into the hiding reaction because their learning is hindered by anxiety, causing impaired concentration, intrusive thoughts and low energy.[8]

In high-risk areas with a high crime rate, where violence is prevalent, parents place less value on sociability and curiosity than parents in low-risk areas.[9] They tend to stress obedience and so nurture a more restricted autonomy.[10] Teenagers in dangerous areas do not see tightly supervising mothers as over-controlling. In fact they prefer this and find it reassuring that their mothers care for them and realize what it is really like in the area. Perhaps this is why some pupils in areas of high deprivation show limited initiative and seek the security of structure and direction. These findings give some insight into the disengagement of some pupils through community security issues.

Anxiety is linked to depression. Depression has been thought to be a form of social yielding to signal submission and so stop any further antagonistic behaviour.[11] If a pupil consistently fails to grab the class's attention they may give up trying. In the same way, embarrassment serves to appease and to show recognition that a norm has been broken.[12] It is a way of communicating that you do not pose any threat and should be left alone.

Conditional love

Parental use of conditional love has been linked with low self-esteem[13] and is possibly a feature in the family background of some pupils in this reaction. Conditional love conveys to pupils that they are not loved for who they are but for what they do. Such conditionality makes the child rigidly take on board parental values but without accepting them as their own; their behaviour is controlled by their desire for approval.[14] This creates acquiescent affiliation and conditional self-emotions where every success and failure causes fluctuations in how they feel about themselves. Any satisfaction following a success is short-lived and every failure creates shame and guilt. Conditionality is associated with poor coping skills, a sense of being disapproved of by parents, and resentment towards parents.[15]

Self-protection

The hiding reaction reflects a concern with self-protection that outweighs the desire for success, resulting in cautious behaviour.[16] Here pupils are concerned with protecting their 'private' esteem. Lacking firm self-knowledge, they may fall into various traps such as setting inappropriate goals, or starting things that are too difficult or too easy. It is important to recognize that the goal of such self-defeating strategies, like withholding effort or procrastination, is ironically self-protection.[17] Shy pupils hang back until they are more comfortable with what is expected.[18] They need to scout out the situation to find out what is expected of them before they will join in.

Shame-proneness

Pupils who are *shame-prone* tend to blame themselves and so are vulnerable to the full force of failure.[19] Shame generalizes beyond the specific behaviour to reflect negatively on the entire self. Any failure triggers self-scrutiny, leading to feelings of unworthiness and helplessness. Failure also comes with feelings of being exposed to an imaginary audience and these feelings can be experienced even in private. This leads to the desire to hide.[20] Shame causes more enduring feelings than embarrassment. Shame-prone people try to fix themselves rather than the problem, as they blame their whole character.

Peer rejection

Withdrawn and immature pupils are particularly vulnerable to peer rejection. Their main problem is their wariness that makes them increasingly submissive.[21] These problems can start as babies, if they are hard to soothe. If their parents react with insensitivity and neglect they may develop insecure attachments that in turn may lead to social withdrawal. They try to avoid rejection through passive, adult-dependent behaviour that restricts their social development.

Peer adversity may transform helplessness into hopelessness by confirming their anxieties. With increasing age, withdrawal becomes more important to the peer group and leads to unpopularity.[22] The more they try to ingratiate themselves, the worse they make it. Parents may make matters worse by overprotecting them. Bullies target peers who are seen to be anxious and isolated,[23] who lack self-confidence and social skills.[24] There is a strong link between social problems such as shyness, peer rejection and bullying and introversion and emotional instability.[25] Peer rejection places pupils at great risk of future truancy. Rejected pupils, especially girls, have been found to be eight times more likely to drop out of school than accepted pupils.[26]

Pupils' proneness to withdraw can be exacerbated or defused depending on how their peer group treats them.[27] Non-threatening peer groups can redirect vulnerable pupils in a more positive direction and disconfirm their anxieties.[28]

Shyness

Anxious and solitary pupils tend to be shy and verbally inhibited even among familiar peers.[29] They would like to mix with peers but avoid them for fear of ridicule. Such pupils who experience peer rejection show socially helpless behaviour, including:

- not taking any initiative in social situations
- giving up easily in the face of social difficulties
- being unassertive
- not persisting with social problem-solving.

Their vulnerability is exacerbated by peer group adversity. Anxious solitude and peer exclusion are mutually reinforcing.

There are two types of shyness that are related to levels of sociability. Shyness is not the same as low sociability. Some pupils are shy introverts with low sociability while others are shy but would like to be sociable. Shyness is a risk factor but it is further exacerbated paradoxically by sociability that creates an approach–avoidance conflict.[30] Such sociable but anxious pupils are vulnerable to misusing drugs and alcohol to help them cope with their social difficulties.

What works and what makes it worse?

Stop and think

What is the worst thing you can do with pupils in this reaction?
What is the best thing you can do with pupils in this reaction?

The Origami energizer

Kwok Hung is a 9-year-old boy with a poor grasp of English. He was withdrawn in class and had a low standing within the peer group. That was until his teacher discovered his skills in origami. She helped him to demonstrate these skills by giving him the key words, such as fold here and so on. He gave a captivating demonstration to the whole class. His standing was greatly enhanced and this brought him out of his shell. This one-off experience was enough to help him, and others, to see him in a new light. It gave him a 'starter' to build upon so that his other positive qualities became visible.

The key internal drainers

- They are dealing with anxiety by avoiding.
- Shy and easily embarrassed.
- They lack social potency.
- They become skilled at discouraging teachers from persisting in their attempts to get them to work.

Their strengths

- Sensitive, watchful.
- Potentially responsive to support.
- Often aware of their problems.

The best teaching style

- Pushy caring.
- Finding ways to protect them through clarity of expectations and supported participation.
- Providing escape routes.
- Offering rewards and satisfaction from activities other than achieving success in the curriculum, such as personal hobbies and interests.

The worst teaching style

- Exposing them.
- Ignoring them.
- Surprising them.

Stance-specific energizers

Engagement – to show you care – what they need

Recap on the affiliation profile.

- They are withdrawn and isolated
- acquiescent, timid, likely to be bullied
- find groups difficult and prefer solitary activities.

Giving short one-to-one sessions to show an interest in their lives, finding out about their hobbies and talents.

Using bubble time and so on to allow them to signal they want to talk to you.

Offering lunchtime clubs. Engaging them in such activities through personalized written invitations.

Trying to re-frame any personal difficulty from a potential embarrassment to a form of their individuality.

Supporting their voice, if necessary by, on occasions, speaking for them or reading out their good work.

Setting up opportunities for them to be kind to others to help reduce their self-focus.

Allowing them to buddy younger peers.

Noting their body language and discussing which situations make them most and least comfortable.

Engagement – what they do not need – avoid

Ignoring them.

Expecting them to show a great deal of initiative.

Allowing their social isolation by letting peers select their own groups and teams.
Asking them to lead a group.
Pandering to any feelings of helplessness and passive forms of coping.

Feedback – to show you believe in them – what they need

Recap on the agency profile.

- They have little self-belief, experience school as out of their control
- are concerned with self-protection, scared to make a mistake, afraid of achievement
- do not believe effort will make any difference.

Dealing with them as privately as possible.
Using written praise as much as possible.
Praising any form of participation.
Giving tangible rewards to combat any praise aversion.
Allocating rewards on a co-operative basis.
Giving rewards for activities beyond the curriculum.
Trying to cultivate a more positive self-appraisal style.
Encouraging them to recognize their strengths.
Helping them to think about themselves from their strengths rather than their weaknesses.
Encouraging them to put down progress to their effort and put down failure to insufficient effort or inappropriate strategies.
Conveying the belief that their ability is not fixed.
Challenging, when appropriate, any vague excuses.
Giving recognition for trying to better their previous performance.
Giving marks based on their effort and participation.

Feedback – what they do not need – avoid

Making comments about their pace of work.
Criticizing the presentation of their work.
Using competitive rewards.
Using public evaluation and comparison.

Structure – to show you trust them – what they need

Recap on the autonomy profile.

- They avoid responsibilities
- hang back until they're sure about what is expected
- use delaying and avoiding tactics
- rarely ask for help.

Giving clear structures and routine.
Making clear to them what is expected.
Letting them know what is coming next.
Negotiating private challenges and responsibilities.
Checking out that they are comfortable with the task and the situation.

Structure – what they do not need – avoid

Reprimanding or punishing unpredictably and without warning.
Making lots of unplanned changes to routines.

Stimulation – to show you enjoy teaching them – what they need

Providing unobtrusive support.
Setting tasks that allow a slow and cautious approach.
Making sure the initial bits of the task are relatively easy or familiar to ensure a successful start.
Giving tight directions and asking them to repeat them to you.
Listing details of the tasks to be done, making sure every task is clear, with no surprises.
Using small group activities where each individual has a clear part to play.
Giving preparation time before asking them questions.
Increasing 'wait time' after questions.
Asking questions that you know they will be able to answer.
Preparing them and giving a head start to let them contribute to the class discussion.
Giving suggestions about ways they can protect themselves, such as saying 'pass'.
Partnering them yourself until they feel confident enough to join in.
Showing them how to get help discreetly.
Helping to scaffold their problem solving, that is just enough to let them sort it themselves.
Creating the possibility of them sharing with the class information that is personally relevant.
Reinforcing any kind of attempt at self assertion or emotional expression.
Providing activities where they can display their strengths and get some status within their peer group.
Pairing with quietly engaging pupils, as mentors.
Encouraging them to compare their performance to others whose level is potentially achievable to them.
Making their contribution to group projects identifiable and indispensable to the outcome, to give recognition and status.

Stimulation – what they do not need – avoid

Giving long periods of individual work, particularly lengthy written work.
Putting them on the spot.
Asking too many questions.
Giving obtrusive support.
Letting them spend too much time in 'passive' entertainment, for example, watching television.
Exposing gaps in their knowledge.
Making their contributions dispensable to the group, particularly when their contribution can be compensated for by superior members.

Stop and think

Have you ever been in a hiding stance? What were the circumstances?
What was done that you found supportive?
Was anything done that drove you further into hiding?
Use the list above to consider your strengths and development needs for dealing with pupils who hide.
To what extent do hiding pupils you know conform to the description above?
What techniques have you used to support them?
Select the strategies that might work for these particular pupils.

14

The exasperating reaction

Josh drove Miss Allan mad by shouting out inappropriate comments and constantly asking silly questions. Miss Allan put him down as a troublemaker. That was until she came to realize how insecure he was and how he craved acceptance from his peer group. She noticed he would respond to any dare, no matter how ridiculous, from his peers. The penny dropped for Miss Allan when one of his classmates, a boy he looked up to, stole money from her handbag and Josh happily took the blame.

This reaction is in the centre of the matrix because it is a hybrid mixture of the other learning stances and reactions. It is particularly open to the subjective views of those defining the behaviour as exasperating. The impact on teachers of a pupil stuck in the exasperating stance is like a slow puncture, not a serious hazard but gradually it gets you down.

Billy is a 10-year-old with Tourette's syndrome. He was exasperating to one teacher who did not know he had the condition; to another teacher who knew of his condition, he was seen as showing 'self-contained fidgeting that can be safely ignored'.

The essence of a 'pest' is that, first, like bad actors, they distract from and interrupt the main action. This could be termed the *distracting* reaction. Second, we assume their behaviour is deliberate. The more we think these pupils are distracting us deliberately, the more exasperated we become and the more personally we take their actions. The more we perceive them as being unable to help it, the less exasperating we find them and the less personally we take it.

Pupils who react this way are the 'if only ' pupils. For example, if only they would be less concerned with other pupils' affairs.

 Stop and think

What is the difference between pupils in the exasperating and opposing reaction?

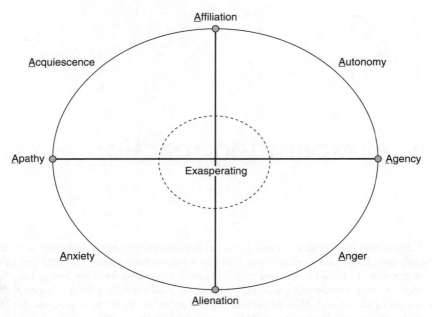

Figure 14.1   The exasperating reaction

Distinguishing characteristics

The exasperating reaction is presented in Figure 14.1.

3A profile

Affiliation
Pupils who spend a lot of time reacting this way tend to see school as a social club and their class as an audience to amuse. They can be interfering and niggling with both teacher and peers. They may be overfamiliar with teachers. They take and use others' things without asking and do not give them back. They show little insight into their behaviour, do not pick up others' cues or hints and are unaware of peers' needs. They seem to be out of step with the rhythm of the class.

Agency
This reaction reflects confusion, where even basic responsibilities can further distract. They seem to fail to learn from mistakes, experience or advice and keep asking the same questions and repeating the same misbehaviour. They can be disorganized and untidy. They fail to listen or pay attention and come across as silly. They will be first with their hands up but do not know the answer. They are often overactive, cannot stop talking and are easily distracted. They fail to manage time well and struggle with timekeeping as they do not plan ahead. They take too long to switch activities. They have

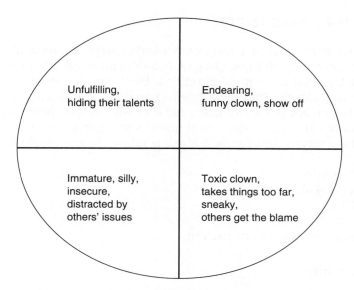

Figure 14.2   The sub types of the exasperating reaction

difficulties understanding how school works and appear unsure of boundaries. They do not bring the right books, often do not know the correct procedures, and seem unable to tell fact from fiction. They can be undependable and full of excuses and empty promises. They may show off as they are keen to impress. Some may be over-competitive and always want to be first.

Autonomy
They appear busy doing nothing and regularly do not finish their work. They do not give straightforward answers. They thrive on drama. They may expect others to do things for them. They can be gullible and naive and become the puppet of the gang. They are impatient and mood dependent. They are inconsistent and teacher rewards and punishments often have only a short-term effect. They are often more interested in being the best rather than doing their best. They are contradictory in that they can be resistant to, but at the same time dependent on, authority. They try to push the limits and nag the teacher to see how much they can get away with.

The exasperating reaction can be further subdivided into sub-types as displayed in Figure 14.2.

Most pupils in the exasperating reaction do not take things too far and know when to stop. A small minority may slip into the opposing reaction, usually when they find it hard to deal with public reprimands. They tend to react badly to such negative public exposure, especially to any 'put down' that creates resentment. *Oppositional exasperators*, in the bottom right-hand quadrant of Figure 14.2, are the low-level irritants that drain teacher morale and form the bulk of school exclusions.

Why do they exasperate?

Pupils who have this reaction could be described as 'hyper-motivated' in the sense that they are driven by multiple motives including approval, achievement, anger and anxiety that pull them in all directions. They want to please everybody but end up pleasing nobody. They do not deliver on their promises that they perhaps should not have made in the first place, but they want desperately to impress. The teacher's exasperation may come from unrealistic expectations. Outlined below are some of the factors underlying this exasperating reaction, including:

- status insecurity
- attention-seeking
- fun-seeking
- impulsivity
- an ambivalent attachment pattern.

Status insecurity

Pupils react this way when they do not know where they stand in the pecking order and they feel insecure and confused. Consequently, their relationships and behaviour revolve around hierarchy maintenance. Their status insecurity can often be seen in their annoyance when others are chosen before them.

Attention-seeking

The term *attention-seeking* could be another label for this reaction. This term however is used to cover a range of behaviours. It depends on the perceptions of those defining the behaviour as attention-seeking.[1]

Pupils learn about their status through the attention structure of the group, where high-status members get looked at more than low-status members.[2]

People who get the most attention in any group are those who are most valued by the group. We assess our status subconsciously through the number of eye gazes we get.[3] Being looked at by others makes us more confident.

Most students therefore enjoy gaining attention through appropriate channels. However, for some, being a nuisance is the only way of getting people to look at them. Any attention is satisfying in the sense that it meets their need to be noticed, if not accepted.

Pupils may be labelled as *attention-seekers*, however, not so much because they are looking for attention as because they are looking for but seen as not *deserving* of attention. Those with high status can call attention to their strengths, and such *attention-grabbing*, like an ambulance siren, is acceptable. We pay attention to people high in the pecking order[4] and get exasperated with people low in the pecking order.

Pupils who find themselves regularly reacting this way are often misunderstood and mistreated by the peer group. *Attention-seekers* typically strive hard to find their place but their desperation forces them to make a mess of their efforts. Sometimes the peer group pick up cues from the teacher that they are seen as pests and they can get trapped in this reputation.

Classes have status hierarchies that facilitate an orderly division of influence among group members, by, for example, allowing or denying different individuals the rights to do certain things. Some high-status individuals are allowed to make decisions and tell others what to do, whereas low-status individuals are expected to defer to others and keep their opinions to themselves.

Individuals' perceptions of their status are usually accurate and match the group's perception of their status, because having too high a view of your status can damage your acceptance in a group.[5] *Status self-enhancers* are those who say a lot in group discussions, assert their opinions forcefully, give unsolicited advice, interrupt others while speaking and try to tell others what to do. People who believe they have higher status than is actually accorded them by the group are disliked, as they are seen as illegitimately demanding privileges and trying to take status from others.

Particularly difficult classes have status self-enhancers whose *status violations* challenge the existing order and provoke conflict. These classes have too many people trying to make decisions for the group and too few people deferring to others.

Stop and think

Who is the biggest attention-seeker in your class?
How do you think the other pupils view classmates in the exasperating reaction?

Fun-seeking

Education provision is organized around the assumption that all pupils have an overriding aim to become high achievers and responsible citizens. Fun is demoted to the status of 'play'. Schools can hold a narrow view of motivation that stresses serious goal orientation and ignores fun. Yet fun is important for creativity and growth. It is essential, particularly for immature pupils.

Most theories see motivation as a drive towards a goal and assume the goal comes first and the means follow. Alternatively, the means can come first. We can enjoy the fun of an activity, whatever the outcome. Sometimes the goal is just an excuse for the activity.[6] Reversal theory suggests that we switch between the serious and playful states. Pupils in the exasperating reaction may be stuck in the playful state and may, for example, enjoy taking risks with silly behaviour particularly when there is a sense of theatre created by an audience.

Impulsivity

Pupils who react this way often show low self-control and push their luck, but without being reckless or aggressive. Impulsivity is a common trait underlying much exasperating behaviour. It is any rapid unplanned response that happens without thinking. Impulsivity comes in many shapes and sizes,[7] and may relate to emotional instability, extraversion or a lack of conscientiousness. Extraverts enjoy impulsive thrill-seeking behaviour. Positive impulsivity is associated with fast information-processing, whereas problematic impulsivity comes from the poor inhibition of competing responses.[8] Emotional instability is related to impulsive antisocial behaviour and low conscientiousness is associated with reckless behaviour,[9] and both personality factors coming together can tip a pupil from the exasperating reaction into the opposing or alarming and draining reaction.

An ambivalent attachment pattern

The roots of an entrenched exasperating reaction may be traced back to an ambivalent attachment pattern in early childhood. Here carers may have been neglecting and unpredictable. The child may have felt unvalued and so became clingy and fretting. As the parental response bore little relation to the child's behaviour, the child could not establish any connection between what they did and their mother's response. All they learned was that attention-seeking behaviour got a reaction eventually.

If their parents were angry they would become coy and disarming in an attempt to placate, often using immature speech and behaviour. They could also become oversensitive to other's moods and so become over-involved, anxious, possessive and jealous. They can hold on to these patterns of behaviour and bring them into school.

What works and what makes it worse?

Stop and think

What is the worst thing you can do with pupils in this reaction?
What is the best thing you can do with pupils in this reaction?

The key internal drainers

- They are out of step with the rest of the class.
- They have status insecurity.
- They deal with their insecurity and confusion by distracting.

Their strengths

- Their high energy levels.
- They are endearing.

Best teaching style

- Faith, hope and clarity to provide certainty to help them to focus and find their place in the group.
- Improving their status.

The worst teaching style

- Confusing them with responsibilities.
- Over-stimulating them.
- Distracting them further.

Stance-specific energizers

Engagement – to show you care – what they need

Recap on the affiliation profile.

- They are over concerned with the affairs of others
- gullible and naive.

Trying to understand why they are exasperating you.
Finding out how others view them.
Trying to assume a playful intent and respond accordingly.
Being patient, counting to 10. Being the broken record.
Setting up collaborative learning with high-status peers.
Separating from certain pupils to avoid potentially toxic combinations.

Engagement – what they do not need – avoid

- Judging them and getting caught up in your own opinion of them.

Feedback – to show you believe in them – what they need

Recap on the agency profile.

- They do not know where they stand in the pecking order
- are desperate to impress
- have low self-control, impatient, reactive, confused
- fail to learn from experience, do not listen or pay attention

Praising publicly for any exceptions to their exasperating behaviour.
Giving immediate rewards, whenever possible.
Offering group points to help raise their peer status.
Using tangible and competitive rewards.
Giving *coded* praise and reprimands via an agreed private code, for example, using the weather or conditions in the room to communicate approval or disapproval.
In private, giving them feedback by describing how their behaviour seems to others.
Providing visual records of their progress to help keep them informed of their learning targets.

Feedback – what they do not need – avoid

Publicly reprimanding them in a way that further undermines their status or reinforces their *pest* image.
Losing your temper and showing your exasperation.
Distracting them by overemphasizing rewards beforehand.

Structure – to show you trust them – what they need

Recap on the autonomy profile.

- They are 'hyper-motivated'
- are resistant to but dependent on authority
- are looking for but not seen to be *deserving of* attention.

Setting limits clearly by:

- displaying rules as an easy reminder
- giving personalized cards with a small number of specific rules as reminders
- checking their understanding of rules by means of a quiz, every now and again
- using rules to highlight the desired behaviours
- explaining why their behaviour fell short of the desired conduct, for example, 'I lose track of what I am saying if you shout out'
- using positive rules, expressed in terms of appropriate behaviour
- limiting rules to the few 'unbreakable' rules
- giving visual indicators of appropriate behaviours, for example, volume controls, interrupt cards
- providing brief non-verbal cues and rule reminders, 'what should you be doing?'
- using reflective rephrasing

- using motivating commands, expressed in clear specific positive terms, kept short and to the point.
- if repeating a command, quietly paraphrase the original command to avoid coming across as nagging.
- limiting the time given to listen to them.

Structure – what they do not need – avoid

Seeking relief from their repetitive tedium by escalating a confrontation to bring things to a head.
Accepting their excuses.

Stimulation – to show you enjoy teaching them – what they need

Making sure the instructions are specific, clear and simple.
Giving time to process instructions, then checking their understanding.
Inducting them in a simple self-starter sequence.
Building in regular visits to the gym or some form of physical activity.
Letting them demonstrate what they know or have learned.
Giving them frequent short tests.
Using strategies to develop their listening skills and attention control, for example, the random use of a tape-recorded message.
Giving advance notice of checking work.
Asking brief, snappy questions to check comprehension and keep them 'on their toes'.
Making regular spot checks on how they are working.
Providing physical manipulative activities to develop their sense of control.
Distracting them with objects to refocus their attention.
Giving a limited number of 'ration' cards that allow them some leeway with problematic behaviour, such as wandering around the room. They have to spend these in a specified time period. The period can be gradually extended or the rationing decreased in the same time period.
Reducing the stimulation in their work space by:

- organizing materials into separate containers
- removing unnecessary materials
- minimizing visual distractions
- keeping all their materials in one place
- highlighting the relevant details
- giving visual instructions
- using gestures and physical prompts, for example, 'fold your arms when ready to give an answer'
- giving instructions via pictorial sequences
- visually clarifying the rules with relevant pictures
- using footprints and mats to let them know, literally, where to stand
- using objects to communicate, for example, a microphone to signal when it is their turn
- using egg timers.

Training them to use these visual cues independently. Incorporating the visual cues into the task.

Helping them develop work habits and routines by, for example:

- providing work schedules in the form of lists to be ticked off
- giving a beginning, middle and end to each task
- insisting they disengage from one activity before they can engage in another
- breaking down long-term deadlines to shorter deadlines
- reducing the time available to complete projects
- helping them plan the order in which they will complete tasks.

Suggesting some secondary activities that may redirect their fidgeting and help them focus, such as drawing (always use colour pencils rather than crayons), playing with Blu-Tack or a relaxation ball, either as a 5-minute break or a parallel activity.

Stimulation – what they do not need – avoid

Overloading them with instructions or with even small class responsibilities (but do choose them for suitable tasks, whenever possible).

Giving complex tasks.

Giving too much choice or instructions, too many transitions, asking too many questions or using too much group work. (But do not deny them equal opportunities.)

Creating an over-stimulating classroom, with too many 'game-like' elements.

Having lots of distracting objects around their work area.

Giving too much passive learning.

Always being available for them.

Oppressing any self-initiated secondary activities that might distract and annoy you, but help their concentration.

Letting them divert you with distracting questions and suggestions.

Giving long-term deadlines.

Stop and think

Have you ever been *exasperating* yourself? What were the circumstances?
What was done that you found supportive?
Was anything done that drove you further into an opposing reaction?
Use the list above to consider your strengths and development needs for dealing with pupils who exasperate.
Think of such pupils.
To what extent do they conform to the description above?
What techniques have you used to support them?
Select the strategies that might work for these particular pupils.

15

The positive learning stances

This chapter profiles each of the three positive learning stances and identifies the best teaching styles and specific energizers for each stance as well as the drainers that should be avoided. It may be thought unnecessary to consider how to motivate pupils who are already engaged. This misses three important points.

First, one of the best ways to engage pupils in the defensive reactions is to raise the engagement of the whole class by maximizing the engagement of those pupils already engaged. In the same way, health strategies have made the biggest impact on problem drinkers by targeting the drinking behaviour of moderate drinkers.

> A rising tide floats all boats.

Second, teachers need to be careful to avoid draining currently engaged pupils. This chapter also shows how teachers can unwittingly push pupils from a positive stance into a defensive reaction. For example:

- Pupils in the quietly engaging stance get on with their learning without any fuss. They can, however, be reluctant to ask for help or put themselves forward and may not be achieving their full potential. Enthusiastic teachers can put them off through an over-intrusive teaching style. The most effective teaching style manages to achieve the balance between letting them get on with it and pushing them enough.
- The energetically engaging stance is taken by pupils whose high energy livens up the class. Sometimes pupils in this stance, however, may stray into the exasperating reaction by, for example, showing off. The most effective teaching style manages to achieve the balance between maximizing autonomy to encourage their enterprise and being directive to keep them on task.
- Pupils who can sustain the harmoniously engaging stance are a paragon of engagement. However, with this group there is a tension between maximizing their positive influence on the rest of the class and exposing them by holding them up as stars.

Third, there are some engaged pupils who have a superficial or pseudo autonomy that is masked by compliance and going through the motions. Their limited engagement will be revealed only when they are left to their own devices for the first time and they, for example, drop out early from higher education.

Why do pupils choose to engage?

In the chapters on the defensive reactions, we explored why pupils disengage. We need also to consider why most pupils choose, most of the time, to take a positive learning stance. This section summarizes the internal energizers that underpin the positive stances, structured in terms of how they meet learners' 3A needs.

Motivated pupils want to learn and think they can.

They meet their need for *affiliation* through their relationships with peers and teachers.

- They have good social and communication skills, in particular the ability to express both positive and negative emotions and to show emotional reciprocity with others. Their emotional intelligence allows them to use these skills to deal with the challenges inherent in the pecking order. These skills are especially important for low ability pupils.
- They have a well developed theory of mind that lets them take another's perspective and helps them understand other people's actions. They have a good capacity for empathy and understand another person's emotions.
- They have friends when they start school and believe other pupils are trustworthy. They are able to keep friends, with whom they develop reciprocity and emotional attunement.
- They can show emotional reliance and get support from others.
- They have an unconditional feeling of regard for themselves.
- The higher their affiliation-based self-esteem the more pro-social they become.

They meet their needs for *agency* through the effective use of what ability they have.

- They can direct attention to activities which provide 'flow' and strengthen their sense of purpose, which amplify any positive feelings and keep their negative emotions in check.
- They participate in extra-curricular activities, especially sport.
- They have a 'growth' view of ability and think it can be increased through effort.
- They put down success to personal, pervasive and permanent factors.
- They are optimistic, have positive expectations and assume any success in one area will spill over to other aspects of school.
- They are good at holding others' attention.
- They can deal with making a fool of themselves in front of their peers.
- They enjoy good status and adopt risky self-enhancing strategies, where they call attention to their strengths.
- They are able to resist peer attempts to involve them in risky behaviour.

- They are concerned more with personal achievement than with the rewards of success. They do not reject rewards, but the rewards are not as essential as the accomplishment itself.

They meet their needs for *autonomy* through their full participation in positive school experiences.

- Their resilience comes from the realization that they have autonomy which allows them to focus their energies on elements of any problems under their control.
- They will have had the chance to exercise control over important aspects of their lives and satisfy their need for control through leadership positions.
- Their resilience reflects the well-adjusted side of the main personality traits.
  - Their agreeableness makes them cooperative.
  - Their conscientiousness renders them determined.
  - Their emotional stability lets them experience positive emotions.
  - Their openness makes them creative and unconventional.
- Their high motivational resilience is reflected in adaptive self-control, including the ability to stay focused, shift attention and persist on tasks, to be as impulsive as possible and as cautious as necessary.
- They have good emotional control that helps them resolve conflict and delay or inhibit their desires.
- They have the capacity to self-reflect and judge their own strengths, to know what teachers want from them and realize how teachers see them.
- They cope with boredom.
- They can switch between being serious and playful.
- They balance academic demands and popularity.
- They express their voice and take initiative.
- They are able to assert themselves to achieve their goals within the requirements to conform.
- They accept responsibility for their learning, take a proactive role and avail themselves of learning opportunities.
- Their energizing emotions broaden their focus and create flexible thinking that helps to keep things in perspective.
- They adopt a mastery or self-improvement attitude to achievement and define success in relation to their own progress.
- They cope well with failure, which they see as a necessary part of learning.
- Their beliefs about the reasons for taking part combine with beliefs about their control over learning.
- They follow through on continuous commitments over several years rather than show fleeting interest in different areas.

Key motivational resilience factors with pervasive outcomes

Some of the features from the above list have a particularly pervasive impact on young people's motivational resilience. They are listed in Table 15.1, with

Table 15.1   Key resilience builders

Key skill	Why so pervasive
The ability to express both positive and negative emotions	Motivates pro-social behaviour, makes them emotionally contagious
Putting success down to personal and enduring skills	Builds robust confidence and persistence that sustains practice, the key to success in all aspects of life
Take the other's perspective and try to understand their actions	Helps cope with unwanted interference from another person that may block their goals
They can deal with making a fool of themselves in front of their peers	Develops a robust confidence and willingness to take risks
The capacity to resist peer attempts to involve them in risky behaviour	Gives pervasive outcomes in terms of self-belief
Showing emotional reciprocity	Enables strong and lasting friendships
Participation in extra-curricular activities, especially sport	Gives high status among peers that builds confidence
Attention holding capacity	Makes them confident and gives status

an explanation of why they are so pervasive and therefore worthy of special attention. These key resilience builders are so pervasive because they press each of the 3A buttons and as such should be key targets for the curriculum.

The quietly engaging stance

> Morven passed through secondary school, almost unnoticed. It was only when she reached university that her parents could see she was really interested in learning. Her mother was puzzled and spoke to her about it. She discovered that Morven, although happy enough in school and highly successful academically, had experienced the formality and routine of school as intrusive and off-putting. Only now was her deep interest in learning blossoming and her true potential being achieved in the more independent climate of university.

Pupils in this stance get on with their learning and do what is asked of them without fuss. They prefer to stay in the background but are the backbone of the class. They are focused in their own heads. They do not go out of their way to earn praise, although they enjoy it when they do. Similarly they do not have a huge need for approval but are distressed by disapproval. They are reluctant to ask for help or put themselves forward.

Distinguishing characteristics

The quietly engaging stance is presented in Figure 15.1.

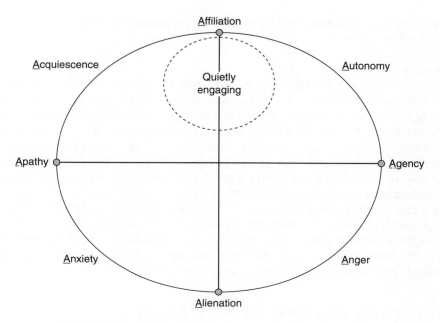

Figure 15.1   The quietly engaging stance

3A profile

Affiliation

This stance is typified by quietly spoken good listeners, who have good, albeit subtle, communication with teachers. They are respectful and well mannered. They can enjoy solitude and may actually prefer independent study. They have a good level of self-awareness and an ability to tune in to the emotional atmosphere. They are able to appraise others' emotions and respond appropriately. They are empathic and have a good understanding of other people's problems. They often show a quirky sense of humour. They show a trusting disposition, and a tender-mindedness. There may be costs to their agreeableness in that they can get distressed by conflict, which can damage their self-esteem.[1]

Agency

Pupils who are regularly in this stance tend to be steady workers with a long concentration span. They think through answers before answering. They are reflective but need to be probed. They approach tasks methodically but may be indecisive and poor at communicating their thoughts. They have good learning organization, planning and strategy use. They have little need to impress and are low on competitiveness. They can be resistant to feedback if they feel they are being intruded upon. They may be deferential and are aware of their shortcomings. They are suited to co-operative classrooms, but may struggle in more competitive situations.[2] Quietly engaging boys may be at a particular disadvantage as they are expected to take part in large competitive groups. They seek out

relationships among facts and like frameworks that integrate the subject matter
into the 'big picture.'

Autonomy
They have a strong mastery, self-improvement attitude and prefer to do well
by their own standards. They are self-reliant. They generally like school
although might not show it. They are calm, predictable pupils who can post-
pone gratification. However they can also be cautious, with a low tolerance of
chaos and risk. They tend to be shy and self-effacing. For example, they will
know the answer but will prefer to let others answer it. Similarly they can be
reluctant to ask for help or to be picked for things. They are selective in what
they attempt. They do not like expressing opinions. They avoid the spotlight,
find it hard to talk about or express themselves and lack spontaneity. As such
they tend to be more of a follower. They are 'embarrassable' and may be concerned in particular about making a fool of themselves in front of their peers.
They can hide, change or repair their feelings and can manage anger well,
although may struggle to express it appropriately.

The mutedly engaging stance/reaction

Pupils can often fall in the overlap between the quietly engaging stance and
hiding reaction. This requires the additional stance/reaction, displayed in
Figure 15.2.

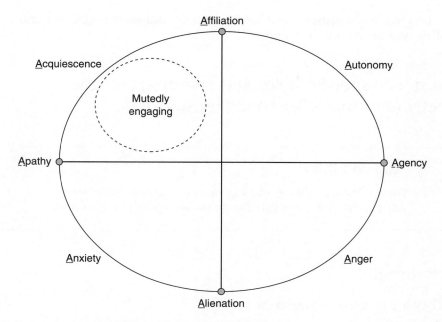

Figure 15.2   The Mutedly engaging reaction-stance

3A profile

Affiliation

Pupils who adopt this stance tend to be considerate, although they maintain a distance and relate on their terms. They find it hard to talk to teachers
they do not know. Consequently, they may take a long time to feel comfortable with the teacher. They are timid, lack social potency and find it
hard to make demands on others, and so will allow others to dominate
them. Such acquiescent affiliation in excess or along with emotional
instability can lead to dependency. They are not sure of themselves, often
apologize and are sensitive to comments from others. They may be over-
dependent and anxious to please.

Agency

They can be concise 'under-elaborators' who are constrained and to the point.
They may be disadvantaged when it comes to tests that require elaborate
answers, both oral and written.

Autonomy

Engagement is tentative and restricted. They do what is asked of them without
much enthusiasm and will not go beyond what they are asked. They do not like
boisterousness and will withdraw from competitive situations. They may be
stuck in their comfort zone and tend to come across as bland and uncritical,

with no clear and strong views. They are rule-bound, over-compliant and over-trusting and need a lot of structure.

The stance-specific styles and energizers for the quietly (and mutedly) engaging stance

Stop and think

What is the worst thing you can do with pupils in this stance?
What is the best thing you can do for/with pupils in this stance?

Their strengths

- They are focused in their own heads.
- Self-aware.
- Respectful and responsible.

Potential internal drainers

- They are self-effacing.
- Reluctant to ask for help or put themselves forward.
- May be disadvantaged in competitive or conflict situations.
- May be indecisive and poor at communicating their thoughts and feelings.

Best teaching style

- Gently persuading and probing.
- Non-intruding and inviting.
- Quietly acknowledging.
- Finding the balance between letting them get on with it and pushing them enough, by, for example, encouraging them to show their talents.

The worst teaching style

- Over-intruding.
- Taking them for granted.

Stance-specific energizers

Engagement – to show you care – what they need

Recap on the affiliation profile.

- They are respectful and co-operative
- may take a long time to get to know; inward looking, can enjoy solitude
- are deferential.

Respecting their need for privacy and distance.
Letting them work alone when they want.
Inviting them to take up tasks rather than waiting for them to volunteer.
Pairing them with more outgoing partners.
Getting to know them gradually.

Engagement – what they do not need – avoid

Creating an over-competitive climate.
Pairing them up with opposing pupils.
Giving unwanted attention.
Expecting them to show a great deal of initiative.

Feedback – to show you believe in them – what they need

Recap on the agency profile.

- They are steady and reliable
- reflective, methodical
- have little need to impress, do not have a strong need for rewards
- may be indecisive.

Maximizing information about their progress.
Giving praise privately.
Praising them in writing.
Praising particularly whenever they ask for help or express an opinion.
Using non-competitive and deferred rewards.
Allocating rewards on a co-operative rather than a competitive basis.

Feedback – what they do not need – avoid

Giving rewards on a competitive basis.
Penalizing them for their low social participation or limited initiative.
Over-praising and reinforcing their duty-driven motivation.
Using tangible rewards that are likely to be experienced as controlling.
Telling them via their report card to 'contribute more to the class'.

Structure – to show you trust them – what they need

Recap on the autonomy profile.

- They have a strong self-improvement attitude
- can be cautious, shy and self-effacing, reluctant to be picked for things or express opinions.
- Giving purposeful but low-key private responsibilities.
- Turning a blind eye to any rare misbehaviour.

Structure – what they do not need – avoid

Stressing what a good pupil should do or would never do, for example, you should not be selfish, in a way which might induce guilt.

Stimulation to show you enjoy teaching them – what they need

Providing tasks requiring a more reflective and slow paced approach.
Negotiating private challenging goals.
Allowing thinking time before expecting an answer.
Probing them to expand on short answers.
Giving opportunities for independent learning and research.
Showing them just enough to let them practise and learn it for themselves.
Suggesting they can ask you questions after class, if they need to check.
Showing them how to group and interconnect knowledge, through, for example, compare/contrast tables, flowchart or concept maps.
Allowing space for periods of non-activity, chances to daydream and to call upon their inner resources.

Stimulation – what they do not need – avoid

Making them the centre of attention.
Pressurizing them into rushed work.
Using time or competitive pressures.
Overusing public tests, like times tables.

The energetically engaging stance

> Robert was in his element in the enterprise class, where he was really encouraged to use his initiative. This was the one time in the week where he swapped his usual exasperating stance for full-on focused engagement. Indeed in this situation, it was Robert who made sure anyone messing about was brought into line.

This could be termed the 'pick me' stance, taken by pupils who liven up the classroom and whose responsiveness makes any teacher feel good. Their full engagement makes it easy for the teacher to find positive things to say about them. Sometimes pupils in this stance can be high maintenance when they become too cavalier in their approach, or stray into the exasperating stance by, for example, showing off too much. They may only work for teachers who work as hard as they do.

Distinguishing characteristics

The energetically engaging stance is presented in Figure 15.3.

3A profile

Affiliation
When in this stance, pupils feel able to be outgoing, enjoy peer activities and work well in groups. They show good conversation and social skills, including turn-taking, and giving greetings and compliments. Their sociability lets them enjoy classroom life. They are sympathetic and generous to others. They are friendly, loyal and easy to get to know and tend to be popular. They manage conflict reasonably

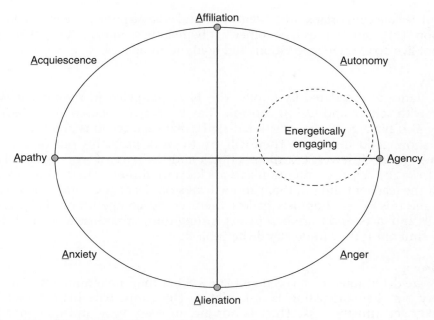

Figure 15.3   The energetically engaging stance

well. They are comfortable with themselves and enjoy a positive identity and reputation. They can, however, be somewhat bombastic or intolerant of others who do not live up to their expectations and hold the group back.

Agency

This stance is populated by pupils who have self-belief in their capacity to cope with school and feel in control. They are active, focused and attentive. They also have good organizational skills, make suggestions about activities and show good initiative. They will try to work problems out or research themes for themselves. Learning is quick and the pace of work is fast. They like to be the centre of attention and are keen to impress. They want to know what the teacher thinks of them and will seek out feedback. They enjoy praise and rewards. Their impulsivity lets them enjoy competition.[3] They enjoy details and facts, and learn best by explaining things to others and this is how they find out if they understand the subject.

Autonomy

They are determined to succeed and know what they are aiming for. They are chatty but their discussion is task-related. They anticipate instructions and quickly get into the task. Their hands are up every time and they give full answers. They see the point in working hard and will ask questions to clarify meaning. They take pride in their work, have a strong sense of purpose and set realistic goals. They spend time regularly in extra-curricular activities and have a wide range of interests. They are open and willingly offer their opinion. They take most things in their stride, although may struggle with losing. They can work through emotional difficulties and will turn to others for support. Their optimism lets them credit success to their effort. It works through positive thinking that allows them to focus their energies on elements of the problems that are under their control. They are team players who see the benefits of rules and know teachers' boundaries. They can be given responsibility, although they can sometimes take over in a group situation.

Stop and think

What is the worst thing you can do with pupils in this stance?
What is the best thing you can do with pupils in this stance?

The stance-specific styles and energizers

Bobby, a 9-year-old, was asked, as a writing exercise, to write a thank you letter to his teacher. He went the extra mile to write as sophisticated a letter as he could to impress Mrs Brown. Mrs Brown could not believe some of the language he had used and asked if his parents had done it for him. Bobby told her he had done it himself, with the help of a dictionary. She saw this as Bobby trying to show off and told him so, saying, somewhat critically, that he should not have needed to use a dictionary for such a simple exercise. Bobby was deflated and confused.

Stop and think

What is going on here?

Points to note

Some pupils are keen to do well to gain attention and praise. Their teachers may be reluctant, however, to make a fuss about them for fear of making them big-headed. Like Mrs Brown, they can unwittingly crush the pupils' natural exuberance. We need to realize that many pupils like Bobby have a healthy need to impress and that need is readily met by teacher encouragement and praise which will not create the monster we fear. Praise, like genuine affection and generosity, never *spoils* pupils. It is only when such *gifts* are used as a compensation for a lack of emotional support or as bribery that they can lead to an unhealthy consumption.

Their strengths

- Their sociability.
- High energy.
- Enterprising.
- Organizational skills.

Potential internal drainers

- They may sometimes want to take over.
- Can be intolerant of others who hold them back.
- May show off.

Best teaching style

- Pacy directing.
- Finding the balance between supporting their autonomy to encourage their initiative and keeping them focused by snappy and convincing directing.
- Promoting their enterprise.

The worst teaching style

- Suppressing their energy, impulsivity and initiative.

Stance-specific energizers

Engagement – to show you care – what they need

Recap on the affiliation profile.
- They are friendly and easy to get to know
- outgoing, sociable and popular.

Letting them talk about their family and listening to their personal stories from home.
Giving them opportunities for leadership and peer supporting roles.

Engagement – what they do not need – avoid

Making assumptions that they are always on task.
Allowing them to be over-competitive and bossy.

Feedback – to show you believe in them – what they need

Recap on the agency profile.
- They are active, focused, work at a quick pace
- have good organizational skills
- are keen to impress and enjoy praise and rewards and will seek out feedback.

Providing rewards on a competitive basis.
Being fulsome and convincing in your praise.
Using moderate and carefully chosen criticism that builds on their strengths to convey the belief that they can do better with more effort.

Feedback – what they do not need – avoid

Stinting your public praise.
Criticizing them for their impulsiveness.

Structure – to show you trust them – what they need

Recap on the autonomy profile.
- They have a strong sense of purpose, good will to achieve
- like to be the centre of attention
- are impulsive and competitive.

Giving high profile responsibilities.
Promoting their organizational skills by giving opportunities to set up activities and events.

Structure – what they do not need – avoid

Inhibiting their enthusiasm with oppressive rules that lack clarity of purpose.
Suppressing their organizational skills.

Stimulation – to show you enjoy teaching them – what they need

Promoting and encouraging their competitive and enterprise spirit.
Providing a busy atmosphere through lots of speed tasks and rapid action.
Giving tasks that involve social contact, novelty, fantasy, critical investigation and extended work.
Providing variety which creates curiosity by being surprising.
Being spontaneous, by changing how you do things, surprising them and keeping them guessing.
Encouraging them to develop their listening skills.

Using simulation and game-like elements to add meaning to what might otherwise become a boring activity.

Making them responsible for generating interest if they find the work boring, by seeking ways to make it more challenging.

Allowing them to construct their knowledge via active participation and interaction, open-ended questioning and discussion, problem-solving and discovery learning.

Using projects, experiments, debates, role play and creative applications.

Challenging a correct answer to condition them against the expectation that a challenge automatically means they're wrong. A 'correct' challenge might be: 'Yes, that's right. How did you know that should be the answer?'

Maximizing their organizational skills.

Providing opportunities to present their ideas to the class and other groups.

Letting them explain things to others.

Stimulation – what they do not need – avoid

Allowing them to get side-tracked.

Insisting that there is only one way to do things.

Healthy versus unhealthy competition

This stance is marked by a competitive spirit and competition will be an important energizer. However it has to be used judiciously. This section outlines a discussion on healthy and unhealthy competition.

Co-operation is working together for a common goal while competition is aiming to outdo others. The effect of competition relative to co-operation depends on the degree of interdependence of the task and how the competition is structured.[4] If the activity needs a lot of teamwork, competition is better. If the tasks are done independently, co-operation and competition have similar outcomes. Inter-group competition can be an extra incentive to help the spirit of affiliation. Overall, pupils prefer co-operative learning situations.[5] Non-competitive peer activities help socialization and the development of relationships.

Healthy competition

Competition is healthy when:

- winning is not heavily emphasized
- there is an equal match
- there are clear rules that make it fair
- participants can gauge their progress, relative to opponents
- tasks are simple, mechanical or repetitive.

Competition gives opportunities for identifying signature strengths and encourages pupils to do their best. It increases enjoyment as long as it is fun. It raises the importance of the goal and gives a sense of affiliation. The competition can increase both the desire to do well and the sense of excitement. It also gives a chance for positive feedback.

Unhealthy competition

Competition becomes off-putting however when:

- winning becomes more important than doing your best
- it encourages striving for selfish goals
- it teaches pupils that others are obstacles to their success.

It is particularly off-putting for insecure pupils to be forced into competition. Competition is unhelpful if it is unrelated to the process of learning and constantly changes the progress to a goal. The worst competitive teaching style is the one that makes pupils believe their worth is dependent on how well they do and failure means falling short as a person.

Unhealthy competition makes pupils:

- more interested in showing they are *the* best rather than achieving *their* best
- show less effort and persistence
- think low ability is the main cause of failure.

Unhealthy competition stops pupils:

- taking responsibility for each other's learning
- supporting everybody's efforts
- recognizing the contribution of others
- giving positive feedback to each other
- working towards a common goal.

Co-operation is always better than unhealthy competition while healthy competition and co-operation have similar outcomes in motor performance.[6]

Stop and think

Where does competition fit into your school, class policy and practice?

The harmoniously engaging stance

At the point of her retirement from 40 years of teaching, Mrs McLelland reflected on the thousands of young people she had taught over her long career. She thought of Jamie, one of many of her star pupils. Teachers and pupils admired Jamie for his qualities and no one seemed to be jealous of him. While he rarely drew unwarranted attention to himself, when he talked, everyone listened. He was never teased even for things he was not very good at. Mrs McLelland remembered, in particular, the time when the class let her down badly and took advantage of a student teacher. Jamie was the only one to retain respect for the student, shamed the rest of the class and saved the day for that student teacher. That student teacher was now making the retirement speech, as Mrs McLelland's head teacher.

Pupils who can sustain the harmoniously engaging stance are a paragon of engagement and light up the class. These are the exceptional pupils whom the teachers would like the inspectors to interview during a school inspection. This stance reflects high motivational resilience and autonomy, illustrated in their ability to handle both power and privilege well.

To reach this stance, pupils need to have the capacity to achieve a balance between:

- individualism and interdependence
- a healthy pride in their own uniqueness with a concern for others
- being independent yet responsible
- being original and bold yet systematic and disciplined
- energy and peace.

> What an antithetical mind – tenderness, roughness – delicacy, coarseness – sentiment, sensuality – soaring and grovelling – dirt and deity – all mixed up in that one compound of inspired clay. (Byron on Robert Burns)

They could be described as *transcendentally engaged* in that they can transcend their circumstances. In stark contrast, the defensive reactions are trapped by the circumstances. It could also be described as *heroically engaged*, when they manage to stay true to themselves in spite of pressures.[7] They are principled and able to stand up for themselves and their beliefs. They are able to think critically.

People at the top of any pecking order are assertive of their individuality, can express themselves authentically and have no problem with being different. Confidence is an important quality of such leaders but humility and self-deprecating humour add to their appeal. People who get the most attention in any group are those who are most valued by the group. *Attention-holding potential* is a useful concept that refers to the attention others pay to a particular person.[8]

Distinguishing characteristics

The harmoniously engaging stance is presented in Figure 15.4.

3A profile

Affiliation
This stance reflects a thoughtful and kind graciousness. They allow others to be themselves, through a non-judgemental attitude. They do not abuse their strengths and privileges. They do not talk overbearingly about themselves or

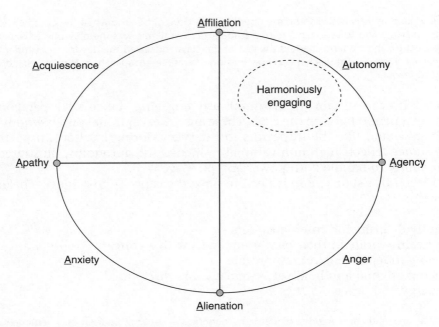

Figure 15.4   The harmoniously engaging stance

interfere with others and so do not disrupt the group activity. They will hold back and self-handicap when appropriate. They take pride in school and contribute positively through a wide range of activities. They are 'magnet' pupils, as others know that they will get on with the work and that they will help them. They can show their feelings when appropriate, which makes them emotionally contagious. Their ability to express both positive and negative emotions motivates pro-social behaviour[10] and nurtures empathy.[11] The combination of this desire to help others and their high self-esteem spurs them to act on behalf of their bullied peers.[12] Their persuasive personality allows them to quickly reach a common ground with others. In this way they draw others into their own rhythms and shape the terms of the interaction.[13]

Agency
This stance reflects high self-belief. They are able to self-evaluate and set their own targets. They show good learning organization, problem-solving and strategy use. They can plan ahead and make choices. They are well informed, creative and imaginative. They see the big picture. They show a 'flow' personality[9] and seek out challenges that stretch them. They 'complexify' routine tasks to make them more interesting. They are often unconventional and show critical curiosity. A cardinal feature is a belief in their capacity to deal with peer pressure, which is a key predictor of pro-social behaviour.[14] Such positive beliefs have pervasive outcomes in terms of popularity, pro-social behaviour and achievement. The capacity to resist pressure, especially to engage in risky activities, makes them particularly assertive. They are open to candid feedback.

Autonomy

They show a mastery attitude and measure success in terms of their own progress. They can work through emotional difficulties and will turn to others for support. They are sensible risk-takers. They can negotiate and question respectfully. They can also voice their opinion, even when in the minority, and disagree with people without falling out. They show trust in others and satisfy their need for control through leadership positions. Their emotional satisfaction comes from using their signature strengths, often to the benefit of others.[15] They are well able to represent themselves, their class and school. They invest their energy in complex goals. Being harmoniously engaging involves:

- mobilizing the group to achieve goals that meet everyone's needs
- clarifying what matters
- feeling part of a bigger picture
- integrating their own goals with group goals
- providing a focal point that helps pull a class together.

These are the pupils who best represent what the group stands for.[16] They accept the role of leader, as the people most effectively contributing to the achievement of group goals.[17]

Their leadership skills include:

- keeping others informed
- proposing objectives
- keeping to the point
- coming up with ideas
- showing the way ahead
- resolving conflict
- seeing connections between ideas
- acknowledging useful contributions.

They are unassuming, do not take themselves too seriously and have a sense of humour, even at their own expense. They enjoy an unconditional feeling of regard for the self, have little need for outside approval and rely on their own values to guide their behaviour.

The stance-specific styles and energisers

 Stop and think

What is the worst thing you can do with pupils in this stance?
What is the best thing you can do with pupils in this stance?

Their strengths

- They are able to handle power and privilege.
- Principled, confident dealing with peer pressure.

Weaknesses

- They may arouse jealousy in others who want to 'knock them off their perch'.

The best teaching style

- Facilitating.
- Find the balance between maximizing their positive influence on the class and avoiding setting them up as stars.

The worst teaching style

- Relying on them and overusing as group leaders.
- Showing favouritism.

Stance-specific energizers

Engagement – to show you care – what they need

Recap on the affiliation profile.

- They are able to express emotions
- their high esteem motivates empathy.

Encouraging them to take the lead.
Helping them set the tone and provide positive role models for others.
Encouraging them to help their peers.

Engagement – what they do not need – avoid

Using them as a leader all the time.
Holding them up as stars.

Feedback to show you believe in them – what they need

Recap on the agency profile.

- They are confident dealing with peer pressure
- unconventional, creative and imaginative.

Giving praise publicly.
Giving deferred rewards for long-term goals.
Providing rewards on a competitive basis.
Encouraging self-assessment through:

- evaluating whether they have learned what was intended
- measuring the quality of their products
- selecting products that reflect their best work
- evaluating the usefulness of the materials used
- deciding what future learning is needed and how that might be realized.

Feedback – what they do not need – avoid

Undermining their pro-social behavior by giving unnecessary rewards.

Structure – to show you trust them – what they need

Recap on the autonomy profile.

- They have confidence with humility
- show natural leadership.

Giving plenty of options.
Relaxing the rules.
Giving them leadership roles, a share of responsibilities and opportunities for decision-making and organizing activities and events.
Making the responsibilities real by negotiating them on their terms.
Allowing them to ask difficult questions about the school and the curriculum.
Giving them discretion in:

- setting work schedules
- working methods
- how to check quality
- when to start and stop
- taking breaks.

Maximizing trust through independent and collaborative learning.
Negotiating the success criteria from the outset.
Giving them *exclusive* responsibility for planning aspects of their own learning.

Structure – what they do not need – avoid

Seeing their assertive, critical and challenging attitude as threatening.
Imposing oppressive restrictions.

Stimulation to show you enjoy teaching them – what they need

Providing multiple task demands, speed tasks and rapid action.
Giving tasks that are challenging, fast paced and involve a lot of social contact.
Using extended work, with variety and novelty.
Giving opportunities for personal and group research projects.
Enabling them to help their peers.
Allowing them to develop their creativity.
Setting problem-solving exercises, channelling risk-taking, giving open-ended opportunities for creative learning, critical investigation and a 'blank sheet' approach.

Asking them what they would like to learn about the topic in question.
Giving them a list of possible questions and asking them to select the most useful ones to answer.
Creating high-pressure competitive situations.
Offering opportunities for public speaking.
Offering opportunities for innovation and creativity.
Setting up collaborative learning opportunities that allow them to have a say in forming groups and working things out.
Setting complex and open ended tasks. Once the task is set giving all authority to the group.
Setting tasks that create curiosity by being surprising and filling a gap in their present knowledge.
Providing sufficient complexity so that outcomes are not always certain.

Stimulation – what they do not need – avoid

Setting repetitive and monotonous tasks, such as lots of copying.
Going at a slow pace.
Always asking them for the answers.

16

Recap, recurring themes and concluding thoughts

This final chapter starts with a recap of the main layers of the motivational matrix before presenting the important themes that have reoccurred throughout the book, and ends with some concluding thoughts.

Recap of the matrix

The unifying theme of this book has been learner needs. The needs matrix is formed by the arc of resilience and its shadow and provides the framework within which we can describe how teachers motivate and pupils respond, namely, the teaching styles and the learning stances. The internal and classroom energizers are the tools pupils and teachers use within the classroom.

This book aims to develop a greater understanding of what makes pupils tick. This comes down to how well they get their 3A needs met. Needs create wants, and wants drive the motives that underpin our behaviour. The 3A needs are team players. If the needs for affiliation, agency and autonomy are all met pupils will be self-motivated and their goals will be self-determined. If these needs are blocked, coerced or crushed, pupils become driven to get their needs met in inappropriate ways.

While all pupils share the same needs, their personalities, experiences and backgrounds lead them to take their own paths to meet those needs. Most pupils want to do their best but, for some, their goals can become restricted, distorted or overwhelmed through a combination of internal drainers, family or peer adversity and how they feel about their school experiences.

The book has explored what helps or hinders pupils' motivation. It considered the internal energizers that shape pupils' motivational resilience, their capacity to get their needs met from within their own resources. It outlined how our 3A needs shape our personality which, in turn, organizes how we meet our needs, and how our need satisfaction then shapes our personality.

Personality has been characterized in terms of how our resiliency and reactivity interact to determine how we adapt. Resilience is a continuum of flexible self-control that is determined by our reactivity. Optimal resilience is achieved at moderate levels of reactivity. The interaction between resiliency and reactivity leads to three personality types, namely, flexible, impulsive and cautious.

As one moves around the resilience *arc*, away from the optimal midpoint, the individual becomes either increasingly cautious and rigid or increasingly impulsive and chaotic. The impulsive/cautious dichotomy becomes increasingly discrete until very low levels of resilience are reached when the two strands merge again at the bottom of the shadow arc of resilience.

Autonomy has been conceptualized as the interactive partner of resilience. As one moves around the arc of autonomy there is an increasing tendency at the extremes to become acquiescent and show restricted autonomy or to become antagonistic and display distorted autonomy. This dichotomy becomes increasingly divergent until the two strands start again to merge in crushed autonomy within the shadow arc of autonomy.

Autonomy is the capacity to balance our two motives to get along (affiliation) and get ahead (agency). Acquiescent affiliation combined with low agency can lead to a restricted autonomy. In stark contrast, antagonistic agency with low levels of affiliation can create a distorted autonomy. Within a balanced set of needs, agency drives autonomy on and affiliation holds it in check. Agency allows us to be ambitious and motivates us to make the most of our talents while affiliation motivates us to take an interest in others and to be co-operative. Autonomy allows us to do both. Affiliation and agency difficulties pull pupils into the dark side of motivation, but it is their autonomy profile that shapes the specific nature of their defensive reaction.

Pupils become increasingly good, as they grow older, at moulding their classroom environments to reflect their personalities and this leads to a degree of continuity in pupil personality. Clearly, however, personality is open to change and is influenced by classroom life. Personality development is a process of growth towards increasing autonomy. Personality, styles and stances are all capable of change.

How well pupils meet their needs is reflected in how they feel about themselves, and this is expressed through their self-emotions. The main function of our emotions is to tell us how we are coping and so motivate us to adapt to whatever context we find ourselves in. Emotions have a rapid response system and each appraisal inclines teachers towards a certain style and pupils to a particular stance. As such, feelings about ourselves are never neutral. Emotions can be energizing, restricting, distorting or draining.

The elements of the self-emotions are both reflections and ingredients of our motivational resilience. The self-emotions provide our personal compass. The three elements of the self-emotions are self-belief (which comes from a sense of agency), self-esteem (which emerges through a sense of affiliation) and self-determination (which is built on our capacity to exercise autonomy).

The book has analysed *what* teachers do to motivate pupils through the classroom energizers. *Engagement* is the energizer through which teachers show they value pupils and is the main way they meet pupils' need for affiliation. *Structure* refers to the clarity of pathways towards the learning outcomes and the boundaries that let pupils know how much autonomy they have. Structure impacts most directly upon pupils' sense of autonomy. *Feedback* gives pupils information about their potential and progress, and impacts most directly on their sense of agency. *Stimulation* comes from teaching and learning approaches that highlight the relevance of activities and challenge the pupils' present capacity, while permitting some control. Each of the energizers impact on all 3A needs, none more so than stimulation.

Teachers focus mainly on engagement and stimulation; they are caring and enthusing. As stimulation has the most pervasive impact on all 3A needs, this is good news indeed. They also increasingly use feedback. The challenge is for teachers to grasp the importance of autonomy support. Teachers tend to see pupils as needing to be cared for and enthused, but not yet as responsible learners who need to be given the autonomy that will let them take control of their own learning. Autonomy support is the key element of teaching style. Motivating teaching uses each of the four classroom energizers together and the fusion, like a multi-layered four-track recording process, is what creates the autonomy support.

Teachers' own motivation, personality and perceptions (that is, teachers' internal energizers) shape *how* they use the classroom energizers to create their teaching styles. The more control and less pressure teachers feel, the more they will be motivated and, in turn, the more autonomy supportive their style will be.

The teaching style arc mirrors the arcs of resilience and autonomy. Motivationally resilient teachers pivot around this style arc, adapting flexibly to pupils as appropriate. Knee-jerk reactions of teachers close to either extreme edge can take them into the dark side of motivation. Such defensive teaching reactions generate the classroom drainers.

What all this feels like for pupils has been described in terms of the classroom climates. Classroom climate is how a class collectively experiences those aspects of classroom life that impact on what it feels like to be a pupil in that classroom, principally the teacher's style. Any classroom climate can be analysed using the lexicon provided by the four *energizers* that interact to meet the 3A needs.

Four types of climate can be described:

1. The *colluding* climate is a restrictive climate that encourages superficial compliance.
2. The *crushing* climate is characterized by a blame culture, resulting in overwhelmed learners.
3. The *coercing* climate is marked by a 'prove yourself' atmosphere that galvanizes opposition.
4. The *motivating* climate is marked by gradual autonomy support that nurtures self-motivated learners.

Pupils need to be informed of their part in creating the climate and engaged in an ongoing dialogue about how they feel about their classroom experiences. This is the best way for teachers to communicate their emotional attunement with their pupils.

The matrix has provided a description of how pupils adapt to the classroom through the learning stances and reactions. These are learned attitudes that pupils adopt in the classroom, shaped by the beliefs and feelings they hold about themselves as learners and by their classroom experiences. The matrix is made up of a positive and negative energy field, and the stances and reactions are like whirlpools within these fields. The dynamism of the learning stances underscores the need for teachers to be flexible in their responses and adapt to the changing stances.

When pupils maladapt to a teaching style through one of the defensive reactions, we call this a behaviour problem and respond with sanctions, which merely suppress the problem or may make it worse. Support interventions should not aim to push pupils in a particular direction but, rather, should try to guide the pupil's propensities in the direction that is optimal for them. To change a child you also need to change the way the class and teacher sees the child.

The stances form as pupils become increasingly aware of status and conditionality in the classroom. Two key stages exist. First, around age 7 when:

- self-control becomes established
- concerns about acceptance increase sharply
- specific evaluations of competence trigger the emergence of the self-emotions.

Second, around age 9 or 10 when:

- explanations of progress stabilize
- pupils begin to realize they can have different feelings simultaneously and so become open to the concept of dynamic stances
- ideas about ability consolidate
- underachievers start to deliberately work below their potential.

These two stages indicate optimal times to work with pupils on their motivation.

The *self-emotions* mediate between ability and engagement, providing part of the explanation as to why some pupils fail to achieve their potential. Pupils' sense of self-esteem, self-belief and self-determination act as intervening variables between the classroom climate and achievement. Teachers impact on achievement via their classroom climate that in turn impacts on these mediators. Learning and teaching are heavily mediated by the atmosphere created by the teaching style. Teachers therefore need to be aware of how their style can impact on learner needs. Rather than think in a paternalistic way about how schools can give pupils self-esteem, schools should be places where pupils are given the space and support to develop their energizing self-emotions. The purpose of schools is pupil self-realization.

Each stance is best dealt with by a subtle adaptation of teaching style rather than an individualized approach. The final part of the book gave some illustrations of how teachers can personalize their approach and find the right *buttons to press* by adapting their style to better match the pupils' learning stances.

Finally we looked at how the styles and stances can dance in or out of step. Motivating teachers have a flexible teaching style that resonates with most of their pupils' stances. They manage to control their knee-jerk reactivity to pupils' defensive reactions. Examples were highlighted of how the over-soothing or over-pushy style can get out of step with the learning stance or reaction. Some examples were also given of how the teaching style can dance in step with the learning stance and can engage and transform the defensive reactions.

> ### Stop and think
>
> Your classroom practice/school policies and practices:
> What has been affirmed?
> What may need fine-tuning?
> What needs to change?
> I/we need to stop … .
> I/we need to start … .
> What could you do right away to consolidate your ideas about motivation?

Recurring themes

This section highlights some of the key themes that have recurred throughout the book, namely, the importance of:

- the context
- peer dynamics
- early intervention
- teacher motivation.
- the balance of power.

The context

While there is much to be gained by a deeper understanding of the internal energizers that drive pupils' motivation from within, it is important to remember that motivation is a quality of the transaction between the learner and the classroom. The 3As are not so much personal qualities as acquired states that are more likely when certain conditions prevail in the classroom.

The classroom needs to give opportunities for pupils to exercise affiliation, agency and autonomy, especially autonomy, which is the key catalyst and the most interactive of the 3As. Motivation is a two-way street. Motivation to learn gradually evolves into an enduring disposition, but for pupils it is shaped by and reflected in the stances they adopt towards a specific context or activity.

Stances cannot be considered independently of the classroom's reciprocal influence on pupils. A pupil's stance is related to their 'standing' in the group and reflects the class's and teacher's posture towards the pupil. Pupils' proneness towards the hiding reaction, for example, can be exacerbated or reduced depending on how their peer group treats them. The opposing reaction cannot be thought of as driven solely from 'within the individual' as it needs some external pressure, like a rule and an authority figure.

For all these reasons there is much to be gained from taking a whole-class approach to motivation rather than becoming too embroiled in the complexities of individual pupils. Classes have their own personality that needs to be acknowledged and nurtured. A key factor in motivating teaching is having a good working relationship with the class. The optimal teaching style engages most of the class and adapts to individuals when they show defensive reactions.

Stop and think

What are the characteristics of a successful class group?
What are the characteristics of an unsuccessful group?
What does it feel like to teach these classes?

Peer dynamics

A pupil's reputation within the peer group is a significant motivational catalyst and peer relationships are crucial to engagement in learning. A major priority and challenge for teachers, therefore, is to facilitate positive peer relationships. This is particularly important for those pupils who are not accepted in the early stages of schooling and are at risk of peer maltreatment in future years. With age, withdrawal from the peer group becomes increasingly important to peers and causes unpopularity. Such chronic maltreatment predicts later disengagement. Supportive peer groups, however, can redirect vulnerable pupils in a more positive direction.

Early intervention

The argument for early intervention has been highlighted throughout the development of the matrix. Some examples are highlighted below:

- While our relationships are critical for resilience, the internal energizers become increasingly important as pupils grow older.[1]
- The propensity towards aggressive behaviour is one of our most enduring traits and early, well-established patterns of aggression do not go away.
- We become increasingly good at adapting to our environment in ways that suit our personality and this has implications for young people who start school with particular personality difficulties.
- The hiding reaction can increasingly impair young people's engage-ability by creating further personal and social problems. If this reaction becomes chronic it will persist through long-term employment instability.
- Any low achievement that may have initially resulted from limited ability can become underachievement due to chronic motivational problems.

Teacher motivation

Motivating teaching demands a huge amount of emotional labour and the more authentic these emotions the better it is for teachers' well-being. It is particularly important for teachers to try to stay connected to their sense of purpose as much as possible. Teachers' motivational resilience influences how flexible their teaching style will be. The chain of motivation starts from work pressure and goes through teachers' perception of pupils' motivation to teachers' own motivation. As the process is kick-started by teachers' perceptions of work pressures, any discussion about pupil motivation must start with the conditions that affect teachers' motivation. You cannot share what you do not have. Pupil autonomy can only flourish in a culture of teacher autonomy.

The balance of power

Power is all about meeting our needs. It is our needs that give our goals their power. If our needs are met our motivation will be self-determined. If our needs are thwarted we become driven to get our needs met in inappropriate ways. We need to move beyond behavioural models that control pupils through rewards and punishments, to models that see pupils' needs, goals, beliefs and feelings as the sources of motivational power.

We saw how in the mother–newborn child relationship, the baby comes pre-programmed to motivate the mother to meet her needs. The mother has to learn to meet the baby's needs while getting on with the rest of her life. The mother gradually achieves a balance of power via reciprocity and trust. Motivating teaching is a similar power dynamic but in the opposite direction. The teacher is in charge but moves towards a more balanced relationship via reciprocity and agreement. When teachers provide autonomy support to pupils, their motivation will be enhanced.

This implies an attitude shift about the nature of authority towards a new social contract between teachers and pupils. Pupils want and thrive on responsibility. For some teachers, the change from a relationship based on compliance to a more reciprocal contract is a significant transformation. Many pupil–teacher transactions remain one-way, reflecting both a restricted understanding of pupil needs and a limited repertoire of energizing strategies. The more pressurized to produce high achievement the further teachers move to a controlling style.

Authority is a key energizer but can also become a drainer. Teachers can reduce the need to exert their authority by embedding its functions into the social processes and class norms. This requires a more participative style that shifts more of the responsibility to the pupils.

Like all good leaders, motivating teachers gradually:

- shape what pupils want to do
- position themselves among rather than above the group
- encourage pupils to see themselves as part of the class
- encourage pupils to see the class's interests as their interests.

Pupils express their personalities differently as a function of the degree of support for their needs, particularly autonomy. Support for autonomy is all about support for being oneself. The more autonomy supportive the climate, the more pupils will express their personality and the more parents will compliment the teacher for bringing the best out of their children. The more pupils feel controlled, the more they shut down and show less of their better self.

The major tension for teachers is to strike a balance between controlling pupils while releasing their potential for self-determination. This can be resolved by establishing authority then 'loosening the reins' to provide increasing opportunities for autonomy. The optimal style involves giving autonomy without undermining their authority. Teachers need to vary the level of autonomy they give pupils, according to pupils' capacity to exercise autonomy, as communicated by their learning stances.

Concluding thoughts

This book has talked a great deal about concepts of mutuality, reciprocity and pecking orders, that is, concepts that describe interpersonal power dynamics. Everyone is motivated to get their needs met and this occurs within some form of power relationship. Motivating others therefore is all about trying to make sure both parties' needs are met through reciprocity.

The colluding and coercing teaching reactions are taken by teachers when they become preoccupied with their own needs, problems or status. Both reactions rigidly focus on the achievement of the teachers' own goals and, consequently, the teachers become less attuned to the needs of the pupils. These teacher reactions might not appear harmful but pupils' perceptions of such approaches trigger defensive reactions in pupils.

Motivating learning boils down to teachers and pupils treating one another with respect and being able to negotiate and agree upon goals which are re-negotiated as pupils mature. Motivation requires teachers to expect responsibility from pupils and this means sharing power with pupils.

Traditional teaching has been challenging to pupils but relatively easy for the teacher. The recommendations in this book to motivate pupils by meeting their needs for autonomy, agency and affiliation will make schools more engaging for pupils but more challenging for teachers. To attract learners out of their comfort zone, teachers have to leave their own.

Motivation is a two-way process and pupils significantly impact on teacher morale. The sooner they are brought into the discussions the better. Pupils have much to say from their 'lived in' perspective of classrooms. This requires schools to create a climate where pupil opinion is valued and where leadership is distributed throughout classrooms as well as staff rooms.

Curricular reforms are starting to ask, 'what kind of child do we want?' as opposed to 'what do we want to teach?' An even better starting point might be to ask, 'what kind of pupils do we have and how can we best guide them towards self-determination?' Rather than direct pupils, according to our values, we should guide them in the optimal direction for them. School is where pupils find out who they are and what they are good at. Education should be about learning how

Figure 16.1   The achievement chain ii

to think critically, not what to think. Our schools' most important goal is to encourage pupils to be who they want to be, not who we think they ought to be. Qualifications are important but what young people do with these when they leave the climate of compulsion will be more telling in the end.

As depicted in Figure 16.1, achievement requires engagement which needs motivation. Pupil motivation is shaped by pupils' self-emotions that are determined by how well their 3A needs are met. This is where schools can have the most impact on achievement. Motivating classrooms enable pupils' 3A needs to provide their own incentives.

> Hence the good school is to be assessed, not by any tale of exam success, however impressive, but by the extent to which it has filled the years of youth with security, graciousness and ordered freedom. (Advisory Report on Secondary Education, 1947)

Appendix 1 How are the 3As met in your school?

Affiliation

What percentage of staff attend staff nights out?
Does the school have a social committee?
What percentage of staff have lunch in the staffroom?
Do staff have their own jar of coffee?
Do staff look forward to staff meetings?
Are there pictures of staff socializing?
Is there a welcome book for new colleagues?
Is there a staff group photograph on display?
Are there examples of staff being relaxed together, for example, dressing-up days?
How often do staff participate in activities with pupils?
Are there many plants around the building?
Is there high-quality furniture in staff areas?
Do managers use the staffroom?
How much sharing is there?
How do others react to the achievement of a colleague?
Do most teachers enjoy and want to work here?
Do people like and get on with each other?
Do people feel comfortable giving presentations to their colleagues?

Agency

Would this be a good student placement?
Does the school welcome visitors to share practice?
Are staff asked to give talks to other schools and conferences?
What percentage of staff are creative and innovative?
Does the climate support questioning and innovation?
Are achievements of staff and pupils highly visible?
Are there opportunities to experiment?
How many staff are doing courses?
Are most teachers up to working here?
Is there much criticism of each other within the team?

Autonomy

Are everyone's ideas listened to?
What percentage of staff can express themselves fully?

How do staff feel when the head asks for a quiet word later?
What percentage of staff look for and get responsibility?
What percentage of staff are ready to take on more responsibility?
What percentage of staff are able to decide on important issues?
What percentage of staff know what to do when they do not know what to do?
Are students and supply staff able to express their opinions in staff meetings?
Are people encouraged to take risks?
Do staff behave the same when the head teacher is not at the staff meeting?
Do most teachers want to work here?
Is there a feeling of vitality across the school?
Do people feel able to be emotionally reliant upon colleagues?

Appendix 2   How motivating is my classroom?

Teacher questionnaire

This checklist is designed to help you focus on factors within your control that impact on your pupils' motivation.

Ideally you should complete the checklist in collaboration with a colleague who is familiar with your classroom.

Circle the number that best applies to your view of the statement.

Affiliation through engagement. Do I	Never	Sometimes	Mostly	Always
1 like teaching this class?	0	1	2	3
2 try to get to know pupils as a person?	0	1	2	3
3 help everyone feel like they belong in this class?	0	1	2	3
4 help pupils sort things out if they get upset?	0	1	2	3
5 let the class have fun and a laugh?	0	1	2	3
6 treat them the way I want them to treat others?	0	1	2	3
Autonomy support through stimulation. Do I				
7 make sure pupils know what to do?	0	1	2	3
8 make the lessons relevant and interesting?	0	1	2	3
9 encourage them to develop their own interests?	0	1	2	3
10 let them choose how to do their work?	0	1	2	3
11 encourage them to try more difficult work?	0	1	2	3
12 let them know there are different ways to do well?	0	1	2	3
Autonomy support through structure. Do I				
13 allow pupils a say in running the class?	0	1	2	3
14 let them take responsibility for their own learning?	0	1	2	3

15	try to be fair to all pupils?	0	1	2	3
16	use the rules clearly and consistently?	0	1	2	3
17	encourage pupils to use their initiative?	0	1	2	3
18	ask pupils what helps them to learn?	0	1	2	3

Agency through feedback. Do I

19	notice and tell when they work hard and do well?	0	1	2	3
20	help them put their progress down to hard work?	0	1	2	3
21	praise achievements other than work, for example, helping others?	0	1	2	3
22	look at how they're doing without comparing to others?	0	1	2	3
23	treat mistakes as a good way to learn?	0	1	2	3
24	encourage pupils to work out how much they're learning?	0	1	2	3

Pupil questionnaire

Does the teacher		Never	Sometimes	Mostly	Always
1	like teaching our class?	0	1	2	3
2	try to get to know me as a person?	0	1	2	3
3	help me feel like I belong in this class?	0	1	2	3
4	help me sort things out if I get upset?	0	1	2	3
5	let us have fun and a laugh?	0	1	2	3
6	treat us the way she wants us to treat others?	0	1	2	3
7	make sure we know what to do?	0	1	2	3
8	make the lessons relevant and interesting?	0	1	2	3
9	encourage us to develop our own interests?	0	1	2	3
10	let us choose how to do our work?	0	1	2	3
11	encourage me to try more difficult work?	0	1	2	3
12	let us know there are different ways to do well?	0	1	2	3

13	allow us a say in running the class?	0	1	2	3
14	let me take responsibility for my own learning?	0	1	2	3
15	try to be fair to all pupils?	0	1	2	3
16	use the rules clearly and consistently?	0	1	2	3
17	encourage me to use my initiative?	0	1	2	3
18	ask me what helps me to learn?	0	1	2	3
19	notice when I work hard and do well?	0	1	2	3
20	help me put my progress down to hard work?	0	1	2	3
21	praise achievements other than work, for example, helping others?	0	1	2	3
22	look at how I am doing without comparing me to others?	0	1	2	3
23	treat mistakes as a good way to learn?	0	1	2	3
24	encourage us to work out how much we are learning?	0	1	2	3

Notes

Chapter 1

1   Connell, 1990, p. 4
2   DeCharms, 1976
3   Skinner et al., 1998
4   Anderman and Maehr, 1994
5   Maehr and Midgley, 1996
6   Vansteenkiste et al., 2005
7   The Scottish Parliament, 2006
8   Brophy, 2004
9   Deci, 1975
10 Ryan and Deci, 2000a
11 Gaylin, 1979

Chapter 2

1   Hogan, 1996
2   Helgerson, 1994
3   Baumeister and Leary, 1995
4   Luthar, 2006
5   Heifetz and Linsky, 2002
6   Wentzel, 2002
7   Furrel and Skinner, 2003
8   Assor et al., 2002
9   Heifetz and Linsky, 2002
10 Hay Group, 2006
11 National Research Council Institute of Medicine, 2004
12 Baumeister, 2005
13 Baumeister, 2005, p. 732
14 Goleman, 1997
15 Baumeister, 2005
16 Adler et al., 1992
17 Judge and Cable, 2004
18 Persico et al., 2004
19 Bandura, 1997
20 Seligman et al., 1995
21 Deci and Ryan, 1985
22 Haidt, 2006
23 Ryan and Frederick, 1997
24 Ryan and Deci, 2000b
25 Ryan et al., 1995
26 Deci and Ryan, 2002
27 Helgeson and Fritz, 1999
28 Ghaed and Gallo, 2006
29 Ryan and Deci, 2000b
30 Kasser and Ryan, 1996
31 Kasser, 2005
32 Guy Browning, *Guardian Magazine*, 12 August 2006, p. 9
33 Pinker, 1997
34 Pinker, 2002
35 Harris, 2007

Chapter 3

1   Hogan, 1996
2   Tett and Gutterman, 2000
3   McRae and Costa Jnr, 1999
4   Assendorf and van Aken, 1999
5   Hart et al., 1997
6   Busato et al., 2000
7   Borg and Shapiro, 1996
8   Furnham et al., 1999
9   Kirkcaldy and Furnham, 1991
10 John et al., 1994
11 Bradlee and Emmons, 1992
12 Costa and McCrae, 1992
13 Shiner and Caspi, 2003
14 Shiner et al., 2003
15 Shiner et al., 2003
16 Costa and McCrae, 1992
17 Havill et al., 1998
18 Francis, 1997
19 Matthews et al., 2000
20 John et al., 1994
21 McCrae et al., 2000
22 Gardner, 1983
23 McCrae and Costa, 2000
24 Hogan, 1996
25 Lucas et al., 2000
26 Matthews and Zeidner, 2000
27 Matthews et al., 2000
28 Suls et al., 1998
29 Bornstein and Cecero, 2000
30 Wolfe and Kasmer, 1988
31 Furnham, 1981
32 Guay et al., 2003

33 Masten and Coatsworth, 1995
34 Caspi and Roberts, 2001
35 Shiner et al., 2003
36 Roberts and Delvechio, 2000
37 Hart et al., 2003
38 Bradley and Corwyn, 2002
39 Lazarus, 2003
40 Luthar, 2006
41 Hart et al., 2003
42 Harris, 2007
43 Leontiev, 2006
44 La Guardia and Ryan, 2007
45 Crittenden, 2005

Chapter 4

1   Aron et al., 2000
2   Shields et al., 2001
3   Ainsworth et al., 1978
4   Crittenden, 1990
5   Ainsworth et al., 1978
6   Crittenden, 2005
7   Crittenden, 2005
8   Bowlby, 1973
9   Rubin et al., 1996
10 Salovey and Mayer, 1989
11 Mischel et al., 1989
12 Parker et al., 2004
13 Petrides et al., 2004
14 Eisenberg and Fabes, 1996
15 Baron-Cohen, 2003
16 Slaughter et al., 2002
17 Olsen et al., 1988
18 Baron-Cohen, 1995
19 Barresi and Moore, 1996
20 Choudhury et al., 2006
21 Bjorkqvist et al., 2000
22 Matthews et al., 2000
23 Baron-Cohen, 2003
24 Dweck, 2000
25 Quihuis et al., 2002
26 Erdley and Dweck, 1993
27 Dweck, 2000
28 Dweck, 2006
29 De Charms, 1968
30 Weiner, 1990
31 Bandura, 1997
32 Bandura, 1999
33 Reivich et al., 1995
34 Ruble et al., 1993
35 Tracy and Robins, 2007
36 Thompson et al., 2004
37 Cheung et al., 2004

38 Walls and Little, 2005
39 Nolen-Hoeksema et al., 1986
40 Shatte et al., 1999
41 Craske, 1988
42 Duda, 1992
43 Dweck, 2000
44 Baldwin and Sinclair, 1996
45 Barron and Harackiewicz, 2000
46 Elliot and Church, 1977
47 Coyne and Lazarus, 1980
48 Seligman et al., 1995
49 Thompson, 1999
50 Parker and Asher, 1993
51 Kirkpatrick and Ellis, 2004

Chapter 5

1   Cheung et al., 2004
2   Block and Block, 1980
3   Eisenberg et al., 2004
4   Prince-Embury, 2007
5   Eisenberg et al., 2004
6   John et al., 1994
7   Asendorpf and van Aken, 1999
8   Hart et al., 1997
9   Robins et al., 1996
10 Block, 2002
11 Hymel et al., 1993
12 John et al., 1994
13 Robins et al., 1998
14 Hart et al., 1997
15 John et al., 1994
16 Block and Gjerde, 1986
17 Kasser et al., 1995
18 Apter, 2001

Chapter 6

1   Frijda, 1986
2   Cole et al., 2004
3   Gibbs, 2006
4   Smith et al., 2007
5   Assor et al., 2005
6   Fredrickson, 2004
7   Fredrickson, 2004
8   Isen, 1990
9   Frederickson, 2004
10 Csikszentmihalyi, 1990
11 Campos et al., 2004
12 Csikszentmihalyi, 1990
13 Csikszentmihalyi and Rathunde, 1998
14 Panksepp, 1998

15 Reivich et al., 2005
16 Oyserman, 2004
17 Ryan and Deci, 2003
18 Frome and Eccles, 1998
19 Stipek et al., 1995
20 Harter, 1993
21 Harter, 1999
22 Stipek, 1981
23 Gurney, 1988
24 Rosenberg, 1979
25 Harter, 1999
26 Markus and Ruvolo, 1989
27 Carver et al., 1999
28 Higgins, 1987
29 Higgins, 1989
30 Higgins and Liberman, 1998
31 Elliot and Harackiewicz, 1996
32 Pintrich and Schunk, 1996
33 Leary et al., 1995
34 Graham and Juvonen, 1998
35 Roffey et al., 1997
36 Swann, 1996
37 Kernis, 1995
38 Taylor, 1990
39 Deci and Ryan, 1985
40 Rogers, 1961
41 Baumeister et al., 1996
42 Baumeister, 1993
43 Bradlee and Emmons, 1992
44 Harris, 2007
45 Pellegrini, 2003
46 Brown and Ryan, 2003
47 Kavussanu and Harnisch, 2000
48 Walls and Little, 2005
49 Roeser et al., 1996

Chapter 7

1   National Research Council Institute of Medicine, 2004
2   National Research Council Institute of Medicine, 2004
3   Paley, 1992
4   Grusec and Redler, 1980
5   Yates and Younis, 1996
6   Fabes et al., 1989
7   Blatchford et al., 2006
8   Hay Group, 2000
9   Deci et al., 2001
10 McLean, 2003
11 Assor et al., 2002
12 Patrick et al., 2002
13 Wentzel, 2002

14 Reeve, 2006
15 Reeve and Jang, 2006
16 Tannenbaum and Schmidt, 1958
17 Reeve, 2006
18 Adair, 2006, p. 42
19 Erikson, 1963
20 Hallam, 2004
21 Vansteenkiste et al., 2005
22 Kasser et al., 2004
23 Csikzentmihalyi, 1990
24 National Research Council Institute of Medicine, 2004
25 RAND Mathematics Study Panel, 2002
26 Wigfield and Eccles, 2000
27 Deci and Ryan, 2002
28 Wandersee and Griffard Phyllis, 1999
29 Seligman, 1998
30 OECD, 2005
31 Seligman et al., 1995
32 Dweck, 2000
33 Brophy, 2004
34 Vansteenkiste et al., 2004

Chapter 8

1   Csikszentmihaly, 1993
2   Crittenden, 2005
3   Rozenblit and Keil, 2002
4   McGregor, 1960
5   Pelletier and Vallerand, 1996
6   Skinner and Belmont, 1993
7   Kruglanski and Webster, 2000
8   Deci et al., 1982
9   Deci et al., 1982
10 Reeve et al., 1999
11 Reeve et al., 1999
12 Pelletier et al., 2002
13 Prensky, 2006
14 Brotheridge and Grandy, 2002
15 Heifetz and Linsky, 2002
16 Barber, 1996
17 Assor et al., 2005
18 Eccles and Midgley, 1989
19 Kaplan and Roth, 2003
20 Assor et al., 2002
21 Mageau and Vallerand, 2003
22 Hay Group, 2000
23 Hay Group, 2000
24 Nicholls, 1989
25 Duda, 2001
26 Ames, 1992

27 Newton et al., 2000
28 Duda, 2001
29 De Botton, 2004
30 Bruner, 1996, p. 143

Chapter 9

1   Cheung et al., 2004
2   Block and Kremen, 1996
3   Eisenberg et al., 2004
4   Eisenberg, 1995
5   Reis et al., 2000
6   Ekman, 1995
7   Vallerand, 1997
8   Buss, 2004
9   La Guardia and Ryan, 2007
10 The Midlands Psychology Group, 2007
11 Brophy, 2004

Chapter 10

1   Baumeister et al., 2003
2   King, 1999
3   Humphrey, 2004
4   Deci and Ryan, 2000
5   Soenens et al., 2005
6   Humphrey, 2004
7   McLean, 2003
8   Seligman et al., 1995
9   Deci and Ryan, 1995
10 Eckerman and Diddow, 1988
11 John et al., 1994
12 Pelligrini and Smith, 1998
13 Nichols and Miller, 1984
14 Brophy, 2004
15 Anderman and Maehr, 1994
16 Crittenden, 2005

Chapter 11

1   National Research Council Institute of Medicine, 2004
2   Maccoby, 1998
3   Apter, 2001
4   Rothbaum and Weisz, 1994
5   Maccoby, 1992
6   Rupp and Vodanovich, 1997
7   Dahlen et al., 2004
8   Wilson, 1973
9   De Botton, 2004

10 Martino and Pallotta Chiarolli, 2003
11 Jackson 2003
12 Francis, 2000
13 Jackson, 2006
14 Kelly and Dunbar, 2001
16 Lazarus, 1999
17 Crick and Dodge, 1994
18 Dodge and Sonberg, 1987
19 Heifetz and Linsky, 2002
20 Dodge et al., 1997
21 Crick and Dodge, 1994
22 Kushe and Greenberg, 1993
23 Baron-Cohen, 2003
24 Hoffman, 1987
25 Cohen and Strayer, 1996
26 Zimbardo, 2007
27 Fenigstein and Vanable, 1992
28 McClelland and Burnham, 1968
29 Paulhus and Williams, 2002
30 Kasser et al., 1995
31 Bushman and Baumeister, 1998
32 Kushe and Greenberg, 1993
33 Hughes et al., 1997
34 Baumeister, 1993
35 Ehrler et al., 1999
36 John et al., 1994
37 Costa and McCrae, 1992
38 Sutton and Keogh, 2000
39 Francatani et al., 2003
40 Davis and Kraus, 1997
41 Sutton and Keough, 2000
42 Bradlee and Emmons, 1992
43 Campbell et al., 2000
44 Sedikes et al., 2004
45 Exline et al., 2004
46 Sedikes et al., 2004
47 Wiggins, 1990
48 Paulhus and Williams, 2002
49 Bushman and Baumeister, 1998
50 Bradlee and Emmons, 1992
51 Scott, 2006
52 Bartholemew and Horowitz, 1991
53 Goleman, 1997
54 Newcomb et al., 1993
55 Patterson et al., 1990
56 Coie et al., 1995
57 Cairns et al., 1989
58 Pope and Bierman, 1999
59 Cota-McKinlety et al., 2001
60 Deci and Ryan, 1985
61 Heifetz, 1994

Chapter 12

1   John et al., 1994
2   Eisenberg et al., 2004
3   Shields et al., 2001
4   Parker and Herrera, 1996
5   Fischer et al., 1997
6   Staub, 1992
7   Crittenden, 2005
8   Gohm, 2003
9   Cheung et al., 2004
10 Keegan et al., 1995
11 Taylor, 1990
12 Beck, 1967
13 Higgins and Liberman, 1998
14 Buss, 2004
15 Ingram, 1998
16 Campbell et al., 1997
17 Cole et al., 1998
18 Ryan and Lynch, 1989
19 McQueen et al., 2003
20 Beyers and Goossens, 1999
21 Ryan et al., 2005
22 Ryan et al., 2005
23 Burleson, 2003
24 Beck, 1967
25 Brown and Harris, 1978
26 Wolfe et al., 1989
27 Ryan and Brown, 2003
28 Matthews et al., 2000
29 Wells, 2000
30 Matthews and Zeidner, 2000
31 Matthews et al., 2000
32 Salmela-Aro et al., 2001
33 Stattin and Kerr, 2001
34 Scheier and Carver, 1993
35 Barber and Harmon, 2002
36 Barber, 1996
37 Blatt, 1995
38 Hewitt and Flett, 1991
39 Habke and Flynn, 2002
40 Shafran and Mansell, 2001
41 Caspi and Roberts, 2001
42 Eisenberg et al., 1995
43 Eisenberg et al., 1995
44 Ehrler et al., 1999
45 John et al., 1994
46 Matthews et al., 2000
47 Shields et al., 2001
48 Ladd and Troop-Gordon, 2003
49 Buhs et al., 2006
50 Rutter, 2000
51 Garmezy, 1997
52 Coie et al., 1995
53 Coie et al., 1995
54 Shiner et al., 2003
55 Rutter, 1994
56 Anderman et al., 1999
57 Galton et al., 1999
58 Lazarus, 1999
59 De Longis et al., 1982
60 Wertlieb, 1997
61 Sandberg et al., 1993
62 Quinton et al., 1990
63 Graham, 1994

Chapter 13

1   Poulton and Milne, 2002
2   Apter, 2001
3   McCall et al., 1992
4   Smith et al., 2004
5   Mandel and Marcus, 1995
6   Oltmanns and Emery, 1995
7   Lazarus, 1999
8   Schwartz and Gorman, 2003
9   Burns et al., 1984
10 Schwartz and Gorman, 2003
11 Buss, 2004
12 Keltner and Boswell, 1997
13 Coopersmith, 1967
14 Deci and Ryan, 1985
15 Assor et al., 2004
16 Swann, 1996
17 Raffini, 1993
18 Cole et al., 2004
19 Thompson et al., 2004
20 Stipek, 1995
21 Patterson et al., 1990
22 French, 1990
23 Olweus, 1993
24 Perry et al., 1992
25 Ehrler et al., 1999
26 Parker and Asher, 1987
27 Magnusson, 1988
28 Gazelle and Rudolph, 2004
29 Gazelle and Rudolph, 2004
30 Rubin and Assendorf, 1993

Chapter 14

1   Mellor, 2006
2   Omark and Edelman, 1976
3   Vertegal and Ding, 2002
4   Chance and Larsen, 1976

5   Anderson et al., 2006
6   Apter, 2001
7   Parker and Bagby, 1993
8   Plutchik and Van Praag, 1995
9   Gullone and Moore, 2000

Chapter 15

1   Suls et al., 1998
2   Wolfe and Kasmer, 1988
3   Wolfe and Kasmer, 1988
4   Stanne et al., 1999
5   Borg and Shapiro, 1996
6   Stanne et al., 1999
7   Zimbardo, 2007

8   Buss, 2004
9   Brophy, 2004
10 Cohen and Strayer, 1996
11 Batson, 1998
12 Salmivalli et al., 1999
13 Hatfield et al., 1994
14 Bandura, 1999
15 Seligman, 2006
16 Oakes et al., 1999
17 Heifetz, 1994

Chapter 16

1   Luthar, 2006

References

Adair, J. (2006) *Motivation and Leadership*. London: Kogan Page.

Adler, P.A., Kless, S.J. and Adler, P. (1992) 'Socialization to gender roles: Popularity among elementary school boys and girls', *Sociology of Education*, 65: 169–87.

Ainsworth, M., Blehar, M., Waters, E. and Wall, S. (1978) *Patterns of Attachment: A Psychological Study of the Strange Situation*. Hillside, NJ: Erlbaum.

Ames, C. (1992) 'Classrooms: goals, structures, and student motivation', *Journal of Educational Psychology*, 84: 261–71.

Anderman, E.M and Maehr, M.L. (1994) 'Motivation and schooling in the middle grades', *Review of Educational Research*, 64(2): 287–309.

Anderman, E.M., Maehr, M.L. and Midgeley, C. (1999) Declining motivation after the transition to (middle) school: schools can make make a difference', *Journal of Research and Development in Education*, 2(3): 131–47.

Anderson, C., Srivstava, S., Beer, J.S., Spataro, S.E. and Chatman, J.A. (2006) 'Knowing your place: self-perceptions of status in face-to-face groups.' *Journal of Personality and Social Psychology*, 91, (6): 1094–110.

Apter, M.A. (2001) *Motivational Styles in Everyday Life: A Guide to Reversal Theory*. Washington, DC: American Psychological Association.

Aron, A., Norman, C.C., Aron, E.N., McKenna, C. and Heyman, R.E. (2000) 'Couples shared participation in novel and arousing activities and experienced relationship quality', *Journal of Personality and Social Psychology*, 78: 273–84.

Assendorpf, J.B. and van Aken, M.A.G. (1999) 'Resilient, overcontrolled, and undercontrolled personality prototypes in childhood: replicability, predictive power and the trait-type issue', *Journal of Personality and Social Psychology*, 77(4): 815–32.

Assor, A., Kaplan, H. and Roth, G. (2002) 'Choice is good, but relevance is excellent. Autonomy enhancing and suppressing teacher behaviour predicts engagement in school work', *British Journal of Educational Psychology*, 72: 261–78.

Assor, A., Kaplan, H., Kanat-Maymon, Y. and Roth, G. (2005) 'Directly controlling teacher behaviors as predictors of poor motivation and engagement in girls and boys: the role of anger and emotions'. *Learning and Instruction*, 15(5): 397–413.

Assor, A., Roth, G. and Deci, E.L. (2004) 'The emotional costs of parents' conditional regard: a self-determination theory analysis', *Journal of Personality*, 72: 1.

Baldwin, M.A. and Sinclair, L. (1996) 'Self esteem and "if … then" contingencies of interpersonal acceptance', *Journal of Personality and Social Psychology*, 71: 1130–41.

Bandura, A. (1997) *Self-Efficacy: The Exercise of Control*. New York: W.H. Freeman.

Bandura, A. (1999) 'Social cognitive theory of personality', in L.A. Pervin and O.P. John (eds), *Handbook of Personality*. 2nd edn. New York: Guilford Publications.

Barber, B.K. (1996) 'Parental psychological control: revisiting a neglected construct', *Child Development*, 67: 3296–319.

Barber, B.K. and Harmon, E.L. (2002). 'Violating the self: parental psychological control of children and adolescents', in B.K. Barber (ed.), *Intrusive Parenting: How Psychological Control Affects Children and Adolescents*. Washington, DC: APA. pp. 15–52.

Baron-Cohen, S. (1995) *Mindblindness: An Essay on Autism and Theory of Mind*. Cambridge, MA: MIT Press.

Baron-Cohen, S. (2003) *The Essential Difference: Men, Women and the Extreme Male Brain*. London: Allen Lane.

Barresi, J. and Moore, C. (1996) 'Intentional relations and social understanding', *Behavioural and Brain Sciences*, 19: 107–54.

Barron, K.B. and Harackiewicz, J.M. (2000) 'Achievement goals and optimal motivation: a multiple goals approach', in C. Sanstone and J.M. Harackiewicz (eds), *Intrinsic and Extrinsic Motivation, The search for optimal motivation and performance*. San Diego, CA: Academic Press.

Bartholomew, K. and Horowitz, L. (1991) 'Attachment styles among young adults: a test of a four-category model', *Journal of Personality and Social Psychology*, 61: 226–44.

Batson, C.B. (1998) 'Altruism and pro social behaviour'. in T.D. Gilbert, S.T. Fiske and G. Lindzey (eds), The Handbook of Social Psychology. Vol. 2. Boston, MA: McGraw-Hill.

Baumeister, R. (2005) 'Rejected and alone', *The Psychologist*, 18(12): 732–5.

Baumeister, R. and Leary, M.R. (1995) 'The need to belong: desire for interpersonal attachments as a fundamental human motivation', *Psychological Bulletin*, 117: 497–529.

Baumeister, R.F. (ed.) (1993) *Self-Esteem: The Puzzle of Low Self-Regard*. New York: Plenum Press.

Baumeister, R.F., Campbell, J.D., Krueger, J.I. and Vohs, K.D. (2003) 'Does high self-esteem cause better performance, interpersonal success, happiness, or healthier lifestyles?', *Psychological Science in the Public Interest*, 4(1): 1–44.

Baumeister, R.F., Smart, I. and Boden, J.M. (1996). 'Relation of threatened egotism to violence and aggression: the dark side of high self-esteem', *Psychological Review*, 103: 5–33.

Beck, A.T. (1967) *Depression: Causes and Treatment*. Philadelphia, PA: University of Pennsylvania Press.

Beyers, W. and Goosens, L. (1999) 'Emotional autonomy, psychosocial adjustment and parenting: interactions, moderating and mediating effects' *Journal of Adolescence*, 22(6): 753–69.

Bjorkqvist, K., Osterman, K. and Kaukiainen, A. (2000) 'Social intelligence – empathy = aggression', *Aggressive & Violent Behaviour*, 5: 429.

Blatchford, P., Bames, E., Rubie-Davies, C., Bassett, P. and Chowne, A. (2006) 'The effect of a new approach to group work on pupil–pupil and teacher–pupil interaction', *Journal of Educational Psychology*, 98(4): 750–65.

Blatt, S.J. (1995) 'The destructiveness of perfectionism', *American Psychologist*, 50: 1003–20.

Block, J. (2002) *Personality as an Affect-Processing System: Toward an Integrative Theory*. Mahwah, NJ: Erlbaum.

Block, J. and Gjerde, P.F. (1986) 'Distinguishing between antisocial behavior and undercontrol', in D. Olweus, J. Block and M. Radke-Yarrow (eds), *Development of Antisocial and Prosocial Behavior: Research, Theories, and Issues*. New York: Academic Press. pp. 177–206.

Block, J. and Kremen, A. (1996) 'IQ and ego resiliency: their conceptual and empirical connections and separateness', *Journal of Personality and Social Psychology*, 70: 349–61.

Block, J.H. and Block, J. (1980) 'The role of ego control and ego resiliency in the organisation of behaviour', in W.A. Collins (ed.), *Minnesota Symposium on Child Psychology*. Vol. 13. Hillsdale, NJ: Erlbaum.

Borg, M.O. and Shapiro, S.L. (1996) 'Personality type and student performance', *Journal of Economics Education*, 27: 3–25.

Bornstein, R.F. and Cecero, J.J. (2000) 'Deconstructing dependency in a five factor world; a meta-analytic review', *Journal of Personality Assessment*, 74(2): 324–43.

Bowlby, J. (1973) *Attachment and Loss*. Vol. 2, *Separation*. New York: Basic Books.

Bradlee, P.M. and Emmons, R.A. (1992) 'Locating narcissism within the interpersonal circumplex and the five factor model', *Personality and Individual Differences*, 13: 821–30.

Bradley, R.H. and Corwyn, R.F. (2002) 'Socio-economic status and child development', *Annual Review of Psychology*, 53: 371–99.

Brophy, J. (2004) *Motivating Students to Learn*. Mahurah, NJ: Erlbaum.

Brotheridge, C. and Grandy, A. (2002) 'Emotional labour and burnout', *Journal of Vocational Behaviour*, 60: 17–39.

Brown, G. and Harris, T. (1978) *Social Origins of Depression*. London: Tavistock.

Brown, K.W. and Ryan, R.M. (2003) 'The benefits of being present: mindfulness and its role in psychological well-being', *Journal of Personality and Social Psychology*, 84: 822–48.

Browning, G. (2006) The Guardian magazine, p. 9, 12 August 2006.

Bruner, J.S. (1996) *Toward a Theory of Instruction*. Cambridge, MA: Harvard University Press.

Buhs, E.S., Ladd, G.W. and Herald, S.L. (2006) 'Peer exclusion and victimisation: processes that mediate the relation between peer group rejection and children's classroom engagement and achievement'. *Journal of Educational Psychology*, 98(1): 1–13.

Burleson, B.R. (2003). 'The experience and effects of emotional support: what the study of cultural and gender differences can tell us about close relationships, emotion and interpersonal communication', *Personal Relationships*, 10: 1–24.

Burns, A., Homel, R. and Goodnow, J. (1984) 'Conditions of life and parental values', *Australian Journal of Psychology*, 36: 219–37.

Busato, V.V., Prins, F.J., Elshout, J.J. and Hamaker, C. (2000) 'Intellectual ability, learning style, personality, achievement motivation and academic success of psychology students in higher education', *Personality and Individual Differences*, 29: 1057–68.

Bushman, B.J. and Baumeister, R.F. (1998) 'Threatened egotism, narcissism, self-esteem, direct and displaced aggression: does self-love or self-hate lead to violence', *Journal of Personality and Social Psychology*, 75: 219–29.

Buss, D.M. (2004) *Evolutionary Psychology, the New Science of the Mind*. 2nd edn. Boston, MA: Pearson.

Cairns, R.B., Cairns, B.D. and Neckerman, H.J. (1989) 'Early school drop out; configurations and determinants', *Child Development*, 60: 1437–52.

Campbell, A., Mincer, S. and Odber, J. (1997) 'Aggression and testosterone; testing a bio social model', *Aggressive Behaviour*, 23(4): 229–38.

Campbell, K.W., Reeder, G.D., Sedikides, C. and Elliot, A.J. (2000) 'Narcissism and comparative self-enhancement strategies', *Journal of Research in Personality*, 34: 329–47.

Campos, J.J., Frankel, C.B. and Camras, L. (2004) 'On the nature of emotional regulation', *Child Development*, 75(2): 377–94.

Carver, C.S, Lawrence, J.W. and Scheier, M.F. (1999) 'Self-discrepancies and affect: incorporating the role of feared selves', *Personality and Social Psychology Bulletin*, 25: 783–92.

Caspi, A. and Roberts, B.W. (2001) 'Personality development across the life course: the argument for change and continuity', *Psychological Inquiry*, 12: 49–66.

Chance, M.R.A. and Larsen, R.R (eds) (1976) *The Social Structure of Attention*. London: Wiley and Sons.

Cheung, M.S., Gilbert, P. and Irons, C. (2004) 'An exploration of shame, social rank and rumination in relation to depression', *Personality and Individual Differences*, 36: 1143–55.

Choudhury, S., Blakemore, S.-J. and Charman, T. (2006) 'Social cognitive development during adolescence', *Social Cognitive and Affective Neuroscience*, 1(3): 163–4.

Cohen, D. and Strayer, J. (1996). 'Empathy in conduct-disordered and comparison youth', *Developmental Psychology*, 32: 988–98.

Coie, J.D., Terry, R., Lennox, K., Lochman, J. and Hyman, C. (1995) 'Childhood peer rejection and aggression as predictors of stable patterns of adolescent disorder', *Development and Psychopathology*, 7: 697–714.

Cole, D.A., Peeke, L.G., Martin, J.M.,Truglio, R. and Seroczynski, A.D. (1998) 'A longitudinal look at the relation between depression and anxiety in children and adolescents', *Journal of Consulting and Clinical Psychology*, 66: 451–60.

Cole, P.M., Martin, S.T. and Dennis, T.A. (2004) 'Emotional Regulation as a Scientific Construct: Methodology, Challenge and Direction for Child Development Research'. *Child Development*, 75(2): 317–33.

Connell, J. P. (1990) 'Context, self, and action: A motivational analysis of self-esteem processes across the life-span'. In D. Cicchetti (Ed.), *The Self in Transition: From Infancy to Childhood* Chicago IL: University of Chicago Press. (pp. 61–97).

Coopersmith, J. (1967) *The Antecedents of Self-Esteem*. San Francisco: W. H. Freeman.

Costa, P.T and McCrae, R.R. (1992) *The NEO-PI-R and NEO FFI. Professional Manual*. Odessa, FL, Psychological Assessment Resources.

Cota-McKinlety, J., Woody, P. and Bell, T. (2001) 'Vengeance, effects of gender, age and religious background', *Aggressive Behaviour*, 27: 343–50.

Coyne, J.C. and Lazarus, R.S. (1980) 'Cognitive style, stress perception, and coping', in I.L. Kutash and L.B. Schlesinger (eds), *Handbook on Stress and Anxiety*. San Francisco, CA: Jossey-Bass.

Craske, M.L. (1988) 'Learned helplessness: self worth motivation and attribution retraining for primary school children', *British Journal of Educational Psychology*, 58: 154–64.

Crick, N.R. and Dodge, K.A. (1994) 'A review and reformulation of social information–processing mechanisms in children's social adjustment', *Psychological Bulletin*, 115: 74–101.

Crittenden, P.M. (1990) 'Internal representational models of attachment relationships', *Infant Mental Health Journal*, 11: 259–77.

Crittenden, P.M. (2005) 'Attachment and early intervention', keynote address at the German Association of Infant Mental Health (GAIMH), Hamburg, Germany.

Csikszentmihalyi, M. (1990) *Flow: The Psychology of Optimal Experience*. New York: Harper Perennial.

Csikszentmihalyi, M. and Rathunde, K. (1998) 'The development of the person: an experiential perspective on the ontogenesis of psychological complexity', in R.M. Lerner (ed.), *Handbook of Child Psychology*. Vol. 1, *Theoretical Models of Human Development*. New York: Wiley.

Dahlen, E.R., Martin, R.C., Ragan, K. and Kuhlman, M.N. (2004) 'Boredom-proneness in anger and aggression: effects of impulsiveness and sensation seeking', *Personality and Individual Differences*, 37: 1615–27.

Davis, M. and Kraus, L. (1997) 'Personality and empathic empathy', in H. Ickes (ed.), *Empathic Accuracy*. New York: Guilford Press.

De Botton, A. (2004) *Status Anxiety*. London: Penguin Books.

De Longis, A. (1984) 'The impact of hassles on health and well-being: inter- and intra-individual approaches', paper presented at the annual meeting of the American Psychological Association, Toronto.

DeCharms, R. (1968) *Personal Causation*. New York: Academic Press.

DeCharms, R. (1976) *Enhancing Motivation: Change in the Classroom*. New York: Irvington.

Deci, E.L. (1975) *Intrinsic Motivation*. New York: Plenum Press.

Deci, E.L. and Ryan, R.M. (1985) *Intrinsic Motivation and Self-Determination in Human Behavior*. New York: Plenum.

Deci, E.L. and Ryan, R.M. (1995) 'Human autonomy: the basis for true self-esteem', in M. Kernis (ed.), *Efficacy, Agency, and Self-Esteem*. New York: Plenum. pp. 31–49.

Deci, E.L. and Ryan, R.M. (2000) 'The "what" and the "why" of goal pursuits: human needs and the self-determination of behavior', *Psychological Inquiry*, 11: 227–68.

Deci, E.L. and Ryan, R. (2002) *Handbook of Self Determination Research*. Rochester, NY: University of Rochester Press.

Deci, E.L., Ryan, R.M., Gagne, M., Leone, D.R., Usunov, J. and Kornazheva, B.P. (2001) 'Need satisfaction, motivation, and well-being in the work organizations of a former Eastern Bloc country', *Personality and Social Psychology Bulletin*, 27: 930–42.

Deci, E.L., Speigel, N.H., Ryan, R.M., Koestner, R. and Kauffman, M. (1982) 'The effects of performance standards on teaching styles: The behavior of controlling teachers', *Journal of Educational Psychology*, 74: 852–9.

Dodge, K.A. and Sonberg, D.R. (1987) 'Hostile attitude biases among aggressive boys are exacerbated under conditions of threat to the self', *Child Development*, 58: 213–24.

Dodge, K.A., Lochman, J.E., Harnish, J.D, Bates, J.E. and Pettit, C.S. (1997) 'Reactive and proactive aggression in school children and psychiatrically impaired chronically assaultive youth', *Journal of Abnormal Psychology*, 106(1): 37–51.

Duda, J.L. (2001) 'Goal perspectives and their implications for health related outcomes in the physical domain', in F. Cury, P. Sarrazin and F.P. Famose (eds), *Advances in Motivation Theories in the Sport Domain*. Paris: Presses Universitaires de France.

Duda, R. (1992) 'Dimensions of achievement motivation in schoolwork and sport', *Journal of Educational Psychology*, 84: 290–9.

Dweck, C.S. (2000) *Self-Theories: Their Role in Motivation, Personality and Development*. Hore: Psychology Press.

Dweck, C.S. (2006) *Mindsets*. New York: Random House.

Eccles, J.S. and Midgley, C. (1989) 'Stage-environment fit: developmentally appropriate classrooms for young adolescents', in C. Ames and R. Ames (eds), *Research on Motivation in Education*. Vol. 3. San Diego, CA: Academic Press. pp. 139–88.

Eckerman, C.O. and Diddow, S.M. (1988) 'Lessons drawn from observing young peers together', *Acta Paediatrica Scandinavica*, 77: 55–70.

Ehrler, D.J., Evans, J.G and McGhee, R.L. (1999) 'Extending Big-Five theory into childhood: a preliminary investigation into the relationship between Big-Five personality traits and behaviour problems in children', *Psychology in the Schools*, 36(6): 451–8.

Eisenberg, N. and Fabes, R.A. (1996) 'Prosocial development', in *Handbook of Child Psychology*. Vol. 3, *Social, Emotional, and Personality Development*. 5th edn. New York: Wiley. pp. 707–78.

Eisenberg, N., Spinrad, T.C., Fabes, R.A. and Reiser, M. (1995) 'The role of emotional regulation in children's social functioning', *Child Development*, 66: 1360.

Eisenberg, N., Fabes, R.A., Murphy, B. and Maszk, P. (2004) 'The relation of effortful control and impulsivity to children's resiliency and adjustment', *Child Development*, 75(1): 231–246.

Ekman, P. (1995) *Telling Lies: Clues to Deceit in the Marketplace, Politics and Marriage*. New York: Norton.

Elliot, A.J. and Harackiewicz, J.M. (1996) 'Approach and avoidance achievement goals and intrinsic motivation: a mediational analysis', *Journal of Personality and Social Psychology*, 70: 461–75.

Elliot, J.E. and Church, M.A. (1977) 'A hierarchical model of approach and avoidance achievement motivation', *Journal of Personality and Social Psychology*, 72(1): 218–32.

Erikson, E.H. (1963) *Childhood and Society*. New York: W.W. Norton.

Erdley, C.S. and Dweck, C.S. (1993) 'Children's implicit theories as predictors of their social judgement' *Child Development*, 64: 863–78.

Exline, J.J., Baumeister, R.F., Campbell, B.J., Keith, W. and Finkel, E.J. (2004) 'Narcissistic entitlement as a barrier to forgiveness', *Journal of Personality and Social Psychology*, 87(6): 894–912.

Fabes, R.A., Fultz, J., Eisenberg, N., May-Plumlee, T. and Christopher, F. S. (1989) 'Effects of rewards on children's pro social motivation: a socialization study', *Developmental Psychology*, 25: 509–15.

Fenigstein, A. and Vanable, P.A. (1992) 'Paranoia and self-consciousness', *Journal of Personality and Social Psychology*, 62: 129–38.

Fischer, K.W., Ayoub, C., Singh, I., Noam, G., Maraganore, A., and Raya, P., (1997) 'Psychopathology as adaptive development along distinctive pathways', *Development and Psychopathology*, 9: 751–81.

Francatani, P.S., Greenman, B.H., Schneider, P. and Manuela, F. (2003) 'Bullying and the Big Five. A study of childhood personality and participant roles in bullying incidents', *School Psychology International*, 24(2): 131–46.

Francis, L.J. (1997) 'Coopersmith's model of self-esteem: Bias toward the stable extravert?', *Journal of Social Psychology*, 137: 139–42.

Frederickson, B.C. (2004) 'The broaden-and-build theory of positive emotions', *Philosophical Transactions Biological Sciences*, 359: 1367–78.

French, D.C. (1990) 'Heterogeneity of peer rejected girls', *Child Development*, 61: 2028–31.

Frijda, N. (1986) *The Emotions*. Cambridge: Cambridge University Press.

Frome, P. and Eccles, J. (1998) 'Parents influence on children's achievement-related perceptions', *Journal of Personality and Social Psychology*, 74: 435–52.

Furnham, A. (1981) 'Personality and activity preference', *British Journal of Social Psychology*, 20: 57–60.

Furnham, A., Jackson, C.J. and Miller, T. (1999) 'Personality, learning style and work performance', *Personality and Individual Differences*, 27: 1113–22.

Furrel, C. and Skinner, E. (2003) 'Sense of relatedness as a factor in children's academic engagement and performance', *Journal of Educational Psychology*, 95 (1): 148–62.

Galton, M., Gray, J. and Ruddock, J. (1999) *The Impact of School Transitions and Transfers on Pupil Progress and Attainment*. London: DFEE.

Gardner, H. (1983) *Frames of Mind: The Theory of Multiple Intelligences*. New York: Basic Books.

Garmezy, N. (1997) 'Reflections and commentary on risk, resilience, and development', in R. Haggerty, L. Sherrod, N. Garmezy and M. Rutter (eds), *Stress, Risk and Resilience in Children and Adolescents: Processes, Mechanisms and Interventions*. Cambridge: Cambridge University Press.

Gaylin, W. (1979) 'Feeling bored', in W. Gaylin (ed.), *Feelings: Our Vital Signs*. New York: Harper and Row.

Gazelle, H. and Rudolph, K.D. (2004) 'Moving toward and away from the world: social approach and avoidance trajectories in anxious solitary youth', *Child Development*, 75(3): 829–49.

Ghaed, S.G. and Gallo, L.C. (2006) 'Distinctions among agency, communion and unmitigated agency and communion according to the interpersonal circumplex, five-factor model and social-emotional correlates', *Journal of Personality Assessment*, 86(1), 77–88.

Gibbs, R. (2006) *Embodiment and Cognitive Science*. Cambridge: Cambridge University Press.

Gohm, C.C. (2003) 'Mood regulation and emotional intelligence: individual differences', *Journal of Personality and Social Psychology*, 84: 594–607.

Goleman, D. (1997) *Vital Lies, Simple Truths. The Psychology of Self-Deception*. London: Bloomsbury.

Graham, P. (1994) 'Prevention', in M. Rutter, E. Taylor and L. Hersov (eds), *Child and Adolescent Psychiatry: Modern Approaches*. Oxford: Blackwell Scientific.

Graham, S. and Juvonen, J. (1998) 'Self blame and peer victimization in middle school: an attributional analysis', *Developmental Psychology*, 34: 587–99.

Grusec, J.E. and Redler, E. (1980) 'Attribution reinforcement and altruism: a developmental analysis', *Developmental Psychology*, 16: 525–34.

Guay, F., Mageau, G. and Vallerand, R.J. (2003) 'On the hierarchical structure of self-determined motivation: a test of top-down, bottom-up, reciprocal and horizontal effects', *Personality and Social Psychology Bulletin* 29(8): 992–1004.

Gullone, E. and Moore, S. (2000) 'Adolescent risk-taking and the five-factor model of personality', *Journal of Adolescence*, 23: 393–407.

Gurney, P.W. (1988) *Self-Esteem in Children with Special Educational Needs*. Routledge.

Habke, A.M. and Flynn, C.A. (2002) 'Interpersonal aspects of trait perfectionism', in G.L. Flett and P.L. Hewitt (eds), *Perfectionism: Theory, Research, and Treatment*. Washington, DC: American Psychological Association. pp. 151–80.

Haidt, J. (2006) *The Happiness Hypothesis: Finding Modern Truth in Ancient Wisdom*. New York: Heinemann.

Hallam, S. (2004) *Homework: The Evidence Institute of Education*. London: University of London.

Harris, J.R. (2007) *No Two Alike. Human Nature and Human Individuality*. New York: Norton.

Hart, D., Atkins, R. and Fegley, S. (2003) *Personality and Development in Childhood: A Person Centred Approach*. Oxford: Blackwell.

Hart, D., Hofmann, V., Edelstein, W. and Keller, M. (1997) 'The relation of childhood personality types to adolescent behavior and development: a longitudinal study of Icelandic children', *Developmental Psychology*, 33: 195–205.

Harter, S. (1993) 'Causes and consequences of low self-esteem in children and adolescents', in R.F. Baumeister (ed.), *Self-Esteem: The Puzzle of Low Self-Regard*. New York: Plenum.

Harter, S. (1999) *The Construction of the Self, A Developmental Perspective*. New York: Guilford.

Hatfield, E., Cacioppo, J.T. and Rapson, R.L. (1994) *Emotional Contagion*. Cambridge: Cambridge University Press.

Havill, V.L., Besevegis, E. and Mouroussaki, S. (1998) 'Agreeableness as a diachronic personality trait', in G.A. Kohnstamm and C.F. Halverson (eds), *Parental Description of Childhood Personality: Developmental Antecedents of the Big 5*. Mahwah, NJ: Erlbaum.

Hay Group (2000) *Research into Teacher Effectiveness; A Model of Teacher Effectiveness*. Report by Hay McBer to the Department of Education and Employment. London: Hay Group.

Hay Group (2006) *Staying on Track: Securing the Performance of Schools after Merger and Amalgamation*. London: Hay Group.

Heifetz, R.A. (1994) *Leadership without Easy Answers*. Cambridge, MA: Harvard University Press.

Heifetz, R.A. and Linsky, M. (2002) *Leadership on the Line*. Cambridge, MA: Harvard Business School Press.

Helgerson, V.S. (1994) 'Relation of agency and communion to psychological well being: evidence and potential applications', *Psychological Bulletin*, 116: 412–28.

Helgerson, V.S. and Fritz, L.F. (1999) 'Unmitigated agency and unmitigated communion: distinctions from agency and communion', *Journal of Research in Personality*, 33: 131–58.

Hewitt, P.L. and Flett, G.L. (1991) 'Perfectionism in the self and social contexts: conceptualization, assessment and association with psychopathology', *Journal of Personality and Social Psychology*, 60: 456–70.

Higgins, E.T. (1987) 'Self-discrepancy: a theory relating to self and affect', *Psychological Review*, 94: 319–40.

Higgins, E.T. (1989) 'Self-discrepancy theory: what patterns of self-beliefs cause people to suffer?', in L. Berkowitz (ed.), *Advances in Experimental Social Psychology*. Vol. 22. New York: Academic Press. pp. 93–136

Higgins, E.T. and Liberman, I. (1998) 'Development of regulatory focus: promotion and prevention as ways of living', in J. Heckhausen and C.S. Dweck (eds), *Motivation and Self-Regulation across the Life Span*. New York: Cambridge University Press.

Hoffman, M.L. (2000) *Empathy and Moral Development: Implications for Caring and Justice*. Cambridge: Cambridge University Press.

Hogan, R.A. (1996) 'Socioanalytic perspective on five-factor model of personality', in J.S. Wiggins (ed.), *The Five Factor Model of Personality*. New York: Guilford Press.

Hughes, J.N., Cavell, T.A. and Grossman, P.B. (1997) 'A positive view of self: risk or protection for aggressive children?', *Development and Psychopathology*, 9: 75–94.

Humphrey, N. (2004) 'The death of the feel-good factor? Self-esteem in the educational context', *School Psychology International*, 25(3): 347–60.

Hymel, S., Bowker, A. and Woody, F. (1993) 'Aggressive versus withdrawn unpopular children: variation in peer and self perceptions in multiple domains', *Child Development*, 64: 879–90.

Ingram, R.E. (1998) 'Self-focused attention and clinical disorders: review and a conceptual model', *Psychological Bulletin*, 107: 156–76.

Isen, A.M. (1990) 'The influence of positive and negative affect on cognitive organization: some implications for development', in N. Stein, B. Leventhal and T. Trabasso (eds), *Psychological and Biological Approaches to Emotions*. Hillsdale, NJ: Erlbaum.

Jackson, C. (2003) 'Motives for "laddishness" at school: fear of failure and fear of the "feminine"', *British Educational Research Journal*, 29: 583–98.

Jackson, C. (2006) *Lads and Ladettes in School*. Maidenhead: Open University Press.

John, O.P., Caspi, A., Robins, R.W., Moffit, T.E. and Stouthamer-Loeber, M. (1994) 'The "little five": exploring the nomological network of the five-factor model of personality in adolescent boys', *Child Development*, 65: 160–78.

Judge, T.A. and Cable, D.M. (2004) 'The effect of physical height on workplace success and income: preliminary test of a theoretical model', *Journal of Applied Psychology*, 89: 428–41.

Kaplan, H. A. and Roth, G. (2003) 'Is autonomy important for all students? Evidence from a longitudinal study', paper presented at the 84th Annual Meeting of the American Educational Research Association, Chicago, Illinois.

Kasser, T. (2005) 'Frugality, generosity, and materialism in children and adolescents', in K.A. Moore and L.H. Lippman (eds), *What Do Children Need to Flourish? Conceptualizing and Measuring Indicators of Positive Development*. New York: Kluwer/Plenum.

Kasser,T. and Ryan, R.M. (1996) 'Further examining the American dream: differential correlates of intrinsic and extrinsic goals', in P. Scmuck and K.M. Sheldon (eds), *Life Goals and Well-Being: Towards a Positive Psychology of Human Striving*. Goettingen: Hogrefe and Huber.

Kasser, T., Ryan, R.M., Couchman, C.E. and Sheldon, K.M. (2004) 'Materialistic values: their causes and consequences', in T. Kasser and A.D. Kanner (eds), *Psychology and Consumer Culture: The Struggle for a Good Life in a Materialistic World*. Washington, DC: American Psychological Association. pp. 11–28.

Kasser, T., Ryan, R.M., Zax, M. and Sameroff. A.J. (1995) 'The relations of maternal and social environments to late adolescents' materialistic and prosocial values'. *Developmental Psychology*, 31: 907–14.

Kavussanu, M. and Harnisch, D.L. (2000) 'Self-esteem in children: do goal orientations matter?', *British Journal of Educational Psychology*, 70: 229–42.

Keegan, D., Greenier, M., Kernis, M.H. and Waschull, S.B. (1995) '"Not all high (or low) self-esteem people are the same". Theory and research on stability of self-esteem', in M.H. Kernis (ed.), *Efficacy, Agency and Self Esteem*. New York: Plenum Press.

Kelly, S. and Dunbar, R.I.M. (2001) 'Who dares, wins: heroism versus altruism in women's mate choice', *Human Nature*, 12(2): 89–105.

Keltner, D. and Boswell, B.N. (1997) 'Embarrassment: its distinct form and appeasement functions', *Psychological Bulletin*, 122: 250–70.

Kernis, M.H. (ed.) (1995) *Efficacy, Agency, and Self-Esteem*. New York: Plenum.

King, K.C., Hyde, J.S., Sowers, C.J. and Buswell, B.N. (1999) 'Gender differences in self-esteem: a meta-analysis', *Psychological Bulletin*, 125: 470–500.

Kirkcaldy, B. and Furnham, A. (1991) 'Extraversion, neuroticism, psychoticism, and recreational choice', *Personality and Individual Differences*, 12: 737–45.

Kirkpatrick, L.E. and Ellis, B.J. (2004) 'An evolutionary-psychological approach to self-esteem: multiple domains and multiple functions', in M.B. Brewer and M. Hewstone (eds), *Self and Social Identity*. Oxford: Blackwell.

Kruglanski, R.W. and Webster, D.M (2000) 'Motivated closing of the mind: seizing and freezing', in E.T. Higgins and R.W. Kruglanski (eds), *Motivational Science Social and Personality Perspectives*. Philadelphia, PA: Taylor and Francis.

Kushe, C. and Greenberg, M. (1993) *Teaching PATHS in your Classroom: The PATHS Curriculum Instruction Manual (Special Needs Version)*. Seattle, WA: University of Washington Press.

La Guardia, J.G. and Ryan, R.M. (2007) 'Why identities fluctuate: variability in traits as a function of situational variations in autonomy support', *Journal of Personality*, 75(6): 1205–25.

Ladd, G.W. and Troop-Gordon, W. (2003) 'The role of chronic peer difficulties in the development of children's psychological and adjustment problems', *Child Development*, 74(5): 1344–67.

Lazarus, R.S. (1999) *Stress and Emotions: A New Synthesis*. New York: Springer.

Lazarus, R.S. (2003) 'Does the positive psychology movement have legs', *Psychological Inquiry*, 14: 93–109.

Leary, M.R., Tambor, E.S.W., Terdal, S.K. and Chokel, J.T. (1995) 'Self esteem as an interpersonal monitor. The sociometer hypothesis', *Journal of Personality and Social Psychology*, 74: 1290–9.

Leontiev, D. (2006) 'Positive personality development approaching personal autonomy', in M. Csikszentmihalyi and I.S. Csikszentmihalyi (eds), *A Life Worth Living*. Oxford: Oxford University Press.

Lucas, R.E., Diener, E., Grob, A., Suh, E.M. and Shao, L. (2000) 'Cross cultural; evidence for the fundamental features of extraversion', *Journal of Personality and Social Psychology*, 79: 452–68.

Luthar, S.S. (2006) 'Resilience in development: a synthesis of research across five decades', in D. Cichettii and D.J. Cohen (eds), *Developmental Psychopathology; Risk, Disorder and Adaptation*. Vol. 3. 2nd edn. Hoboken, NJ: John Wiley and Sons. pp. 739–95.

Maccoby, E.E. (1992) 'The role of parents in socialising children. A historical overview', *Developmental Psychology*, 28: 1006–17.

Maccoby, E.E. (1998) *The Two Sexes: Growing Up Apart, Coming Together*. Cambridge, MA: Harvard University Press.

Maehr, M.L. and Midgley, C. (1996) *Transforming School Cultures*. Boulder, CO: Westview.

Mageau, G.A. and Vallerand, R.J. (2003) 'The coach–athlete relationship: a motivational model', *Journal of Sport Sciences*, 21: 883–904.

Magnusson, D. (1988) *Individual Development from an Interactive Perspective: A Longitudinal Study*. Hillsdale, NJ: Erlbaum.

Mandel, H.P. and Marcus, I.S. (1995) *Why Children Underachieve & What to Do about It: Could Do Better*. Darby, PA: Diane Publishing.

Markus, H. and Ruvolo, A. (1989) 'Possible selves: personalised representatives of goals', in L. Pervin (ed.), *Goal Concepts in Personality and Social Psychology*. Hillsdale, NJ: Erlbaum. pp. 211–41.

Martino, W. and Pallotta-Chiarolli, M. (2003) *So What's a Boy? Addressing Issues of Masculinity and Schooling*. Buckingham: Open University Press.

Masten, A.S. and Coatsworth, J.D. (1995) 'Competence, resilience, & psychopathology', in D. Cicchetti and D. Cohen (eds), *Developmental Psychopathology*. Vol. 2, *Risk, Disorder, and Adaptation*. New York: Wiley. pp. 715–52.

Matthews, G. and Zeidner, M. (2000) 'Emotional intelligence, adaption to stressful encounters, and health outcomes', in R. Bar-On and J.D.A Parker (eds), *Handbook of Emotional Intelligence*. New York: Jossey-Bass. pp. 459–89.

Matthews, G., Schwean, V.L., Campbell, S.E., Saklofske, D.H. and Mohamed, A.A.R. (2000) 'Personality, self-regulation, and adaptation: a cognitive-social framework', in M. Boekaerts, P.R. Pintrich and M. Zeidner (eds), Handbook of Self-Regulation. New York: Academic Press. pp. 171–207.

McCall, R., Evahn, C. and Kratzer, L. (1992) *High School Underachievement*. Newbury Park, CA: Sage.

McClelland, D.C. and Burnham, D.H. (1968) 'Power is the great motivator', Harvard Business School Press.

McRae, R.R. and Costa Jnr, P.T. (1999) 'A five factor theory of personality', in L.A. Pervin and O.P. John (eds), *A Handbook of Personality*. New York/London: Guilford Press.

McCrae, R.R. and Costa, P.T. (2000) 'Conceptions and correlates of openness to experience', in R. Hogan, J.A. Johnson and S.R. Briggs (eds), *Handbook of Personality Psychology*. San Diego, CA: Academic Press.

McCrae, R.R., Costa, P.T. Jr, Ostendorf, F. and Angleitner, A. (2000) 'Nature over nurture: temperament, personality and life span development', *Journal of Personality and Social Psychology*, 78(1): 173–86.

McGregor, D. (1960) *The Human side of Enterprise*. Boston: McGraw-Hill.

McLean, A. (2003) *The Motivated School*. London: Paul Chapman Publishing.

McQueen, A., Getz, J.G. and Bray, J.H. (2003) 'Acculturation, substance use and deviant behavior: examining separation and family conflict as mediators', *Child Development*, 74: 1737–50.

Mellor, N. (2006) 'Attention seeking: the paradoxes of an under researched concept', *Educational and Child Psychology*, 23(1): 94–105.

Mischel, W., Shoda, Y. and Rodriguez, M.L. (1989) 'Delay of gratification in children', *Science*, 244: 933–38.

National Research Council Institute of Medicine (2004) *Engaging Schools: Fostering High School Students' Motivation to Learn*. Washington, DC: National Academies Press.

Newcomb, A.F., Bukowski, W.N. and Pattee, L. (1993) 'Children's peer relations, a meta analytic review of popular, rejected, neglected, controversial and average sociometric status', *Psychological Bulletin*, 113: 99–128.

Newton, M., Duda, J.L. and Yin, Z. (2000) 'Examination of the psychometric properties of the perceived motivational climate in sport questionnaire-2 in a sample of female athletes', *Journal of Sport Sciences*, 18: 275–90.

Nicholls, J. and Miller, A. (1984) 'Development and its discontents. The differentiation of the concept of ability', in J. Nicholls (ed.), *The Development of Achievement Motivation*. Greenwhich, CT: JAI.

Nicholls, J.G. (1989) *The Competitive Ethos and Democratic Education*. Cambridge, MA: Harvard University Press.

Nolen-Hoeksema, S., Girgus, J.S. and Seligman, M.E.P. (1986) 'Learned helplessness in children: a longitudinal study of depression, achievement, and explanatory style', *Journal of Personality and Social Psychology*, 51: 435–42.

Oakes, P., Haslam, S.A. and Turner, J.C. (1999) 'The role of prototypicality in group influence and cohesion: contextual variation in the graded structure of social categories', in S. Worchel, J.F. Morales, D. Paez and J.C. Deschamps (eds), *Social Identity, International Perspectives*. London: Sage.

Olson, D.R., Astington, J.W. and Harris, P.L. (1988) 'Introduction', in J.W. Astington, P.L. Harris and D.R. Olsen, *Developing Theories of Mind*. Cambridge: Cambridge University Press.

Oltmanns, J.F. and Emery, R.E. (1995) *Abnormal Psychology*. Upper Saddle River, NJ: Prentice-Hall.

Olweus, D. (1993) Victimisation by peers: antecedents and longterm outcomes, in K.M. Rubin and J.B. Assendorf (eds), *Social Withdrawal*, Inhibition and Shyness in Childhood. Hillsdale, NJ: Erlbaum. pp. 315–41.

Omark, D.R. and Edelman, M.S. (1976) 'The development of attention structure in young children', in M.R.A. Chance and R.R. Larsen (eds), *The Social Structure of Attention*. London: Wiley.

Organisation for Economic Co-operation and Development (OECD) (2005) *Formative Assessment: Improving Learning in Secondary Classrooms*. Paris: OECD.

Oyserman, D. (2004) 'Self-concept and identity', in M.B. Brewer and M. Hewstone (eds), *Self and Social Identity*. Oxford: Blackwell.

Paley, J. (1992) *You Can't Say, You Can't Play*. Cambridge, MA: Harvard University Press.

Panksepp, J. (1998) 'Attention deficit hyperactive disorders, psychostimulants and intolerance of childhood playfulness: a tragedy in the making?', *Current Directions in Psychological Science*, 7: 91–8.

Parker, J.D.A., Bagby, M.B. and Webster, C.B. (1993) 'Domains of the impulsivity construct: a factor analytical investigation', *Personality and Individual Differences*, 15: 267–74.

Parker, J.D.A., Creque, R.E. Snr., Burnhart, D.L. and Harris, J.L. (2004) 'Academic achievement in high school. Does emotional intelligence matter?', *Personality and Individual Differences*, 37: 1321–30.

Parker, J.G. and Asher, S.R. (1987) 'Peer relations and later personal adjustment; are low accepted children at risk', *Psychological Bulletin*, 102: 357–89.

Parker, J.G. and Asher, S.R. (1993) 'Beyond group acceptance: friendship and friendship quality as distinct dimensions of children's peer adjustment', in D. Perlman and W.H. Jones (eds), *Advances in personal Relationships*. Vol. 4. London: Jessica Kingsley Publishers. pp. 261–94.

Parker, J.G. and Herrera, C. (1996) 'Interpersonal processes in friendships: a comparison of abused and non abused children's experiences', *Developmental Psychology*, 32: 1025–38.

Patrick, H., Anderman, L.H. and Ryan, A. (2002) 'Social motivation and the classroom social environment', in C. Midgley (ed.), *Goals, Goal Structures, and Patterns of Adaptive Learning*. Mahwah, NJ: Erlbaum. pp. 85–108.

Patterson, C.J., Kupersmidt, J.B. and Griesler, P.C. (1990) 'Children's perception of self and of relationships with others as a function of sociometric status', *Child Development*, 61: 1335–49.

Paulhus, D.C. and Williams, I.C. (2002) 'The dark triad of personality: narcissism, Machiavellianism and psychopathy', *Journal of Research in Personality*, 36: 546–56.

Pellegrini, A. (2003) 'Bullying and peer status', *Journal of Experimental Child Psychology*, 85: 257–65.

Pelligrini, A. and Smith, P.K. (1998) 'Physical activity play: the nature and function of a neglected aspect of play', *Child Development*, 69: 577–98.

Pelletier, L.G. and Vallerand, R.J. (1996) 'Supervisors' beliefs and subordinates' intrinsic motivation: a behavioral confirmation analysis', *Journal of Personality and Social Psychology*, 71: 331–40.

Pelletier, L.G., Se' guin-Le' vesque, C. and Legault, L. (2002) 'Pressure from above and pressure from below as determinants of teachers' motivation and teaching behaviors', *Journal of Educational Psychology*, 94(1): 186–96.

Perry, T.G., Perry, L. and Kennedy, E. (1992) 'Conflict and the development of anti social behaviour', in C. Shantz and W.W. Hartup (eds), *Conflict in Child and Adolescent Development*, New York: Cambridge University Press.

Persico, N., Postlewaite, A. and Silverman, D. (2004) 'The effect of adolescent experience on labour market outcomes. The case of height', *Journal of Political Economy*, 112: 1019–53.

Petrides, K.V., Frederickson, N. and Furnham, A. (2004) 'The role of trait emotional intelligence in academic performance and deviant behavior at school', *Personality and Individual Differences*, 36: 277–93.

Pinker, S. (1997) *How the Mind Works*. New York: W.W. Norton.

Pinker, S. (2002) *The Blank Slate*. New York: Viking.

Pintrich, P.R. and Schunk, D.H. (1996) *Motivation in Education Theory, Research and Application*. Englewood Cliffs, NJ: Merrill Prentice Hall.

Plutchik, R. and Van Praag, H.M. (1995) 'The nature of impulsivity: definitions, onotology, genetics, and relations to aggression', in E. Hollander, D.J. Stein (eds), *Impulsivity and Aggression*, Chichester: John Wiley and Sons. pp. 7–24.

Pope, A.W. and Bierman, K.L. (1999) 'Predicting adolescent peer problems and antisocial activities: the relative roles of aggression and dysregulation', *Developmental Psychology*, 35(2): 335–46.

Poulton, R. and Milne, B.J. (2002) Low fear in childhood is associated with sporting prowess in adolesence and young adulthood, *Behaviour Research and Therapy*, 40(10): 1191–97.

Prensky, M. (2006) *Don't Bother Me Mom, I'm Learning! How Computer and Video Games are Preparing your Kids for 21st Century Success and How You Can Help!* St. Pauls, MN: Paragon House.

Prince-Embury, S. (2007) *Resiliency Scales for Children and Adolescents*. San Antonio, Tx: Harcourt Assessment.

Quinhuis, G., Bempechat, J., Jiminez, N. and Boulay, P. (2002) 'Implicit Theories of Intelligence across academic domains: A study of meaning making in adolescents of Mexican descent', in J. Bempechat and J. Elliot (eds), *Learning in Culture and Context: Approaching the complexities of achievement motivation in student learning*. San Francisco, CA: Jossey Bass.

Quinton, D., Rutter, M. and Gulliver, L. (1990) 'Continuities in psychiatric disorders from childhood to adulthood in the children of psychiatric patients', in L. Robins and M. Rutter (eds), *Straight and Devious Pathways from Childhood to Adulthood*. Cambridge: Cambridge University Press.

Raffini, J. (1993) *Winners without Losers: Structures and Strategies for Increasing Student Motivation to Learn*. Boston, MA: Allyn and Bacon.

RAND Mathematics Study Panel (2002) *Mathematical Proficiency for All Students: Toward a Strategic Research and Development Program in Mathematic Education*. Rep. No. MR 1643.0 – OER. Santa Monica, CA: Author.

Reeve, J. (2006) 'Teacher as facilitator. What autonomy supportive teachers do and why the students benefit', *Elementary School Journal*, 106: 225–36.

Reeve, J. and Jang, H. (2006) 'What teachers say and do to support autonomy during a learning activity', *Journal of Educational Psychology*, 98(1): 209–18.

Reeve, J., Bolt, E. and Cai, Y. (1999) 'Autonomy-supportive teachers: how they teach and motivate students', *Journal of Educational Psychology*, 91: 537–48.

Reis, H.T., Sheldon, K.M., Gable, S.L., Roscoe, J. and Ryan, R.M. (2000) 'Daily well-being: the role of autonomy, competence, and relatedness', *Personality and Social Psychology Bulletin*, 26: 419–35.

Reivich, K., Gillham, J.E., Chaplin, T.M. and Seligman, M.E.P. (2005) 'From helplessness to optimism; the role of resilience in treating and preventing depression in youth', in S. Goldstein and R.B. Brooks (eds), *Handbook of Resilience in Children*. New York: Kluwer Academic/Plenum. pp. 223–37.

Roberts, B.W. and Delvechio, W.F. (2000) 'The rank order consistency of personality traits for children to old age; a quantitative review of longitudinal studies', *Psychological Bulletin*, 126: 3–25.

Robins, P.W., John, O.P. and Caspi, A. (1998) 'The typological approach to studying personality', in R.B. Cairns, I. Bergman and J. Kagan (eds), *Methods and Models for Studying Individual Type*. Thousand Oaks, CA: Sage.

Robins, R.W., John, O.P., Caspi, A., Moffitt, T.E. and Stouthamer-Loeber, M. (1996) 'Resilient, overcontrolled and undercontrolled boys: three replicable personality types in early adolescence', *Journal of Personality and Social Psychology*, 70: 157–71.

Roeser, R.W., Midgley, C. and Urdan, T.C. (1996) 'Perceptions of the school psychological environment and early adolescents' psychological and behavioural functioning in school: the mediating role of goals and belonging', *Journal of Educational Psychology*, 88: 408–22.

Roffey, S., Tarrant, A. and Majors, B. (1997) 'Friends, who needs them? What do we know and what can we do?', *Educational and Child Psychology*, 14(1): 34–48.

Rogers, C.R. (1961) *On Becoming a Person*. Boston, MA: Houghton Mifflin.

Rosenberg, M. (1979) *Conceiving the Self*. New York: Basic Books.

Rothbaum, F. and Weisz, J. (1994) 'Parental caregiving and child externalising behaviour in non clinical samples: a meta-analysis', *Psychological Bulletin*, 116: 55–74.

Rozenblit, T. and Keil, S. (2002) 'The misunderstood limits of folk science: an illusion of explanatory depth', *Cognitive Science*, 26: 521–62.

Rubin, K.H. and Assendorf, J.B. (eds) (1993) *Social Withdrawal, Inhibition and Shyness in Childhood*. Hillsdale, NJ: Erlbaum.

Rubin, K.H., Bukowski, W. and Parker, J.G. (1996) 'Peer interactions, relationships, and groups', in W. Damon and N. Eisenberg (eds), *Handbook of Child Psychology*. 5th edn. Social, Emotional, and Personality Development Series. New York: John Wiley and Sons. pp. 617–700.

Ruble, D.N. (1993) 'The role of gender-related processes in the development of sex differences in self-evaluation and depression', *Journal of Affective Disorders*, 29: 97–128.

Rupp, D.E. and Vodanovich, S.J. (1997) 'The role of boredom prone induced self reported anger and aggression', *Journal of Social Behaviour and Personality*, 12: 925–36.

Rutter, M. (1994) 'Stress research: accomplishments and tasks ahead', in R. Haggerty, L. Sherrod, N. Garmezy and M. Rutter (eds), *Stress, Risk, and Resilience in Children and Adolescents*. Cambridge: Cambridge University Press.

Rutter, M. (2000) 'Resilience reconsidered: conceptual considerations, empirical findings, and policy implications', in J.P. Shonkoff and S.J. Meisels (eds), *Handbook of Early Childhood Intervention*. 2nd edn. New York: Cambridge University Press.

Ryan, R.M. and Brown, K.W. (2003) 'Why we don't need self-esteem: on fundamental needs, contingent love, and mindfulness', *Psychological Inquiry*, 14(1): 27–82.

Ryan, R.M. and Deci, E.L. (2000a) 'The darker and brighter sides of human existence: basic psychological needs as a unifying concept', *Psychological Inquiry*, 11: 319–38.

Ryan, R.M. and Deci, E.L. (2000b) 'Self-determination theory and the facilitation of intrinsic motivation, social development and well-being', *American Psychologist*, 55: 68–78.

Ryan, R.M. and Deci, E.L. (2003) 'On assimilating identities to the self: a SDT perspective on internalization and integration within cultures', in M.R. Leary and J.P. Tangney (eds), *Handbook of Self and Identity*. New York: Guilford Press. pp. 253–74.

Ryan, R.M. and Frederick, C.M. (1997) 'On energy, personality, and health: subjective vitality as a dynamic reflection of well-being', *Journal of Personality*, 65: 529–65.

Ryan, R.M. and Lynch, J. (1989) 'Emotional autonomy versus detachment: revisiting the vicissitudes of adolescence and young adulthood', *Child Development*, 60: 340–56.

Ryan, R.M., Deci, E.L. and Grolnick, W.S. (1995) 'Autonomy, relatedness, and the self: their relation to development and psychopathology', in D.C. Cicchetti and D.J. Cohen (eds), *Developmental Psychopathology*. Vol. 1, *Theory and Methods*, 618–55. New York: Wiley.

Ryan, R.M., La Guardia, J.G., Solky-Butzel, J., Chirkov, V. and Kim, Y. (2005) 'On the interpersonal regulation of emotions: emotional reliance across gender relationships and cultures', *Personal Relationships*, 12: 145–63.

Salmela-Aro, K., Pennanen, R. and Nurmi, J.-E. (2001) 'Self-focused goals, what they are, how they function and how they relate to well-being', in P. Scmuck and K.M. Sheldon (eds), *Life Goals and Well-Being: Towards a Positive Psychology of Human Striving*. Goettingen: Hogrefe and Huber.

Salmivalli, C., Kaukiainen, A., Kaistaniemi, L. and Lagerspetz, K.M.J. (1999) 'Self-evaluated self-esteem, peer-evaluated self-esteem, and defensive egotism as predictors of adolescents' participation in bullying situations', *Personality and Social Psychology Bulletin*, 25: 1268–78.

Salovey, P. and Mayer, J.D. (1989) 'Emotional intelligence imagination', *Cognition and Personality*, 9: 185–211.

Sandberg, S., Rutter, M., Giles, S., Owen, A., Champion, L., Nicholls, J., Prior, V., McGuiness, D. and Drinnan, D. (1993) 'Assessment of psycho-social experiences in childhood: methodological issues and some illustrative findings', *Journal of Child Psychology and Psychiatry*, 34: 879–97.

Scheier, M.F. and Carver, C.S. (1993) 'On the power of positive thinking. The benefits of being optimistic', *Current Developments in Psychological Science*, 2(1): 26–30.

Schwartz, D. and Gorman, A.H. (2003) 'Community violence exposure and children's academic functioning', *Journal of Educational Psychology*, 1: 163–73.

Scott, S. (2006) 'Improving children's lives, preventing criminality', *The Psychologist*, 19(8): 484–7.

Sedikes, C., Rudich, E.A., Gregg, A.P., Kumashiro, M. and Rusbult, C. (2004) 'Are normal narcissists psychologically healthy? Self-esteem matters', *Journal of Personality and Social Psychology*, 87(3): 400–16.

Seligman, M.E.P. (1998) *Learned Optimism*, New York: Pocket Books.

Seligman, M.E.P. (2006) *Authentic Happiness*. New York: Free Press.

Seligman, M.E.P., Reivich, K., Jaycox, L. and Gillham, J. (1995) *The Optimistic Child*. New York: Harper Perennial.

Shafran, R. and Mansell, W. (2001) 'Perfectionism and psychopathology: A review of research and treatment', *Clinical Psychology Review*, 21: 879–906.

Shatte, A.J., Reivich, K., Gillham, J.E. and Seligman, M.E.P. (1999) 'Learned optimism', in C.R. Snyder (ed.), *Coping: The Psychology of What Works*. New York: Oxford University Press. pp. 161–81.

Shields, A., Ryan, M. and Cicchetti, D. (2001) 'Narrative Representations of Caregivers and Emotional Dysregulation as Predictors of Maltreated Children's Rejection by Peers', *Developmental Psychology*, 37: 321–37.

Shiner, R.L. and Caspi, A. (2003) 'Personality difficulties in childhood', *Journal of Clinical and Child Psychology*, 44(1): 2–32.

Shiner, R.L., Masten, A.S. and Roberts, J.M. (2003) 'Childhood personality foreshadows adult personality and life outcomes two decades later', *Journal of Personality*, 71(6): 1145–70.

Skinner, E.A. and Belmont, M.J. (1993) 'Motivation in the classroom: Reciprocal effects of teacher behaviour and student engagement across the school year', *Journal of Educational Psychology*, 85: 571–81.

Skinner, E.A., Zimmer-Gembeck, M.J. and Connell, J.P. (1998) 'Individual differences and the development of perceived control', *Monographs of the Society for Research in Child Development*, 63 (2–3, Whole No. 204).

Slaughter, V., Dennis, M.J. and Pritchard, M. (2002) 'Theory of mind and peer acceptance in pre-school children', *British Journal of Developmental Psychology*, 20: 545–64.

Smith, C., John Dakers, J., Dow, W., Head, G., Pirrie, A. and Sutherland, M. (2004) 'A systematic review of what pupils, aged 11–16, believe impacts on their motivation to learn in the classroom', the EPPI Centre Social Science Research Unit, Institute of Education, University of London.

Smith, E.R., Seger, C.R. and Mackie, D.M. (2007) 'Can emotions be truly group level? Evidence regarding four conceptual criteria', *Journal of Personality and Social Psychology*, 93(3): 431–46.

Soenens, B., Vansteenkiste, M., Duriez, B., Luyten, P. and Goossens, L. (2005) 'Maladaptive perfectionistic self representations: the mediational link between psychological control and adjustment', *Personality and Individual Differences*, 38: 487–98.

Stanne, M.B., Johnson, D.W. and Johnston, R.T. (1999) 'Does competition enhance or inhibit motor performance: a meta-analysis', *Psychology Bulletin*, 125: 133–54.

Stattin, H. and Kerr, M. (2001) 'Adolescents' values matter', in J.-E. Nurmi (ed.), *Navigating through Adolescence: European Perspectives*. New York and London: Routledge Falmer.

Staub, E. (1992) 'The origins of caring, helping and non aggression; parental socialisation, the family system, schools and cultural influence', in P.M. Oliner, L. Barron, L.A. Blum, D.L. Krebs and M.Z. Smolensk (eds), *Embracing the Other, Philosophical, Psychological and Historical Perspectives on Altruism*. New York: New York University Press. pp. 390–412.

Stipek, D.J. (1981) 'Children's perceptions of their own and their classmates' ability', *Journal of Educational Psychology*, 73: 404–10.

Stipek, D.J. (1995) 'The development of pride and shame in toddlers', in J.P. Tangney and K.W. Fischer (eds), *Self-Conscious Emotions: The Psychology of Shame, Guilt, Embarrassment, and Pride*. New York: Guilford Press.

Stipek, D.J., Rechia, S. and McLintic, S. (1995) 'Self-evaluation in young children', *Monograph of the Society for Research in Child Development*, 57 (1/84, serial no.226).

Suls, J., Green, P. and Hillis, S. (1998) 'Emotional reactivity to everyday problems, affective inertia and neuroticism', *Personality and Social Psychology Bulletin*, 24: 127–36.

Sutton, J. and Keogh, E. (2000) 'Social competition in school: relationships with bullying, Machiavellianism, and personality', *British Journal of Educational Psychology*, 70: 443–56.

Swann, W.B. (1996) *Self Traps: The Elusive Quest for Higher Self Esteem*. New York: Freeman.

Tannenbaum, R. and Schmidt, W.H. (1958) 'How to choose a leadership pattern'. *Harvard Business Review*, March–April. 36(2): 95–101.

Taylor, S.E. (1990) *Positive Illusions: Creative Self-Deception and the Healthy Mind*. New York: Basic Books.

Tett, R.P. and Gutterman, H.A. (2000) 'Situational trait relevance, trait expression and situational consistency. Testing a principle of trait activation', *Journal of Research in Personality*, 34: 397–423.

The Midlands Psychology Group (2007) 'Questioning the science and politics of happiness', *The Psychologist*, 20(7): 484–7.

The Scottish Parliament (2006) Report on pupil motivation, by the Education Committee.

Thompson, T. (1999) *Underachieving to Protect Self-worth. Theory, Research and Interventions*. Aldershot: Ashgate.

Thompson, T., Alomans, R. and Davidson, J. (2004) 'Shame-proneness and achievement behaviour', *Personality and Individual Differences*, 36: 613–27.

Tracy, J.L. and Robins, R.W. (2007) 'The psychological structure of pride: a tale of two facets', *Journal of Personality and Social Psychology*, 92(3): 506–25.

Vallerand, R.J. (1997) 'Toward a hierarchical model of intrinsic and extrinsic motivation', in M.P. Zanna (ed.), *Advances in Experimental Social Psychology*. Vol. 29. San Diego, CA: Academic Press. pp. 271–360.

Vansteenkiste, M., Simons, J., Lens, W., Sheldon, K.M. and Deci, E.L. (2004) 'Motivating learning, performance, and persistence: the synergistic role of intrinsic goals and autonomy-support', *Journal of Personality and Social Psychology*, 87: 246–60.

Vansteenkiste, M., Simons, J., Lens, W., Soenens, B. and Matos, L. (2005) 'Examining the impact of intrinsic versus extrinsic goal framing and autonomy-supportive versus internally controlling communication style upon early adolescents' achievement', *Child Development*, 76: 483–501.

Vertegaal, R. and Ding, Y. (2002) 'Explaining effects of eye gaze on mediated group conversations: amount or synchronisation?' *Proceedings of CSCW 2002 Conference on Computer Supported Collaborative Work (41–48)*. New Orleans, LA: ACM Press.

Walls, T.A and Little, T.D. (2005) 'Relations among personal agency, motivation and school adjustment in early adolescence', *Journal of Educational Psychology*, 97(1): 23–31.

Wandersee, T. and Griffard Phyllis, P. (1999) 'Challenges to meaningful learning in African-American females at an urban science high school', *International Journal of Science Education*, 21(6): 611–32.

Weiner, B. (1990) 'History of motivational research in education', *Journal of Educational Psychology*, 82: 616–22.

Wells, A. (2000) *Emotional Disorders and Metacognition: Innovative Cognitive Therapy*. Chichester: Wiley.

Wentzel, K.R. (2002) 'Are effective teachers like good parents? Teaching styles and student adjustment in early adolescence', *Child development*, 73: 287–301.

Wigfield, A. and Eccles, J. (2000) 'Expectancy-value theory of achievement motivation', *Contemporary Educational Psychology*, 25: 68–81.

Wiggins, J.S. (1990) 'Agency and communion as conceptual coordinates for the understanding and measurement of interpersonal behaviour', in D. Cichetti and W. Grove (eds), *Thinking Critically in Psychology*. Minneapolis, MN: University of Minnesota Press.

Wilson, C. (1973) *New Pathways in Psychology*. London: Victor Gollancz.

Wertlieb, D. (1997) 'Children whose parents divorce: life trajectories and turning points', in I. Gotlib and B. Wheaton (eds), *Stress and Adversity over the Life Course: Trajectories and turning points*. Cambridge: Cambridge University Press. 179–96.

Wolfe, R.N. and Kasmer, J.A. (1988) 'Type versus trait: extraversion, impulsivity, sociability, and preferences for cooperative and competitive activities', *Journal of Personality and Social Psychology*, 34(5): 864–71.

Wolfe, V., Gentiles, C. and Wolfe, D. (1989) 'The impact of sex abuse on children. A PTSD formulation', *Behaviour Therapy*, 20: 215–28.

Yates, M. and Younis, J. (1996) 'A developmental perspective on community service in adolescence', *Social Development*, 5: 85–111.

Zimbardo, P. (2007) *The Lucifer Effect: How Good People Turn Evil*. New York and London: Random House.

Index

Added to a page number 'f' denotes a figure and 't' denotes a table